Contested Identities

PRINCETON MODERN GREEK STUDIES

This series is sponsored by the Princeton University Program
in Hellenic Studies under the auspices of the
Stanley J. Seeger Hellenic Fund

Contested Identities

GENDER AND KINSHIP IN
MODERN GREECE

Edited by
Peter Loizos and
Evthymios Papataxiarchis

PRINCETON UNIVERSITY PRESS
PRINCETON, NEW JERSEY

Copyright © 1991 by Princeton University Press
Published by Princeton University Press, 41 William Street,
Princeton, New Jersey 08540
In the United Kingdom: Princeton University Press,
Chichester, West Sussex

Library of Congress Cataloging-in-Publication Data

Contested identities : gender and kinship in modern Greece /
edited by Peter Loizos and Evthymios Papataxiarchis.
p. cm.—(Princeton modern Greek studies)
Includes bibliographical references and index.
1. Kinship—Greece. 2. Marriage—Greece. 3. Friendship—
Greece. 4. Sex Role—Greece. 5. Women—Greece—
Social conditions. 6. Greece—Social life and customs.
I. Loizos, Peter, 1937–   . II. Papataxiarchis, Evthymios.
III. Series.
GN585.G85C66   1991   306.83'09495—dc20   90-47780   CIP

ISBN 0-691-09460-8 (cl.)—ISBN 0-691-02859-1 (pb.)

This book has been composed in Linotron Caledonia

Princeton University Press books are printed on acid-free paper
and meet the guidelines for permanence and durability of the
Committee on Production Guidelines for Book Longevity of the
Council on Library Resources

Printed in the United States of America by Princeton Academic Press

3   5   7   9   10   8   6   4   2

To John Campbell

μέ ἀγάπη καί ἐκτίμηση

CONTENTS

ACKNOWLEDGMENTS

THIS VOLUME grew out of a conference in Mytilene, September 1986, to mark the foundation of the Social Anthropology Department of the University of the Aegean. We thank the many persons who made that conference possible, and the participants, particularly Ernestine Friedl, for their intellectual stimulation.

We must also thank the contributors to this volume for their patience. The reviewers for Princeton University Press did much to improve the book, and Gail Ullman has encouraged us from the start. Lauren Lepow in her copyediting was a model of tact and helpfulness. Marina Iossifides, Panayotis Panopoulos, and Athanasios Yiounis prepared the index, and Marios Sarris did a perceptive job of additional proofreading. The editors' warm thanks to them all. Papataxiarchis must acknowledge a British Council Fellowship that enabled him to come to London to do editorial work, and he is grateful to Costas Douzinas, Theodore Paradellis, Alexandra Bakalaki, Eva Kalpourtzi, and Ileana Antonakopoulou for encouragement and support throughout the project. Our informants, numbers of Greek women and men, who tolerated our inquiries deserve our thanks not least. Jean Canfield, at L.S.E., typed many drafts of our papers, and managed the task of integrating varied typescripts into an editable form with patience and good grace, and we thank her warmly.

TRANSLITERATION

We have not imposed a uniform system of transliteration from Greek to English upon our authors, some of whom have rendered certain Greek words as they are pronounced in local dialects, rather than as they would appear in written Athenian standard Greek.

Contested Identities

Introduction

GENDER AND KINSHIP IN MARRIAGE
AND ALTERNATIVE CONTEXTS

Peter Loizos and Evthymios Papataxiarchis

ETHNOGRAPHERS of Greece, *pace* Friedl (1962) and Campbell (1964), have been, until recently, almost entirely preoccupied with marriage and have analyzed a single idea of maleness and femaleness as expressed in the context of conjugal procreation. The dominant norm of procreation-within-marriage has been adopted as the frame of reference in ethnographic analysis, as if it had been forgotten that cultures vary greatly in the degree to which they encourage women and men to follow one and only one idea of what is appropriate to their sex.[1] This emphasis on marriage has decisively shaped anthropological thinking on kinship and gender in Greece, the core theme of this volume.

Within this analysis, Greece has been described by anthropologists as a society largely based on kinship.[2] Investigators have singled out familism as the most important orientation in Greek life, thus justifying the priority that most ethnographers have given to kinship. Insofar as marriage leads to the reproduction of kinship, kinship has been regarded as a fundamental principle of relatedness and a powerful idiom of action. Kinship informs the complex of "honor and shame" values and all actions oriented to prestige (Peristiany 1965a). It also embraces spheres of activ-

---

[1] Indeed, some cultures, and often those which are small-scale, tribal, preliterate, and pronatalist, seem to offer only one model: all men and all women should marry and have children. In many of these cultures, those who remain unmarried are pitied, if not scorned—there is Lévi-Strauss's (1973) well-known and amusing passage on the wretchedness of bachelor life among the Nambikwara Indians—while persons who continue to show a sexual preference for their own kind might be regarded with amazement, disgust, incredulity. In some of these cultures, not only have informants claimed that such practices did not occur, but it seems as if they could not even imagine them (Ortner and Whitehead 1981:81 and 111n.1).

[2] Extreme concern with kinship has given rise to an overapplication of descent theory and the "discovery" of lineages where they did not exist. For example, there has been discussion of "patrilineal emphasis," "patrilines," and "lineages" (Aschenbrenner 1976:216–217) where the reality was just a matter of surnamed groups, and "dual patrilineal and matrilineal descent lines" (Hoffman 1976:333) where men and women simply inherited names and property through the father's and mother's side respectively.

ity outside marriage; in structural-functionalist terms, it is the basis of the institutional domains of economics, politics, and religion.

Many ethnographers have also noticed that within marriage kinship is implicated in the construction of gender, and that both kinship and gender are, as Yanagisako (1987) has suggested, "mixed metaphors" of personhood. Indeed, "gender" cannot be an autonomous topic, for both femaleness and maleness are defined in terms of kinship. Women, for example, are thought to embody the "natural" prospect of sexual reproduction and the very sentiment of kinship. Women's personhood is realized within the limits of kinship-phrased and domestically oriented action. And as women seem to be locked within the terms of kinship, their personhood can be expressed in relational terms only. Where women as mothers are identified with the domestic sphere, men are more indirectly involved with it.

This volume seeks to transcend these traditional interests. We want to bring forward new evidence from current research on gender roles and representations in contemporary Greece and to account for patterns of variation. In recent ethnographic work (Dubisch 1986a; Caraveli 1986; Herzfeld 1985a; Hirschon 1989), a greater prominence is given to social and symbolic aspects of gender as the framework that encompasses conjugal procreative life. Ethnographers of Greece have increasingly become aware that, with regard to gender, whole institutional areas of social life and important sources of thought and action have been ignored. Greece is a "complex" society, that is, a society in which some of the functions of kinship are performed by other formal institutions, but also one in which there are contexts other than marriage, diverse models of identity and personhood that cannot be understood within frameworks made for the study of "simple" societies.

This plurality of contexts, within marriage and outside it, is one organizing principle of this book. Our authors document gender roles and ideas about maleness and femaleness, and they account for these variations in terms of comparisons and contrasts between contexts. Indeed, they demonstrate that gender ideas contrasting with those of the mainstream model do emerge outside marriage; and that in the nonconjugal models kinship is implicated in the construction of gender rather differently from the way it is in the dominant one.

We give a lot of emphasis to the terms *model* or *discourse*, which we use interchangeably, and *context*. Here, we employ *context* to suggest spheres of activity in which ideas of gender can be identified. We are committed, therefore, to dealing primarily with ideas manifested in action, ideas that inform roles and relations as actually observed. Contexts, however, may vary in degree of institutionalization and may range from discrete *domains* (Collier and Yanagisako 1987)—such as the household or the convent, with their distinct sets of values and, often, formal rules—to sets of practices of a more informal and transient nature, such as the interethnic courtship that arises from tourism. A gender model or discourse is the set of ideas that informs the activity of each sex in a particular context. Gender discourses vary in accordance with the context in which they are established, and the less instituted the context, the more problematic is their delineation. In this volume the authors report on fully instituted discourses that have been based on long-standing, literate traditions of marriage and monastic celibacy; less formal discourses on the margins of established religious traditions; and leisure practices and fragments of discourse that are either provisional or on the way to fuller institutionalization.

In the first part of this introduction, we approach the dominant discourse on gender that is traced (by all authors) in the gender domains of married life and in combination with kinship patterns which vary according to the type of marital residence involved. In the second part, contrasting discourses are discussed in the context of the coffee shop, the *kafeteria*, and the convent. These subordinate discourses are approached either through the study of their implications for friendship, kinship, and conjugality, or more directly through the analysis of their core concepts. We also address the themes of variation in gender representations within marriage, particularly those which focus on women's roles, and in patterns of friendship, and we attempt to explain these variations in terms of the different types of postmarital residence and kinship.

Our main emphasis in this introduction is on the comparison of the gender models and ideas that ethnographic research has so far outlined, with a focus on the relative significance of kinship in the construction of gender. As a basis of action and personhood, kinship is implicated differently and often contrastingly in various contexts, the most significant contrast being that between marriage, on the one hand, and convent and coffee shop on the other. While in the former domestic kinship is the dominant metaphor of gendered personhood, in the latter that form of kinship is either transcended or negated.

The Domestic Model of Gender

The domestic model of gender is a set of ideas about men and women in married life and can be depicted in what married people say about and do in marriage. As an ideal, it encapsulates the values of marriage, while in practice it informs male and female conjugal and domestic roles and provides standards for social life in general. In Greece, marriage is of supreme value because it is regarded as a necessary condition of procreation and, therefore, of the continuation of life and, in a more metaphysical sense, of the self through the perpetuation of family names and the persons of the parents.[3] Besides normally requiring a religious ritual, marriage is also an event with economic and political implications and has been influenced by both church and state. From various ethnographic reports, it seems that the idea of the "household" (*nikokirio*) is the single most significant element in the formal regulation of marriage. The focus on the house derives from it. Nikokirio is an economically and politically autonomous, corporate, conjugal household: this is the ideal social environment to which men and women can bring their distinct identities and abilities to create a new family.[4]

The "household" model seems to be conceptually demarcated from religious ideas about female and male nature.[5] It is particularly stressed, sometimes as a status symbol (Papataxiarchis 1990; Sant Cassia forthcoming), in communities where the church has historically taken on the role of cultural and political representation as well as that of spiritual leadership, especially during the Ottoman era (Pantazopoulos 1967; Papadopoulos 1967), and has acted as arbiter of customary law on marriage and kinship. There is no doubt that as a "folk" ideology the domestic model derives its potency from long-standing and continuous promotion by the church.

Most ethnographers agree that women and men are attached differently to the ideals of formal conjugality and corporate marriage. Since women's "destiny" is to give birth and bring up children (du Boulay 1986), it seems that women's only option is to marry and to identify with a household of procreation. The house and the children are the imperative concerns around which married women organize their lives. Men's attachment is more flexible and indirect since their destiny is more ambiguous and overshadowed by extrahousehold concerns. However, the role of household head (*nikokiris*) is often a vital condition of assuming an active profile in public life (see Loizos 1975a:112–113; Salamone and Stanton 1986; Papataxiarchis 1988).

The stress on the conjugal household as an institution indissolubly dedicated to procreation is strikingly confirmed by a close investigation of issues of illegitimacy and divorce. First, in contrast to Iberian communi-

[3] The emphasis on conjugal procreation has origins that point back to the early teachings of the Orthodox Church on gender, sexuality, and the destiny of human beings. This came out in the debate about the identity of God and the attempt of the early church to cast God as a Father (Pagels 1979; but see also Heine 1987).

[4] On the imperative nature of marriage, see Campbell (1964); du Boulay (1986); Hirschon (1989:106–109).

[5] This emphasis can be seen in the work of ethnographers who emphasize the actual content of practices and relations in marriage, rather than the conceptual foundation of marriage on religious symbolism.

ties (Pina-Cabral 1986; O'Neill 1987; Brettell 1985), Greece presents a near-zero record in cases of procreation outside wedlock. Ethnographers do not report the existence of even the occasional illegitimate child, let alone the systematic occurrence of extramarital birth.[6] Second, Greeks view divorce with unusually strong disapproval, and, to judge from the ethnography, it has been uncommon (du Boulay 1974:133–134).[7] It is interesting that the divorce cases reported by Papataxiarchis (1988) involved childless couples in the first years of marriage. Campbell (1964:186–187) mentions two cases of marriage that broke down before they were consummated, and Loizos heard of a similar case during his fieldwork. Informal separations may in some circumstances have substituted for divorce proper, but more recently the increase in urban divorce rates suggests important changes in the meaning of marriage that may well affect the countryside in due course.[8]

Two aspects of the conjugal model should be stressed at the outset: first, the central role played by kinship in the definition of female and male identities; and, second, the representation of the sexes as being in a relationship of complementarity, mutual dependence, and ideal equality. It is becoming a commonplace in anthropology that gender and kinship should be the subjects of a unified analysis (Collier and Yanagisako 1987). This approach is promising in the Greek context, where the pervasiveness of kinship in married life, in the constitution of gender identities, in economic cooperation and political negotiation, and in ritual action has been established by many ethnographers. Roger Just, however, in his contribution here, notices how important it is to distinguish levels of kinship. In the endogamous community of Meganisi, kinship appears as a powerful and morally binding idiom because it touches everyone in the locality. Yet when its efficacy in the organization of economic or political tasks is put to the test, its capacity to function as a structural principle of action is limited to the domestic sphere. The idiom of kinship requires the corporate properties of marriage and household to be the basis of organized life.

In married life, therefore, we have a positive articulation between ideas of domestic kinship and gender, employed as mixed metaphors. Womanhood and manhood are expressed in the relational terms of domestic kinship. Women are perceived as "mothers," "house-mistresses," and "wives"; men as "householders," or "fathers." Gender attributes are

[6] Handman (1983:91) reports eight cases of illegitimate children since 1930.

[7] In Pouri, divorce occurs after 1970 and, according to Handman (1983:170), represents a new form of women's rebellion against maltreatment in marriage.

[8] A more ambiguous attitude toward divorce is reported for the big cities. A little more than one-third of those interviewed in a survey conducted among 366 households in the wider metropolitan area of Athens approved (Presvelou and Teperoglou 1980).

linked to domestic kinship roles.[9] Womanhood means nurturing, cooking, cleaning: activities that reflect women's unique psychology, their ability to love as mothers. Manhood means providing for the household, representing or defending kinship loyalties in line with men's psychological capacity for rational calculation and overarching responsibility. There is notable variation, however, to which we shall return.

On another level, cognatic kinship ideology and the conjugal model of gender are characterized by images of complementarity and interdependence between men and women. There is a symmetrical recognition of mother's and father's sides in kinship classification. In native ideas on procreation, the womb is of at least the same significance as the sperm; children bear attributes of both parents since they are thought to be of two bloods.[10] In terms of roles, the household requires both a husband and a wife found in a relation of ideal equality and complementarity, their participation organized in sex-specific spheres of activity.[11] The successful running of the household brings prestige to both sexes and allows both connections between private interests and public life.[12]

GENDER AND KINSHIP VARIATIONS IN VIRILOCAL, UXORILOCAL, AND NEOLOCAL MARRIAGE

Marriage in Greece is not, however, structurally uniform. There are three distinct types of marriage, characterized by postmarital residence—virilocal, uxorilocal, and neolocal. Each of these is accompanied by different sorts of emphasis (skewing, or bias) in the organization of kinship and in the contribution of gender to notions of relatedness.[13] This is particularly the case in the creation of matrilateral and patrilateral biases, and in the construction of relations of relative equality, or inequality, between wife and husband.[14]

---

[9] Characteristic of the phrasing of women's personhood in kinship terms is the remark made by Salamone and Stanton (1986:99): "The concept of individual (that is, non-familial) personal accomplishment is alien to the women of Amouliani."

[10] "Half-siblings from the same mother are said to be closer than those from the same father, for they come from 'the same womb' " (du Boulay 1983:258).

[11] In du Boulay's words, "There is in the traditional village view an ideal equality between the sexes which enabled the villages to see marriage as a symbiosis, and enabled a woman to transcend her fallen nature by means of her spiritual nature and create with her husband a relationship of equals" (du Boulay 1983:258). This is a symbolic kind of equality. Du Boulay (1974), Hirschon (1989:143), and Salamone and Stanton (1986:103) stress the complementarity in the conjugal bond.

[12] See Salamone and Stanton (1986:98).

[13] Dimen and Friedl (1976) discuss variation in the actualities of kinship and social organization in terms of regional and geographical specificities. For an analytically rigorous taxonomy of postmarital residence in the Greek context, see Casselberry and Valavanes (1976).

[14] Du Boulay (1983) attributes the variations of the marriage patterns to the indivisibility/

First, there are communities in which married sons reside in the immediate vicinity of their natal households, usually after a short period of coresidence with their parents. Virilocality and the requirements of male cooperation in pastoralism, trade, or family agriculture promote an agnatic emphasis in kinship. The special value put onto maleness and male-male relatedness makes inequality between husband and wife the norm. Men dominate, at least in appearance, but usually in reality too (Friedl 1986). Property, names, and reputations are basically under male control and are transferred from father to sons.[15] Women are in a classic state of muteness, as they are "reduced" to their reproductive biology, and they have two crucial but limiting roles: effective housekeeping and bearing sons. The shepherding communities of northwest Greece (Campbell 1964) and mountainous Crete (Herzfeld 1985a) and the feud-oriented communities of southern Peloponnese (Andromedas 1962; Lineton 1971) are classic examples of this type. The patterns described by Friedl (1962) and du Boulay (1974) combine virilocality with agriculture, and here female subordination is less marked.[16]

Second, at the opposite pole are the communities that practice uxorilocality. Here, women's dowries are houses built near their natal homes, so that neighborhoods tend to be clusters of matrilaterally related women (and their male kin). Property and names are transferred through gendered lines, from mother to daughters and from father to sons, and women often get the lion's share of family property and dominate in the administration of these properties as well as in the arrangement of marriages. A matrilateral bias characterizes kinship in these societies. The symbolic and practical importance of the woman as the mistress of the house comes to have a structural character, as does the concomitant prominence of special friendship between men who are not kin. The

divisibility of the economic sphere of activity, in which men rule, from the house. In agricultural contexts where land is the focus of male economic activity and therefore indivisible from the house, men seem to identify fully with it. In maritime and urban communities, men do not work the land, and therefore "the principle of continuity embodied in the house and land—no longer being inevitably identified with the men—might, under pressure of circumstances, shift to the women" (254). In both cases, however, the values of male superiority hold.

[15] The closer identification of men with the household is depicted in the Ambeliotes' traditional description of boys as being "in the house" (du Boulay 1983:252) and girls as destined to a "strong hearth" (253). Women as the weaker side were mobile and "on the whole moved to the men" (254).

[16] On the virilocal pattern, also see Couroucli (1985) for the Ionian islands, Bialor (1976:232–235) for northwestern Peloponnese, Aschenbrenner (1976:215) for southern Peloponnese, and Dimen (1986) for Epiros. For Mani, see also Alexakis (1980). In Mani, Allen (1976:184) contrasts the emerging pattern of uxorilocality among migrants in the city with traditional virilocality that survives in the village and mentions a "patrilineal bias" (188) in kinship.

largely matrifocal communities of the Aegean Basin can be regarded as representative of this type (Dubisch 1976; Kenna 1976a; Bernard 1976; Vernier 1984; Beopoulou 1987; Papataxiarchis 1988).[17]

There is a third recognizable type, intermediate between the other two, which, when understood historically, may prove to be a point of transition in movements between the two poles we have just described. In these cases, we find the representation of kinship as fully bilateral, with only rather small areas of life where men can argue for their superiority as a sex, and small and rather unimportant areas of behavior organized to stress male-male links or anything resembling agnatic descent. These systems tend to neolocal marital residence and full partible inheritance of land. A good example is described by Loizos (1975b). Hirschon's material represents a departure from this intermediate type and is, indeed, close to the matrifocal pattern. Du Boulay (1974, 1983) describes a transition from the previously virilocal to the neolocal type.

These variations are a necessary framework especially for those who want to compare different Greek cases. In the rest of this introduction, we will use the pattern of kinship variations in different types of marriage as an explanatory framework in order to account for variations of gender roles and representations within marriage and outside it. We will start with the analysis of contrasting ideas about womanhood and women's expressive roles in marriage.

REPRESENTATIONS OF WOMEN AND WOMEN'S SELF-EXPRESSION IN MARRIED LIFE

The study of women has been the single most important ingredient of the anthropology of gender. Among others, two issues have received the attention of ethnographers of Greek life: first, representations of womanhood in the context of married life, and second, the muting, or restriction of women in a manner that contradicts the adult status they achieve in marriage.

Representations of Women

Many ethnographers, including some of our coauthors, stress the symbolic handicap with which women start their domestic careers. In brief,

---

[17] On the matrilocal pattern, also see the section on the ethnography of the Aegean islands in the Dimen and Friedl (1976) collection, and particularly the contibutions by Hoffman (1976) and Bernard (1976:295–297). On Kalymnos, see also Casselberry and Valavanes (1976). Handman (1983:100–102) describes a village community in Pelio (Thessaly) that combines uxorilocality with a form of male domination that is usually encountered in virilocal contexts.

"Women are viewed as polluted because of their bodily functions, and as dangerous by virtue of their sexuality" (Dubisch 1983:196). These indigenous assumptions originate in levels of discourse (for example, the New Testament) external to the mainstream model of domesticity, yet it has been argued that they are of considerable influence within marriage as well.[18] It is on these grounds that women are kept away from significant aspects of public life as well as placed under ritual restriction. On the other hand, marriage initiates a process of gradual redemption: by assuming the role of "mistress of the house" (*nikokira*) and eventually demonstrating their ability to control household boundaries and transform polluting disorder into domestic order, women mold their own nature and eventually redeem themselves from their symbolic handicaps as "daughters of Eve" (du Boulay 1974, 1986; Hirschon 1978:79–86; Dubisch 1983, 1986c; Rushton 1983).[19]

Juliet du Boulay has played a key role in formulating the thesis that "redemption" is the means of transcending "nature" in womanhood. In this volume, she takes her analysis one step further to consider gender domains in ritual life and, further, the relation among gender, cosmos, divinity, nature, and social life. Du Boulay confirms that married women are protagonists in life-crisis rituals and stresses that the female mourner in her capacity "to live not for herself but for others" can transform sin into forgiveness and redeem the dead. Therefore, women as married persons with domestic responsibilities transform their identity by redeeming those on whom they depend.

Even more striking and original, however, are her thoughts on the symbolic foundations of the conjugal model. How is gender in the cosmos of divinity and nature elaborated in ritual spheres of domestic life?[20] Du Boulay argues that the villagers of Ambeli are influenced by different levels of thinking that originate in the Old and New Testaments, as well as in pre-Christian discourse, which present women variously as subordinates, honorary superiors, and spiritual mediators. Yet when she considers closely one of those levels and analyzes the gender attributes of the sun and moon in pre-Christian discourse, she establishes a pattern of homologies between the representations of gender in natural cosmology and those that inform ritual action. In both dimensions, women are

[18] For a comprehensive description of gender and symbolism in religious discourse, see Campbell (1964); du Boulay (1974:100–120). In both classic studies, the discursive contexts of religious symbolism and marriage are dealt with in separate chapters.

[19] The representation of women as both *Panayia* (the All Holy) and Eve corresponds to what Giovannini (1981) describes as the structural duality of being simultaneously the Madonna and the whore in Catholic communities.

[20] Also see Stewart (1985) on the role of supernatural belief in modern Greek life.

aligned with ideas of process and growth within settled, stable structures that are symbolically identified with men.

It could be argued that the representation of women as more fluid, volatile creatures relates to another image of women as emotional, particularistic, and fundamentally unstable elements in systems that ultimately depend on men's more solid, stable, and enduring psychological characters. Jill Dubisch, however, in her contribution criticizes the analysis of gender in terms of the opposition between "sentiment and structure." She contends that in a neolocal context which combines dowry, same-sex lines of name and property transfer (Kenna 1976a, 1976b; Vernier 1984), and a matrilateral emphasis in kinship, female kinship and sentiment adopt a structural significance. We think that the differences of theoretical interpretation between du Boulay and Dubisch are partly explained by the sharp contrast in marital residence and the organization of kinship which they describe for the communities they studied.

Women's Self-Expression

In Greek ethnography, women are often described as being marginal and muted. It is men, being endowed with godlike attributes such as intellect, who seem to embody *logos* (that is, intelligent reasoning, rationality) and eloquence, and who, therefore, articulate the "common good," the universalistic concerns that enhance order and promote welfare. By "nature" women are gossips, their speech inherently damaging and divisive.[21] Therefore, proper women have to keep their expressive potential suspended between controlled, modest manifestations of emotion and silence. Yet this does not mean that they are altogether deprived of the capacity to express themselves, but rather that they are led to indirect, nonverbal means. This is, at least, Ardener's (1975) contention when he distinguishes between discursive capacity, found at the paradigmatic level of language, and the actual, verbal manifestation of meaning that can be found on the surface, syntagmatic level. Certain groups, such as women, who find themselves in a "muted position" are sometimes forced to express themselves indirectly by use of symbolism in art, myth, or ritual, rather than through confrontational exposition in a direct challenge to hegemonic ideas.

This point has been debated in a recent collection on gender and power in Greece. Dubisch (1986b) asked how far women's view of themselves and of the relations between the sexes differs from that of men, and she mentioned the possibility that women might have a "muted

---

[21] On gossip, see du Boulay (1974:201–229). For a critical perspective, see Herzfeld (1990).

model" of gender. She cited the case of a woman who apparently would have been content not to bear children. In the same volume, Juliet du Boulay rejected the possibility that in Ambeli (Euboea) women had a view of gender which differed significantly from that of men. Moreover she insisted that "there is no girl in the society who does not wish to become a housewife," and that men could not be usefully understood in that village to derive an advantage from exploiting their assertions of their formal superiority to women.

In this volume, three of our coauthors address the issue, returning to Ardener's thesis. Herzfeld boldly contends that in the virilocal context of shepherding, the primary options open to Greek women are to engage in undermining gossip or submissive silence. Women's silences, however, represent a problem for the study of the creation of meaning (Herzfeld's "poetics") in contexts of female interaction. Herzfeld proposes a solution that rests on the concept of disemia (Herzfeld 1982).[22] Women are often found in outward conformity to (yet inward protest against) the androcentric norm. They adopt a male idiom of contest in order to ridicule it; in mourning they overemploy "ritualized speech" to protest against maltreatment by male affines;[23] or they pursue more outward gestures of obedience to the code of sexual concealment, gestures that by means of their ambiguity turn into open assertions of domestic power. These instances indicate women's ability to capitalize on their exaggerated exhibition of submissiveness and turn it into a projection of female identity. Herzfeld's contention is that through irony women can "creatively deform" the disadvantages of their muted position.

Yet what sort of "poetics" is this? In the Cretan case women have to subvert male definitions through their ambiguous nonverbal comportment in order to reach self-presentation, or else borrow from the male stock of formal discourse and verbal exaggeration, thus, in effect, legitimizing it. Their criticism seems to be "inchoate" and to lack substance. The image of women "performing" their lack of performance in order to deflate men's performative pretensions nicely demonstrates the contingency of the "poetics of womanhood" proposed by Herzfeld.

Ardener has stressed the great significance of symbolic and ritual forms of expression for women. Women's participation in ritual and religious contexts is examined in the contrasting cases of virilocality and uxorilocality by Danforth and Dubisch. In the Macedonian village of Ayia Eleni, wives reside with their husband's family after marriage. Their domestic position is weak, and tension often develops within the triangular relation of mother, son, and incoming daughter-in-law. In his contribution, Dan-

[22] See also Herzfeld (1987).
[23] See Caraveli (1986).

forth examines the social and symbolic implications of women's membership in the cult group of Saint Constantine for the resolution of intrafamil-
ial conflict. The *Anastenaria* is a trance and procession ritual that
functions as a system of treating psychogenic illness among women (see
Danforth 1983, 1989). The afflicted woman expresses her resentments in
the form of illness, which is subsequently diagnosed as "possession" by
Saint Constantine. She then participates in a ritual association, whose
members practice firewalking, and the singing of a special narrative poem
that "works through" a conflict situation similar to the woman's own, but
exemplified by the tribulations of the saint, under whose protection the
woman now lives.[24] Danforth locates the conflict as primarily between
the female in-laws, and, in complementarity to Herzfeld's cautiousness,
he emphatically stresses the social efficacy of women's ritual action. The
song's symbolic statements convert domestic conflict into harmony, and
the postperformance situation is structurally transformed to accord with
the image of domestic symmetry enacted in the ritual. In a virilocal context, participation in ritual, when available to such women, has more
marked effects than does the mere application of irony to the condition
of women's subordination.

It is well established in the ethnography of Greece that religion offers
"public" space for women, with symbols that accommodate and sanction
female domestic power and a definite release from muteness (Dubisch
1983; Hirschon 1983, 1989; du Boulay 1986; Rushton 1983).[25] The acknowledgment of the mother role in the religious image of Panayia, the
All-Holy Woman, i.e., Mary as Mother of Christ, is a classic example of
religious symbolism in the service of women's domestic interests. Dubisch in her contribution (see also Dubisch 1987) discusses women's involvement in religious pilgrimage to the Panayia of Tinos, a major place
of worship in the Aegean. Women pilgrims identify with the Panayia as a
suffering mother and with a powerful image that arouses sentiments of
admiration and respect and carries prestige. Women use religious symbolism to create in an explicit and public manner meanings that further
reinforce them as the centers of domestic life.

How can we make sense of these varying representations of gender in
married life? And what kind of exegesis can be offered to account for the
sharp contrast between the religious poetics of womanhood discussed by
Dubisch and the rhetorical poetics of silence and irony presented by

---

[24] Such protests by wives in frustrating relationships with their husbands or mothers-in-
law remind us of the famous "sex war" aspect of women's *Zar* cults in the Horn of Africa
(Lewis 1971).

[25] For the impact of religious symbols, ideas, and values on secular life in modern
Greece, see Hirschon (1989:192–206). Hirschon (1983:116) stresses that among the urban
dwellers of Piraeus "the integration of religion and daily life is most striking."

Herzfeld? Here, we contend that the type of marriage, along with the subsequent degree of identification of each of the sexes with the household and domestic kinship, is a crucial factor underlying variations both in constructs of womanhood and in women's ability to express meanings about themselves.

Indeed, in virilocal contexts (Herzfeld, Danforth, du Boulay) men seem to identify more closely with the household and use their identification in prestige-oriented action more than women, who at marriage experience a dislocation from, and a consequent diminution of, their natal kinship-based identity and are drawn into muteness. Women are represented as mobile elements in a world of male stability, and their poetics, when they exist, are inchoate, contingent, and of a corrective nature. In uxorilocal settings, on the other hand, women throughout their lives identify with households that are linked through female kinship, while men, especially of plebeian status, experience a certain detachment from domestic life. Such women, then, are regarded as part of "structure."[26] Women as *representatives* of their households can more easily move from silence to prestige-oriented religious action, acting as links between the domestic and the divine, and engage in the explicit, affirmative poetics of womanhood described by Dubisch.

To put it differently, the more prominent women are within domestic kinship, the more womanhood is represented exclusively in kinship terms and their religious poetics merely confirm them in the prestigious roles of mother (*mana*) and mistress of the house (*kira*). However, principles other than domestic kinship come to shape gender and personhood, and these topics are discussed in the next sections.

CONTEXTS OUTSIDE MARRIAGE

We can now turn to consider gender ideas and relations in contexts outside marriage, starting with convent and coffee shop and moving into kafeteria and interethnic courtship in an order of declining institutionalization. The convent is a fully instituted domain with a distinct set of formal rules and elaborated practices that ultimately derive from published codes. This is less true for the coffee shop, which has historically declined from a center of religious heterodoxy (Hattox 1985) into a leisure place for men. At the other pole are the more recent and transformational contexts. The kafeteria is a new kind of establishment for young people and manifests a Western profile, while interethnic courtship, which is linked to the development of tourism, seems to lack any institutional status at all. The contexts outside marriage discussed in this book can be

---

[26] See Papataxiarchis (1988); also Dubisch (this volume).

further contrasted in terms of same-sex and intersex relatedness. As we shall see, this is suggestive of the nature of gender representations outside marriage.

The Convent

Our limited knowledge of the convent at first hand indicates that it is a marginal institution. Today the clergy are neither plentiful nor in particularly good standing with the laity. We suggest, however, that the importance of monasticism, in its symbolic and exemplary role, has been considerable in Greek culture. Ethnographers have said little about monastic life, partly, we suspect, because the convents and monasteries are removed from the communities they study. The institution's "absence" from village life, owing to its physical distance from it, has meant that its conceptual importance has gone relatively unremarked. Yet monasticism offers distinct and important ideas about female and male that we cannot afford to ignore.

In Orthodox theology celibacy is an option for the individual that, once the world of conjugality has been renounced, offers both an elevated spiritual condition and a distinctive communal life. In the patristic period, the early Christian Church argued strongly that celibacy was a superior life, but it was early recognized that most lay people would be unable to follow such a "heroic" path. We are not suggesting that the spiritual superiority of the celibate is now so widely acclaimed. Frequent jokes from villagers indicate that they are not convinced by monastic claims of chaste living.[27] However, there are some aspects of villagers' self-representations that suggest the deep rootedness of Orthodox teachings on body, soul, and sexuality. Thus the assertion of women that they are "Eves" (du Boulay 1974; Hirschon 1978) and the common statement that sexual intercourse, even between married couples, is "sinful" are surely indications that monastic ideas have played an important part in molding secular consciousness of gender and sexuality.

In practical terms, the worlds of the laity and of the celibate monastics are interdependent; for although monasteries and convents could, in principle, be self-sufficient in food production, they rely for recruitment on the profane activities of householders. Monks and nuns have been born into families that have reproduced sexually; the monastic world depends for its perpetuation upon the activities of those who have chosen the "lower" life. But the dependence is reciprocal, and perhaps "balanced," since the lay communities expect the celibates to provide them with religious specialists. Though Orthodox village priests are usually

---

[27] The chaste monk is a common target for villagers' humor.

married and so participate in the profane world of household and kinship reproduction, they can be ordained only by those who live the celibate life. The Protestant churches of the West developed the idea of unmediated religiosity so that all believers could live as "one body in Christ" or a unified "community." In Orthodoxy the "two worlds" remain separate yet connected, but unequal and asymmetric, for while the laity by a positive effort can transcend the limitations of their flaws through fasting and piety (Rushton 1983; du Boulay 1974), the monastics have chosen the "elevated" path, and an increased involvement in the "world of the flesh" must be negatively evaluated. The married priest participates in both "worlds," but he may later renounce his own family-through-marriage to join the "higher" monastic calling. Having made his marriage bed, he need not continue to lie in it. A monastic, however, may not become a married priest—the "higher calling" cannot officially and legitimately be downgraded to the "lower" one.

The Coffee Shop

The coffee shop (kafenio) is gradually receiving the ethnographic attention it deserves as a core institution in Greek social life (Photiades 1965; Herzfeld 1985a; Papataxiarchis 1988). We can distinguish many different types of coffee shops that reflect regional tastes and styles, but all have a single theme in common—men drinking together, in pairs or in drinking parties (parea). Papataxiarchis (this volume) examines the code of commensality and its manifestation of dyadic, emotional friendship. For men, commensality in the coffee shop represents both a personal ethos and a worldview. In coffee shop–related activities of a competitive nature such as drinking, gambling, or rhyme contests, just as in animal theft, men demonstrate strong masculine motives. These are usually expressed in a vocabulary of motive that focuses on the notion of kefi, one sense of which is a state of pleasure wherein men transcend the pettiness of a life of calculation.[28]

Coffee shop and tavern suggest ideas that contrast with those of household and immediate locality or neighborhood. The latter are closed units, the sites of reproduction for individual families that exert strong demands over members to commit their energies and resources to family welfare. "Household" stands then in competitive opposition to what is communicated and transacted between men in places of recreation. In such places, the dominant ethos is kerasma (only poorly translated as "treating") and the creation of "open" friendship groups that do not recruit through the compulsory moral ties of kinship or affinity, but rather through the per-

---

[28] Aspects of the notion of kefi have been analyzed by Caraveli (1982, 1985).

sonal choices of *simpathia* (fellow-feeling). From coffee shop discourse we learn that there are really two kinds of men: domesticated men, who are more or less tame, and men's men, who are more or less free, and sometimes, of course, a little wild. Peristiany noted in 1965 that highland Cypriots were sometimes prepared to hazard a very great deal on the turn of a card, and Loizos in a lowland village saw men gamble away thousands of pounds in a few hours. Indeed, the question of whether a potential bridegroom was inclined to gamble was thought to be one of the most serious questions to be investigated by matchmaking households in Argaki, West Cyprus. Gambling and being a good provider did not mix. Whether in sheep stealing, gambling, or outdoing others in commensal generosity, the Greek male who asserts himself does so in conscious opposition to the demands of conjugality and its restrictions. Countering the ethos of sober, responsible, and domesticated husbands and fathers is one in which men are inclined to say that they are men first and husbands second, for while it is still important to be known as a "good provider," a man's man must not allow himself to become crushed by the burdens of conjugal responsibility.[29]

Transformational Contexts: Kafeteria and Fringe Marriage

Cross-sex companionship has been reported to be rare and occurring in groups (*parees*), usually before marriage, among university or high school students or in ritual contexts such as the weekly promenade (*volta*).[30] Married men and women rarely became involved in friendships since this would arouse suspicion of adulterous intention. Yet Zinovieff and Cowan suggest in their contributions that the development of tourism and the considerable influence of Western European values and practices have enlarged the scope for intersex relatedness outside marriage and have even led to the emergence of institutional outlets for it.

A recent and prominent example of a public leisure space that is distinguished in composition and character from the mainstream coffee shop is the kafeteria. Its atmosphere is "European," as are the drinks offered, and it is attended by unaccompanied women and youths as well as men. The presence of kafeterias in small towns decisively enlarges the scope of

---

[29] See Dubisch (1986a:20); also Friedl (1986).

[30] This is an excellent context in which to consider another level of variation that is linked to the obvious facts of social maturation and generational difference. Young unmarried men and women stress different aspects of gender from those insisted upon by the parental generation, and the young people may themselves differ on values (Lever 1986). Hirschon (1983:121), for example, describes how young men tease elderly female pilgrims who visit regional shrines to combine worship with recreation.

intersex friendship and courtship and promotes new ideas about the sexes.

A spatial metaphor contrasts both coffee shop and kafeteria with household activity, the former described as taking place "outside" the latter. The outward movement characterizes emancipated men (which is something of a commonplace) as well as incorporates the "outside" into women's identity. This is an important ideological transformation for women, and Cowan studies it when the emergence of the new discourse is debated.

The same metaphor can be employed to describe the context of interethnic courtship. In her contribution, Sofka Zinovieff examines male sexual predation in the particularly cosmopolitan environment of a small town dependent on tourism. *Kamaki* (spearfishing), which suggests the sexual "hunting of women," is organized in the context of male friendship and commensal companionship and is directed outward to female tourists. Besides fulfilling male sexual fantasies and providing substantive material for narratives of masculinity, these usually ephemeral encounters give local men of low status the opportunity to upgrade themselves by denigrating their female companions as well as the latter's Western cultural background. In some cases, however, these interethnic heterosexual liaisons turn into culturally "fringe" marriages despite the contradictory representations of the women involved as "easy," "free," and "victims" of male cunning, yet also potential mothers of local men's children. These marriages might owe a lot of both their vitality and their vulnerability to their placement in the liminal zone of culture contact where neither partner is constrained by certain rules that otherwise govern behavior: young men by pressure to marry women they have sex with, young women by stigma of such relationships (since they occur far from home). They further represent men's decision to opt out of the dominant model of early marriage and make a marriage that is more compatible with the coffee shop, a "late marriage" founded upon greater spontaneity and significant experience.

GENDER RELATIONS OUTSIDE MARRIAGE: DISSIMILAR PATTERNS OF FRIENDSHIP

Among the relations that are clearly separated from married life and often occur outside the household, friendship is, no doubt, the most significant and deserves a special discussion. Such discussion should make clear the ways in which ideas about the possibilities of friendship exist for each sex and how, as ideas, they are related to those of kinship and affinity. For any community, we should ask whether friendship is thought of in contrast with kinship, or whether it is superimposed on it. Does one make friends from among one's universe of kin, but not with unrelated people? Or is friendship subordinated to kinship, so that kinship is always and everywhere conceived of as superior to friendship? And, finally, what sense can we make of friendship in a comparative framework that puts gender questions at the center of inquiry and tries to link friendship to types of postmarital residence? In order to suggest, albeit very tentatively, where such questions might lead, we sketch in some contrasts in friendship patterns in four Greek communities.

In Campbell's (1964) account of the transhumant/pastoralist Sarakatsani, there is the strong suggestion that kinship and affinity make such overwhelming claims upon individuals that friendship with unrelated persons is little more than an essentially economic contract. The sense in which the shepherds become clients of cheese makers and lawyers, whom they transform into godparents for their children and *koumbari* for themselves, suggests a formal, restricted relationship with little emotional warmth. Nor does Campbell indicate that friendships between unrelated persons play much part in the shepherds' lives. If a married or unmarried Sarakatsani woman were to form a close friendship with another unrelated woman, it would seem a kind of "betrayal" of both her consanguinal kin and her affines; and friendships between unrelated men and women presumably would arouse the immediate suspicion of adultery. Given that "affines do not laugh and joke together," it seems that all emotional support and intimacy is to be obtained from consanguines, or from one's spouse.

Robinette Kennedy's (1986) picture of the village of Hatzi in western Crete seems to describe another male-dominated virilocal society, but here there appear to be well-developed ideas of friendship between unrelated women. Kennedy argues that women have important friends who are not otherwise related by kinship or affinity and with whom they share a common predicament: that they married outside their natal village. Although we cannot analyze the data from Hatzi in sufficient detail to make a thorough comparison with the Sarakatsani, we note some contrasting features. The Sarakatsani are separated from unrelated persons by the rigors of a competitive pastoral economy where the requirements of pasture and water make unrelated families into rivals; while Hatzi is a settled village where villagers live by mixed agricultural activities and some craft work, and members of the same sex are offered space to come together outside kinship. If we assume that kinship is organized with the sort of agnatic biases reported by Herzfeld (1985a) for Glendi, we can see that women are dealing with a kinship world already strongly ordered in terms of men valuing men. Perhaps the reported woman-woman friendships are, as Kennedy suggests, countervailing institutions that give women a chance to *choose* a personal relationship based upon trust and without the burdens of kinship and affinal obligation found in an otherwise highly structured and demanding life.

It is partly this kind of explanation that Papataxiarchis in his contribution proposes for the importance of male "friends of the heart" in uxorilocal Mouria. Here, kinship and neighborhood relations are constructed on armatures of matrikin: the most important ties for women are mother-daughter ties. Women in Lesbos see themselves as having all they need of support, relationship, and intimacy from such ties, and as their neighborhoods are likely to include other matrilateral consanguines, individual women live within quite dense, local networks of coresident kin that compete for prestige with other set of matrikin within the wider community. In Lesbos, it is men who find the burdens of affinal membership to some extent oppressive, and in the coffee shop they seek out *unrelated* men as "friends of the heart." Papataxiarchis further places "heart-friendship" in the wider context of ideas about the male person to account for the stress on emotional purity in friendship and its demarcation from exchange. He notices that friendship is linked to an "antistructure" as it is informed by ideas that juxtapose masculinity to both domestic and supradomestic hierarchical structures. We do not suggest, therefore, that the experiences of men in Mouria are similar to those of women in Hatzi, yet in some respects their structural situations and friendship patterns seem symmetrical: same-sex friendship offers the individual means to cope with the structural demands of domestic kinship.

To turn to a neolocal case, in the Cypriot village of Argaki (pseudonym: "Kalo"), married persons of either sex could enter into friendships based on "liking" with unrelated persons of the same sex. This was not perceived as any kind of "betrayal" of kinship or affinity. Kinship in Argaki had been formerly skewed by virilocality toward agnation, yet in 1970, neolocality was common and neighborhoods tended to focus on female kinship ties (Loizos 1975). The demands of affinity itself were much more relaxed than, for example, among the Sarakatsani. However, friends would have had to be highly circumspect if, for example, they wished to make unsecured loans of money, or loans without interest, for kin tended to warn each other against possible "exploitation" (*ekmetalevsis*) by friends (Pitt-Rivers 1971:139). As in Lesbos, there were cliques of men whose drinking, gambling, general conduct, and coffee shop conversation seemed to assert their own spontaneity, generosity, and valuing of friendship. This was notable, since this was a community where people attacked each other by the term *sinferontologi* (pursuers of "selfish" self-interest). Such attitudes can be usefully regarded as a kind of implicit critique of subordination to marriage and its responsibilities. Against them were ranged other men who regarded gambling, heavy drinking, and coffee shop bravado as dangerous luxuries or "uncivilized" behavior.

Friendship, therefore, seems to be linked to marriage in two ways. First, in a negative way: since friendship seems to be expressed outside marriage, it is free of kinship and provides the context in which problems related to conjugality are dealt with. Friendship flourishes best perhaps in territory left uncolonized by householding. The more the values of kinship and marriage prevail and organize extradomestic life, as among the familistic Sarakatsani, the less significant friendship can be. The significant but not elaborated friendships in Argaki available to men, and to women, represent a case in which kinship relaxes enough to leave scope for friendship. Second, structural disadvantage in marriage is also a key factor in the development of same-sex friendship among low class, domestically marginal men in uxorilocal, matrifocal Mouria, and among dislocated, kinless, unmarried women in virilocal Hatzi. Indeed, once space for the development of friendship is available, the greater the disadvantage, the more marked the friendship tends to be.

IDEAS OF GENDER AND KINSHIP OUTSIDE MARRIAGE: CONTESTED MEANINGS AND HETERODOXIES

Our contributors examine representations of gender outside marriage to get at ideas that go beyond gender orthodoxy and vary in degree of discursive clarity and in the subsequent challenge they constitute to the mainstream model. They include fragments of discourse that are established outside marriage yet touch the margins of married life, as well as more elaborated and rooted ideologies that constitute real alternatives for the few who do choose.

In the first category are the fragments of feminist discourse examined by Cowan and the ambiguous semantics of fringe marriage discussed by Zinovieff. Cowan captures the very beginning of an important ideological transformation when the emergence of the new kafeteria discourse is debated. From the viewpoint of those men and women committed to the domestic model, "going out for coffee" means entering a dangerous world where female vulnerability can be exploited, promoting the sensual side of womanhood, and putting conjugal harmony at risk in the pursuit of "pleasure" rather than "duty." A virtuous woman is expected to show no public interest in such a place. For the young enthusiasts of the new institution, having coffee in the kafeteria suggests equality between the sexes, female independence, relaxation and sociability, and an opportunity for a woman to associate with others not in sexual terms, as an object of men's desires, but simply as a "human being." Cowan notices that these perceptions resemble feminist discourse. This emerging ideology of woman as autonomous being, in control of her body, represents a challenge to household-focused representations of womanhood. Zinovieff's analysis suggests similar transformations.

The development of this secular consciousness of womanhood that is juxtaposed to the domestic model while leaving room for the reproduction of kinship leads to a public clash with gender orthodoxy. Of course, this is an aspect of a much wider phenomenon. Expensive coffee shop activity such as drinking and gambling is challenged as endangering the welfare of the household; and nuns' relatives stigmatize those women's decision to enter into partnership with Christ and jeopardize the reproductive ambitions of their natal households. Yet it seems that coffee shop and convent discourses are in retreat while the more "modern" ideas are advancing. It is in the latter case, we believe, that the open contestation can lead to subversion from within, to new synthesis, and indeed can foreshadow significant transformations in the meaning of marriage toward a more "open" type. In this respect, the confrontation of gender meanings might constitute alternative ideologies or separate discursive worlds. However, this is a slow process. In general, women who hold views antithetical to householding can hardly survive in the highly judgmental community of the Greek village. It is the urban, cosmopolitan environment that gives refuge to their desire for autonomy.

At this stage the more comprehensive alternatives are provided by convent and coffee shop. These seem to be fully fledged heterodoxies rather than partial alternatives to the hegemonic model. How are they distinguished as autonomous discursive domains, conceptually demarcated from domestic kinship, and how can we account for the complete opposition they offer? In pursuit of a tentative answer, we consider the articulation of gender and kinship in the anticonjugal discourses of convent and coffee shop.

Du Boulay argues in her contribution that the "other world" of the dead in Greek culture is portrayed as inherently spiritual in composition and sharply opposed to the social world of the living. This aligns with the tendency of other cultures to create constructs in which biological kinship is negated (Bloch 1987). Indeed, a stress on nonmateriality and a distance from domestic kinship seem to characterize the gender domains of convent and coffee shop and to constitute them as "other worlds" within "this world." Otherness in contrast to "married life" draws on the metaphor of spirituality and is conceived in direct opposition to conjugality. The "other worlds" of male coffee shop commensality and female monastic celibacy are removed from, and often in opposition to, domestic life.

Let us start with the convent. From the nuns' point of view, love of offspring and of spouse is a material love that supports procreation and is represented in particularistic linkages symbolized by the material substance of blood. Yet as blood displays a certain mutability (see du Boulay 1984) dependent on conduct, the nuns can envisage the transformation of biological, secular kinship. Nuns go on employing aspects of kinship—for instance, kinship terms—yet as Iossifides notices, they transcend the secular meaning of kinship by applying a code that manifests a spiritual version of love and requires the subordination of body to spirit. First, besides being spiritual in nature, the love of God stresses the common humanity of women, and its sustained application is a condition of women's participation in the divine world and of establishing spiritual linkage to divinity. Salvation rather than procreation is the nun's chief desire. Second, the nuns follow their path to salvation by stressing purity. Attitudes to food are suggestive. Bread should be prepared by a postmenopausal woman; food should be plain, so that it will not excite the taste, and scant to the point of austerity. It should be consumed without conversation, with only readings from the Bible as accompaniment. The strict observance of fasting further disciplines the body. In short, the "suppression" of food parallels the suppression of sexuality. The nuns speak with some intensity of their wish to die sooner rather than later, so that their union with Christ, their life's goal, can be attained more swiftly. This is surely the most dramatic reversal of the conventional desire within the profane community for long life. The nuns wish to leave a world in which biology and sexuality are equated with sinfulness and sickness of the soul. The community constructed in the convent, then, uses the metaphors of kinship and consanguinity only to empty them of their profane meanings, to subvert the flesh by reversal and denial.

Coffee shop discourse, on the other hand, is characterized by a conceptual demarcation and opposition to domestic kinship. The sentiments of male solidarity focus on voluntary, open, deeply egalitarian relatedness that is incompatible with kinship. The very transcendence of reciprocity in "heart-friendship" and the emphasis on sameness, measured in terms of masculine feelings, suggests this incompatibility on a structural level. In coffee shop discourse, furthermore, notions of the household, conjugality, and domestic interest are used as metaphors of calculation and materiality and are found in opposition to the idea of kefi, the spirit of joyful commensality. The coffee shop discourse in this respect is openly antihousehold.

The conceptual demarcation of both convent and coffee shop discourse from the domestic model is certainly linked to the type of relations found in both alternative contexts. Indeed, same-sex relatedness is the rule. This excludes heterosexuality and procreation and contrasts sharply with biological kinship. We shall return to the theme of gender and of sexuality between persons of the same sex in the concluding essay.

In a recent collection on kinship and gender, the editors argue that "gender and kinship are mutually constructed. . . . they are realized together in particular cultural, economic and political systems" (Collier and Yanagisako 1987:7). From the perspective of Greek ethnography, we see that while in certain contexts kinship and gender *are* implicated together as a mixed idiom of domesticity and personhood, in other contexts outside marriage *they are constructed in mutual exclusion and opposition the one to the other*. Within the domestic sphere, kinship implicates gender. Yet in contexts such as the coffee shop or the convent, gender at the symbolic level turns against domestic kinship and the household or into a desexed form of personhood that aims to negate the biological and to transcend it.

ACKNOWLEDGMENTS

This paper has grown out of discussions that were initiated in the symposium "Current Horizons in the Ethnography of Greece" organized by the University of the Aegean. We wish to thank Alexandra Bakalaki, Maurice Bloch, Janet Carsten, Jane Cowan, Jill Dubisch, Chris Fuller, Michael Herzfeld, Lisette Josephides, Roger Just, Jonathan Parry, Maria Phylactou, and Sofka Zinovieff for their suggestions and comments. We also want to thank Jean Canfield and Jenny Ivey for skillfully typing versions of the introductory and concluding essays.

PART I

Gender and Kinship in Married Life

Chapter 1

GENDER, KINSHIP, AND RELIGION: "RECONSTRUCTING" THE ANTHROPOLOGY OF GREECE

JILL DUBISCH

BOTH GENDER STUDIES and feminism have been a powerful force within anthropology in the last decade, and the anthropological study of gender has now received a more or less legitimate place within the field. Yet, like the power of women themselves, the significance of such studies has yet to be fully realized or incorporated within the anthropological enterprise as a whole. There is still a tendency to treat gender as "just another topic" and feminism as "just another point of view" within a larger context still dominated by male discourse. Clifford and Marcus's recent and influential book *Writing Culture*, for example, deliberately excludes feminist perspectives from its collection of essays, an exclusion particularly difficult to comprehend when one reads in a footnote in James Clifford's introduction to the volume that "many of the themes I have been stressing above are supported by recent feminist work" (Clifford 1986:19). An additional observation that "feminism had not contributed much to the theoretical analysis of texts" (20) also seems weak, given the considerable body of feminist work within literary criticism and the supposed influence of literary criticism on the anthropological analysis of ethnographies as texts. Statements such as this illustrate the lack of incorporation of feminism into many theoretical debates within anthropology, as well as the fact that all too commonly the study of gender is seen as simply serving to correct an "absence" (Clifford 1986:18; cf. Strathern 1988:62) and not as a serious challenge to existing ways of thought.[1]

But the task of a feminist anthropology (or at least of an anthropology that takes feminism seriously) is more than simply "filling in the gaps" in the ethnographic record, more than simply paying attention to women's activities or pointing out that women as well as men have goals, exercise power, and make decisions regarding their lives. Important as these tasks

[1] The introduction to the Clifford and Marcus volume is a good example of the view that women are still "the other" and that a representative of this "other" (i.e., a "feminist") must come along, bearing something labeled "feminist analysis" for it to be incorporated (as one other "point of view") in an enterprise such as the one the volume represents.

are, if we limit our inquiry by such parameters, we leave many of the androcentric assumptions and biases of the field intact and fail to realize the theoretical potential that a feminist-informed study of gender holds (cf. Collier and Yanagisako 1987:6).

The revolutionary potential of a feminist perspective has been, in some respects, at least, more explicitly recognized in fields such as literary criticism than it has in anthropology. Jonathan Culler, for example, suggests that "feminist criticism undertakes, through the postulate of a woman reader, to bring about a new experience of reading and to make readers— men and women—question the literary and political assumptions on which their reading is based" (Culler 1983:51). By assuming a female reader, such criticism challenges the idea that the perspective of the male critic is sexually neutral while "a feminist reading is a case of special pleading." "The more convincing its critique of phallic criticism, the more feminism comes to provide the broad and comprehensive vision, analyzing and situating the limited and interested interpretations of male critics. Indeed, at this level one can say that feminist criticism is the name that should be applied to all criticism alert to the critical ramifications of sexual oppression" (55–56). In other words, to the extent that it makes us more conscious of *all* points of view, and, more important, of the fact that all criticism proceeds from *some* point of view, "feminist" criticism becomes the model for criticism itself.

While the methods of literary criticism are not necessarily, or even desirably, transferable to the study of anthropology, what these quotations suggest is the power that a female-centered discourse may have for helping anthropology to "deconstruct" its conceptions of gender and society and for reconstituting them in new and fruitful ways. Specifically, such an approach can challenge male-centered ethnographic constructions of the social order, constructions in which women appear only as a "special case" and/or when they pose "problems" for men (Tiffany 1984; see also Dubisch 1986b; Strathern 1988).

At the same time, as Strathern points out, the study of gender and/or women (not necessarily the same, though the two are often conflated) does not in and of itself entail a feminist approach (Strathern 1988:36). Nor, of course, is there a single feminist approach, in anthropology or any other field. In addition, despite the large number of works dealing with women and gender that have been produced by anthropologists in recent years, the relationship between feminism and anthropology is sometimes an uneasy one. As Strathern puts it, " 'Feminism,' that is, the feminist component of this or that theoretical approach, takes system or structure for granted. It does not pretend to an independent (holistic) theory of society as such. Its ends are not those of representation, and system, being taken for granted, is not replicated as the *aim* of scholarly practice" (1988:25; footnote omitted). For Strathern, "It is in the radical nature of much feminist scholarship that potential lies for anthropological scholarship" (27). On the other hand, Flax, in her analysis of feminism and postmodernism, calls for "locating our theorizing within and drawing more self-consciously upon the wider philosophic contexts of which it is both a part and a critique. In other words, we need to think more about *how* we think about gender relations or any other social relations" (1987:623; emphasis added).

For the anthropologist working in Greece, such observations offer a special challenge, a challenge that results from both the current state of Greek ethnography and the contemporary concerns of the discipline of anthropology as a whole. The anthropology of Greece, as the introduction to this volume points out, is currently in a stage of "rethinking." Anthropologists studying Greek society are forced to face the ethnographic and theoretical problems posed by declining rural communities, the growth of cities, increased anthropological awareness of regional variations within Greece, and (for anthropologists who are not themselves Greek) their own relationship to Greek scholarship and scholars. In addition, much of the current work in Greece seeks to break out of (or at least significantly modify) some of the categories and concepts that have hitherto defined and confined the study of gender and kinship in the past, concepts such as "honor and shame," and "public and private."[2]

These developments, of course, are not unconnected with larger issues within the field of anthropology as a whole. One recent work has labeled the current situation of anthropology an "experimental moment" (Marcus and Fischer 1986). Concerns with interpretation, deconstruction, reflexivity, and writing and texts, as well as the tendency toward the breakdown of traditional disciplinary boundaries with resulting anthropological excursions into literary criticism, philosophy, and social history, have led to confusion about the direction of the field, and sometimes to a sense that all previously agreed-upon paradigms are in a process of collapse, a sense which can produce exhilaration or dismay (or both), depending upon one's point of view.

Thus the task facing anthropologists working in Greece is twofold. First, there is the basically empirical enterprise of discerning and describing the ethnographic variations that occur within Greece, a task which requires not only continuing fieldwork in a variety of communities but also attention to the direction, causes, and consequences of social change and a sharpened sense of the specific problems upon which we need to focus. This enterprise is aided (or perhaps made more complex)

---

[2] For discussions of these issues in the context of Greece, see Danforth (1983); Herzfeld (1980, 1987, 1989); Hirschon (1989).

by the second task, which is the "rethinking" of such categories as kinship
and gender and of the theories we use to analyze them. One catalyst in
such rethinking has been the approach (or approaches) loosely labeled
"interpretative anthropology." Interpretive anthropology, according to
Marcus and Fischer, "operates on two levels simultaneously: it provides
accounts of other worlds from the inside, and reflects about the episte-
mological groundings of such accounts" (1986:26; see also Rabinow and
Sullivan 1979; 1987). This in turn reflects recent postmodern concerns
with "deconstructing" notions of "truth, knowledge, power, the self, and
language that are often taken for granted within and serve as legitimation
for contemporary Western culture" (Flax 1987:624). Within anthropology, postmodernism and deconstruction (along with critical reflexivity,
which I regard as an essential part of both) offer a challenge to existing
paradigms; they can lead to more critical analysis, as well as to new and
fruitful ways of collecting and analyzing the material of our field. Anthropologists studying Greece thus face a dilemma: on the one hand, we need
more data on such topics as kinship and gender roles; on the other hand,
questions have been raised about the categories we use for collecting
such data and the frameworks we employ in analyzing them.

   This paper seeks to explore these issues by using ethnographic material
on gender in Greece in order to suggest some of the ways in which many
of our discussions of social structure, in Greece and elsewhere, are dominated by male or male-centered discourse. Specifically I will be examining the ways in which anthropology sees men as both creating and constituting society, while women are "only" women. My goal is twofold: (1)
to further our understanding of gender and kinship in the Greek context,
and (2) to suggest some of the wider implications of this ethnographic
material for anthropology as a whole. The two areas I will examine are
kinship and religion. (I deliberately avoid stating my goal as the examination of "women in kinship systems," or "woman and religion," for reasons that will become apparent below.) My examination will also include
some discussion of myself and my own fieldwork experiences and their
relationship to a critical understanding, for I believe that reflexivity is
especially important when we are dealing with issues of gender. Not only
does every fieldworker have a gender identity acquired as a member of
her or his own society, but this identity interacts in complex ways with
gender in the society being studied.[3] Such interactions can, when rec-

---

[3] On women's experiences doing fieldwork in Greece, see Clark (1982); Friedl (1970).
Giovannini's (1986) account of fieldwork in a Sicilian town is also of interest here.
   It is interesting to note that it is often assumed (particularly when a male fieldworker is
accompanied by his wife) that women's gender identities have a universal quality, resulting,
presumably, from their assumed common biologically determined nature (Tiffany 1984).

ognized and analyzed, lead to important insights. In addition, female anthropologists must deal with the further complication of their socializa-
tion into a male-dominated field—a field whose views of gender have, in
the past at least, and to some extent in the present as well, been shaped
by male discourse (Tiffany 1984:4).

KINSHIP, GENDER, AND SOCIAL STRUCTURE

There has been an increasing recognition in anthropology that descriptions of kinship systems are generally male-centered.[4] John Campbell's
now-classic discussion of the Greek Sarakatsani shepherds is a good illustration of this. Although he speaks of "the Sarakatsani," Campbell describes the kinship system from a male point of view: "a man's four grandparents," a man's "obligations and interests," the recognition of collateral
relatives in "a man's own generation" (Campbell 1964:36).[5] This does not
mean that Campbell (or other ethnographers writing about Greece and
the Mediterranean) have ignored women in their discussion of kinship
systems—only that men have provided the reference point for analysis.
Women's place in such systems has generally been approached in terms
of their relationships to men. A woman is one man's daughter, another's
sister, another's wife, and finally—and most significantly—she is the
mother of sons. Such analyses may also emphasize the "expressive" role
of women. As Campbell sees it, for example, the mother "expresses the
integrity and solidarity of the group" (1964:165). Campbell's analysis
brings out another feature of many male-centered discussions of kinship:
the paired contrasts male/female::instrumental/expressive::action/senti-
ment. Women play a moral and symbolic role, a role whose "passive"
aspects contrast with the more "active" and "structure-determining"
roles of men. Yet as Campbell himself suggests, it is the mother who is
the pivotal figure in the survival of the extended family, for once the
mother is gone, the extended family does "not survive long" (165). (The
issue of women and "sentiment" will be discussed more fully below.)

In addition, although in many areas of Greece the customary spatial
and temporal arrangements of Greek village life lead to women's spend-

---

Such assumptions may also be shared by our informants, and they are seldom subjected to
critical analysis. On gender "identity" itself as a problematic concept, see Strathern (1988).

[4] See, for example, Gough (1971, 1975).

[5] To be fair to Campbell, he does begin his chapter on kinship by talking of "the blood
kinsmen of a man (or woman)" but then in a footnote adds, "Except where there is ambiguity I shall not repeat this cumbersome qualification" (1964:36). The issue is not so easily
set aside as a mere matter of linguistic convenience, however. The analysis that follows is,
despite occasional qualifications, still male-centered.

ing much of their time with other women,[6] little attention has been given to women's relationships with each other as an important feature of the rural Greek social system.[7] One exception to this occurs, significantly, when relationships between women are a "problem"—that is, in discussions of the conflicts which occur between mother and daughter-in-law in situations of patrilocal residence. Men's relationships with men, on the other hand, relationships often expressed in the "public" context, are more likely to be observed and analyzed, especially by male fieldworkers who may not have easy access to the world of women (see, for example, Herzfeld 1985a; also Brandes 1980).

It might be countered that the situation described above is a result of the ethnographic data themselves, rather than a product of bias on the part of the anthropologist. And it is certainly true, for example, that the relationship between a woman and her mother-in-law can be a source of tension within households, at least in those areas of Greece where patrilocal residence is the norm. But the notion that ethnographic data can be observed in purely "objective" fashion is one which has increasingly come to be questioned by many anthropologists.[8] Reexamination of previously collected bodies of data has highlighted the extent to which the anthropologist's biases can structure the description that he (or she) presents. Kathleen Gough's reanalysis of Evans-Pritchard's material on Nuer kinship, for example, has given us a new view of women's role in Nuer society (Gough 1971). Challenging our own assumptions, then, and trying out different ways of "seeing" offer one kind of "check" on both the collection and analysis of ethnographic material.

One means that has been suggested to overcome a male-centered view of kinship systems is to see women as actors, that is, as individuals who seek in culturally structured ways to achieve desired ends (Rosaldo and Lamphere 1974:9). Such an approach rejects the view of women as interchangeable parts in social systems in which men are the prime movers and decision makers, and it recognizes that women have their own strategies and goals. These individual strategies develop within socially defined contexts.[9] The goals may be collective (for example the advancement of the family—see Salamone and Stanton 1986) or they may be personal (such as the establishment of friendships—see Kennedy 1986).

---

[6] This is not true in all areas of Greece, however. Mari Clark reports that in the village she studied near Methana, men and women spend considerable time together as families (personal communication).

[7] For an exception, see Kennedy (1986).

[8] On critical and reflexive trends in anthropology, see Karp and Kendall (1982); Marcus and Fischer (1986). On Greece, see Herzfeld (1987).

[9] The realization of these goals may sometimes be sought through such means as nagging, gossip, and magic. See Dubisch (1986b) for a discussion.

The strength of an actor-oriented approach (most often utilized in analyses of economic and political activities) is that it grants a "creative" role to women. It also acknowledges the flexibility, open-endedness and negotiability of social rules and the "ambiguity, contradiction and conflict" that Beidelman has suggested are the "essence of social life" (Beidelman 1980:30). Therefore it has been important in helping to "fill in the gaps" and in changing to some extent the way that anthropologists perceive women (and for that matter, men) in society. But such an approach can also reinforce some of the biases inherent in the study of kinship and gender. An actor-oriented approach sets up a contrast between system and action: the social system is often seen as defined and/or shaped by men, and, within this system, women act (or react). Though women's actions are shaped and made predictable by this system, these actions are often portrayed in ethnographic accounts as personal, and to some extent idiosyncratic, rather than as creating or constituting the system itself. (Or if they are so viewed, it is often in a passive sense, as in the "exchange" of women in which men have the active and creative role.) Rethinking our ideas about gender and structure, then, requires moving beyond an actor-oriented approach (whether "unisex"—though usually this means "male"—or focused on women) and questioning some of the more general concepts upon which ethnographic description rests.

WOMAN IN THE FIELD

I myself first began to question the standard ethnographic descriptions of women during my initial fieldwork experience in Greece.[10] I arrived in Greece in 1969, settling into a small village on the Aegean island of Tinos to do research for my doctoral dissertation. I was twenty-six years old at the time and newly married. The study of women as a topic within anthropology had barely begun. In fact, I had difficulty defending my research subject (the thesis that women in rural Greece might hold values and views of their social system which differed from those of men) to my (all male) department at the University of Chicago. I thus arrived in Greece with a dual set of expectations. The first—derived from my reading and reinforced by the responses of my department to my proposal—was that I would find a society in which women led restricted lives and in which they acquiesced to the general societal judgment regarding their weaker and less worthy nature. The other—the expectation that had led me to formulate my proposal—was that behind this facade of repression,

[10] Field research for my dissertation was carried out in 1969–1970 under a fellowship and grant from the National Institute of Mental Health. The dissertation itself was on migration (Dubisch 1972), but my interest in gender has since led to several other publications on that topic (Dubisch 1974, 1983, 1986a).

I would find another world, one more clearly and positively shaped by the women themselves. Not surprisingly, I found neither of these expectations to be entirely true.

From the beginning of our stay in the village, women were the main instigators of our social contacts and significant sources of information about village life. During the day, while the men were in the fields or working at jobs outside the village, the village was populated mainly by women. Women would invite us into their houses as we strolled through the streets. Over the requisite trappings of hospitality—coffee, *gliko* (fruit jam), cookies—they would seek, with polite determination, to draw us out: Who were we? Who were our families? Why were we in the village? How long had we been married? Did we have any children? And so on. Then, often without questioning on my part, they volunteered information about their own families, showing me photographs of their children, siblings, and parents, telling me which ones were married, which lived in Athens, what work they did. It did not take me long to realize that far from being the modest retiring creatures some of my reading had led me to believe they would be, most of these women were strong and lively and forward. They scolded and nagged their husbands, made jokes about sexual matters, and confidently took charge of household affairs.

I learned several things from these interactions, and I learned them as much from the questions the women asked me as from what I asked them. For it was through the nature of the questions themselves—questions about my family, my husband, children—that women revealed to me what they considered the most important features of social life. And in addition I learned that these women, the important instigators and maintainers of social contacts, felt sorry for me. I was young, childless, and far from home. But most of all, I was a long way from my mother. "Don't you miss your mother?" I was frequently asked. They never asked about my father (except occasionally to inquire what he did for a living), nor did they seem concerned that my husband might miss his mother as well.

VILLAGE KINSHIP: THE MOTHER-DAUGHTER TIE

As I was introduced to, and guided through, village social life by these women, I observed that much of the daily functioning of such social life depended upon them. Residence in this village was generally neolocal, and there was no consistent pattern of village endogamy or exogamy (cf. Friedl 1962), so that mothers and daughters often remained in the same community. Women ideally received a house as a dowry, though whether or not this occurred in particular cases depended on a family's resources.

If a married couple was unable to have their own house, they generally moved in with the wife's parents. The only cases I found of patrilocal residence involved young women who came from other villages on the island or from other areas of Greece, that is, women who had married exogamously into the village (cf. Casselberry and Valavanes 1976).

What struck me in particular was the strong tie between mother and daughter, a relationship I had not seen discussed in the ethnographic literature on Greece.[11] When I probed villagers about the preferred sex of a child, a not uncommon response was "A boy for the father, a girl for the mother." The first daughter was customarily named after the mother's mother, the second after the father's mother, a common pattern in the Cycladic Islands (cf. Hoffman 1976; Kenna 1976a). The daughter learned the tasks essential to her future role from her mother and grandmother, and began at an early age to help around the house. Later, when the daughter had her own household, she would still return to her mother for aid when she needed it. Unless she migrated to Athens, a girl remained with her mother until she married, and a youngest daughter might be retained in the maternal household a little longer than the others, her mother reluctant to let her go. A son, on the other hand, usually broke his ties to his mother to some extent when he did military service. Even if he returned to his mother's house after that, mother and son were never quite as close. When a woman and her married daughter lived in the same village, there was frequent visiting back and forth. With the birth of the daughter's children, the bond between mother and daughter took on a further dimension. Especially strong ties could develop with a daughter's daughter, and there were several young village girls I learned to associate with their grandmothers before I met their mothers, so much time did the child and the older woman spend together. Children living in Athens were often sent to the village to visit their grandparents, and in my current research at the Church of the Annunciation at Tinos, I have noticed many instances of grandmothers visiting the shrine with a grandchild. Because women were the major agents of social interaction between families, they exerted a matrilateral influence on the interaction of kin in a system usually described as formally bilateral, or (in some regions at least) with tendencies toward patrilineality. This "matrilateral bias" became most apparent in situations of migration. When a woman who had migrated to Athens married a man from another part of Greece, ties were more likely to be maintained with her own community than with his. Such ties included visiting the village reg-

[11] Some of the material on the mother-daughter tie was originally developed in a paper entitled "The Mother-Daughter Tie in Mediterranean Social Structure," presented at the American Anthropological Association meetings, Houston, Texas, 1976.

ularly and perhaps retaining or buying a house there. Village men in Athens married to nonvillage women, on the other hand, were more likely to find themselves visiting their wives' home communities. The fact that women were usually freer than their husbands to leave Athens, and to take their children for long visits at their mothers' houses in the village, added further reinforcement to such ties. In such situations, then, the combination of the institution of the dowry house, the importance of the mother-daughter tie, and women's role in arranging social interactions led to migrant women's retaining, and being retained by, their home community to a greater extent than were men. And in all cases of migration, it was the women of the family who made arrangements for visiting, sent food and other gifts back and forth, made telephone calls and sent letters, and took charge of the ceremonial events (such as baptisms and memorial services) that helped keep migrants tied to village life.

"Kin Work": Structure and Sentiment in Village Life

Micaela di Leonardo has given a name to activities such as those described above. She calls them "kin work." In a study of American families, di Leonardo found that kin work, the tasks that sustain family networks, is, like housework, a woman's task. And it is this contact across households that fulfills American expectations of family life. But because there is a tendency to emphasize "individual women's responsibilities within households and on the job, we reflect the common picture of households as nuclear units, tied perhaps to the larger social and economic system but not to each other" (1987). There are two important implications to this. One is that this view of households as independent units obscures an important female role. The other is that we construct that view a certain way precisely because we do not see women as constituting part of the interconnecting "system."

What I would like to suggest is that di Leonardo's concept of kin work can also be applied to Greece, where women often play an important role as the organizers of social interactions between families.[12] The relationship between mother and daughter is pivotal in kin work, serving to socialize a woman into such work, and providing a major linkage that such work maintains.

There has been a tendency in the ethnography of Greece to present the mother-daughter relationship as simply an emotional one (see, for example, Friedl 1962:54), or in terms of "honor and shame," emphasizing the inheritance of *dropi* (the sense of "shame") from mother to daughter

---

[12] The nature and extent of women's kin work appear to vary somewhat from one region of Greece to another.

(see, for example, Campbell 1964). If we confine our analysis of the relationships between women (in Greece or elsewhere) only to this, we
perpetuate an ideology of gender that sees women and their relationships
as "natural," bound by feelings, and in some sense "passive," while men
and their relationships are "cultural," constituting structure, resulting
from action (see Ortner 1974; also Ortner and Whitehead 1981; Mac-
Cormack and Strathern 1980). Since "sentiment" carries the connotation
of something "inferior" (and indeed "womanish" in the denigrating sense
of the term), we are led into a circular reasoning that equates women and
feeling, seeing the one wherever the other exists and thus relegating
both to outside the system, connected to it only through men (cf. Tompkins 1981).

In addition, the universality of biological maternity has often led us to
see "motherhood" as both universal and natural (an assumption that may
be shared by our informants) and to overlook or downplay the ways in
which, in all societies, it is culturally constituted. This is reinforced by
the Western view of emotions as "natural," a notion increasingly subject
to challenge. As Catherine Lutz puts it, "At first blush, nothing might
appear more natural and hence less cultural than emotions. . . . These
views can be treated, however, as items in a cultural discourse whose
traditional assumptions about human nature . . . constitute what we take
to be the self-evident nature of emotion" (Lutz 1988:3).

This view has implications for anthropological theories of kinship,
which, as Collier and Yanagisako point out in their critique of gender and
kinship, commonly have proceeded from a contrast between the domestic and the politico-jural domains, the former invariant and "built upon
the affective ties and moral sanctions of the mother-child bond" (Collier
and Yanagisako 1987:4). This bond is assumed to be "everywhere constrained by affective and moral convictions generated by the universal
experience of 'mothering' necessary for the biological survival of helpless
infants" (5; reference omitted).

My own analysis of the mother-daughter tie suggests that rather than
seeing such a tie as "natural" and arising out of "sentiment," we must
consider the ways in which both the relationship and the emotions associated with it are culturally constructed and determined. I propose that
as an alternative to the "sentimental" view of the mother-daughter tie,
we view the relationship as pivotal in the structuring of the kinship system, at least in certain areas of Greece (and the kinship system itself as
an important part of social structure).[13] This tie is not "simply" "personal"

---

[13] Some of the islands, in particular, seem to have more strongly "female-centered" kinship systems. I consider other ties with female kin (i.e., with the mother's mother, with
sisters, and with sisters' children) as stemming structurally from the mother-daughter tie.

and a consequence of "natural" affection but is culturally constructed and bears a structural significance which may be equal to (if not in some respects greater than) that of relationships between men.[14] Moreover, if kinship relationships are not seen as confined to the domestic unit alone (as there has sometimes been a tendency to see them in the ethnography of Greece), then the broader role of women in kinship structures becomes more clear. Or, to phrase it in terms of the arguments being presented here, our conceptions of what comprises the kinship structure change precisely because we view women's interactions with other women not as somehow "within" the system but as constitutive of the system. And if sentiment is the personal experience of socially structured relationships, then the implicit contrast of sentiment and structure (the personal and the social) is no longer convincing. Lines of "sentiment" must be seen as lines of "structure." In such a context, it becomes clear that the village women's observations that I must miss my mother were not expressions of "natural" sentiment (and hence, by implication, universal) but rather statements about what they considered a central social relationship and the (socially appropriate) feelings assumed to be associated with it. Not to have my mother with me was to be truly socially displaced.[15]

Additionally, the emotional is generally associated with the private (see Lutz 1988:3). Thus part of the failure to take women seriously as centers and organizers of social systems may be a result of the tendency to focus on the public realm as the source of power in social life (cf. Friedl 1986 [1967]). Since domestic life tends to be devalued in Western society, and since there is a tendency both to separate the domestic from the "real" social world and to perceive the domestic world as in some sense "natural" and unproblematic, the significance of women's "domestic" roles for the society as a whole may be overlooked.[16]

My experiences with Greek women during fieldwork thus led me not simply to an expanded conception of the role of women in village social life, but to a rethinking of the ways in which we define and analyze social systems themselves. This rethinking is further illustrated by some more recent observations on women and religion in Greece.

Whether this can be considered a valid assumption will need to be decided by future research.

[14] We cannot know this with certainty, of course, until we begin to apply to Greek kinship some of the perspectives I have suggested here.

[15] It is interesting to compare this to Abu-Lughod's discussion of how her father accompanied her on her first visit to her field site among the Bedouin. His presence proved that she came from a respectable family which cared about her, and thus allowed her to be appropriately socially "placed" (Abu-Lughod 1987).

[16] The anthropological debate over this issue has produced an extensive literature. For a recent general discussion, see Strathern (1988); on Greece, see Herzfeld (1987).

WOMEN AS "FOLK": DEFINING RELIGION IN GREECE

Studies of the relationship between religion and gender roles have generally focused on the part that religion plays in defining and justifying these roles (e.g., Sanday 1981) and/or the roles that women play within specific religious traditions (e.g., Hoch-Smith and Spring 1978; Holden 1983). As the Introduction to this volume points out, consideration of the Orthodox Church's views on gender and sexuality is an important starting point for discussions of both gender and religion in Greece. In the ethnographic accounts, women's relationship to the Orthodox religion has been portrayed in a variety of sometimes conflicting ways. For example, although Campbell discusses the role of the *Panayia* (Madonna) as a model for the female role, his description of religion among the Sarakatsani proceeds almost entirely from a male point of view.[17] Susanna Hoffman (1976) suggests that in Greece women and religion are almost antithetical to each other. Juliet du Boulay, on the other hand, who sees religion as indispensible in our understanding of gender roles in Greece, views women as associated with both Eve and the Panayia, who represent, respectively, the two poles of feminine character (du Boulay 1986). Danforth has pointed out that women are the main performers in ritual and other duties toward the dead (Danforth and Tsiaras 1982), and in my own fieldwork experience, I noted that village women had other important religious duties as well, duties which only they could fulfill. Women light the oil lamps in front of the family icons, pray for their children, care for churches and graves, and in general connect their families to the spiritual world (Dubisch 1983, 1989; see also Hirschon 1983, 1989).

During more recent research at the Church of the Madonna of the Annunciation (*Evangelistria*) on the island of Tinos,[18] the home of a famous miracle-working icon, I came to further consideration of the relationship between gender and religion. The church draws thousands of pilgrims each year, the majority of them women. These women come to pay their respects to the Panayia, to request her help, and to fulfill vows. They bring with them all manner of offerings, not the least of which is themselves. Some women walk barefoot all or part of the way to the church, while others crawl the entire distance on their knees, sometimes carrying a child on their backs. They bring candles, flowers, icons, oil, and items they have embroidered or crocheted. On busy days they fill the church, filing by the icon of the Panayia, kneeling in front of the icon

[17] Again, this is not meant to imply that Campbell does not include women in his discussion of religion, only that the discussion is presented in terms of a male subject.

[18] Research at the Church of the Annunciation on Tinos was carried out in 1986 and 1987 under a research grant from the Fulbright Foundation and a Faculty Research Grant from the University of North Carolina at Charlotte and the UNCC Foundation.

to pray, resting and sleeping in the courtyard of the church. There are young women and old ones. They come singly, with their families, in organized groups. And they come to pay their respects to a female figure, the Panayia, who is not only all holy and the mother of God (*Theotokos*), but, at this church in particular, a symbol of the nation of Greece itself, since the miraculous icon was purportedly discovered during the turbulent years of the Greek struggle for independence (see Dubisch 1988, 1990).

Thus although the church hierarchy is male, and the formal, prescribed rituals in church are carried out by men, most of the on-going religious activity outside church (in houses, at grave sites, on the pilgrimage journey), as well as certain activities conducted within churches (maintenance of shrines, individual devotions and offerings), are carried out by women, giving religious practice in Greece a "feminine" cast.

The greater participation of women in religion and the predominance of Mary in worship have been noted in other parts of the Mediterranean as well. One explanation which has been suggested for this phenomenon is that women find in Mary an appropriate model for emulation, one which, with its emphasis on purity and motherhood, accords with their own social roles. Hence religious participation not only is congruent with those roles but enhances them as well (cf. Dubisch 1987). There is, however, no parallel religious figure to draw men. While women can identify with Mary and her suffering as a mother, Christ's virtues are not necessarily those associated with the ideal masculine role (Campbell 1964; for a different view, however, see Herzfeld 1985a). In addition, the church's attempt to exercise restraints on sexuality, the institution of confession, and the necessity to submit to the authority of the priest, it has been argued, all combine to keep men away from church, both in Greece and in other parts of the Mediterranean as well (see Brandes 1980; Campbell 1964; Christian 1972; Herzfeld 1986).

Despite this "feminine" cast to religion in daily life, however, religion in Greece, like kinship, is usually portrayed as a male system, a system by which women are constrained and within which women act, but one nonetheless that they do not help to define or create. Within such a framework, discussions of women's religious activities expand our understanding of women's roles—thereby "filling in the gaps"—but do not radically alter our conception of the system itself. In defense, it can be argued that the church hierarchy (in both Catholic and Orthodox countries) is, after all, male, and that male priests control the key rituals such as communion, baptism, and marriage upon which the religion rests. Here, again, however, we may be falling into circularity by beginning with a male-centered framework of analysis and hence concluding with one as well. Not only do women not always agree with everything the male-dominated religion teaches them (see, for example, Caraveli 1986), but to the women who perform them, their own ritual activities are an essential part of their religion, for upon these rituals the health and well-being of their families, as well as the welfare of the dead, depend. In addition, women are responsible for many of the nonsacred aspects (food preparation, cleaning, etc.) of holiday celebrations such as Easter, and it is their work that gives these celebrations much of their richness and tone. Women's activities in this respect are a kind of spiritual equivalent of kin work (see, for example, Lobel 1985). But precisely because they are *women's* activities, and because they are perceived as "domestic," they are presented as "within," or peripheral or complementary to, a system that is, implicitly or explicitly, structured by men.[19]

It is particularly curious that this should be so in the area of religion, for the anthropological study of religion in state societies has long taken as a basic starting point for analysis the distinction between official religion and the religion of the "folk," between the "Great Tradition" and the "Little Tradition."[20] In such analysis, local systems of religion are analyzed *as* systems, even when they are located "within" a church hierarchy that has technical authority to perform rituals and define belief. In the ethnography of Europe there exists a large body of literature that explores the complex relationship between these local systems and higher structures of authority, both contemporaneously and historically.[21] Why then, do we not portray "folk" or popular religion in Greece as a predominantly female activity, conducted and to some extent created by women, contrasting in important respects with the male-dominated official church? If religious activities are the spiritual equivalent of kin work, serving to connect the social units of this world to the next (just as ties among women define and connect families), the idea begins to make a considerable amount of sense.

At the same time, we must be careful not to let such an analysis lead us back into the very trap I have suggested that a serious and radical concern with gender should lead us to avoid. The notion of "folk" or "popular" religion implicitly prioritizes, and the view of Greek women as principally responsible for the activities of "folk" religion carries the danger of placing women once more "inside," constrained by a male structure, in this case the church. So perhaps a better way of stating the implications of what I am suggesting here is that we should examine how

[19] For a discussion of women's "extra-domestic" ritual roles, and for somewhat differing views on whether they are an extension of domestic roles, see Hirschon (1983, 1989); Danforth and Tsiaras (1982).

[20] These terms are usually associated with Redfield (1960). For an analysis of popular religion in Greece that includes a discussion of women's activities, see Dubisch (1990).

[21] See, for example, William Christian's work (1972, 1981, 1984).

analysis of gender and religion leads to "deconstruction" of the very notion of religion itself, to a focus on practice and experience, and to a critical reanalysis of a folk/official dichotomy.

GENDER AS CRITIQUE: IMPLICATIONS FOR THE ANTHROPOLOGY OF GREECE

This paper has sought to suggest some of the ways that the study of gender can do more than "fill in the gaps" in a hitherto incomplete ethnographic record. Rather, such study can change the very way we construct our subject matter. This in turn carries important implications for future research, as well as for the conclusions that have been drawn from research done in the past. An example of this "deconstruction" (or, perhaps more appropriately, "reconstruction") can be seen in the changing view within gender studies of the public/private distinction. This distinction, while initially offering a fruitful approach for the analysis of gender and power (see, for example, Rosaldo 1974), has now come to be seen as a stumbling block to a more complex understanding of both kinship and gender roles (see especially Collier and Yanagisako 1987). I have suggested here, for example, some of the ways in which ideas about public and private may lead us to overlook the structural significance of kin work. As another example, we might consider the way in which men's activities in the public arena, in Greece and in other societies, are often taken as demonstrations of male power and the importance of men's activities. But if we follow Friedl's suggestion that we look beyond the appearance of prestige to the realities of power (Friedl 1986 [1967]), we are led to a different perspective, one which suggests that men's public performances, rather than being an indication of their power, may be a manifestation of their lack of power in a central institution of social life, that is, within the domestic realm. This view has been expressed by anthropologists working in Spain (Driessen 1983), France (Reiter 1975), Portugal (Pina-Cabral 1986), and Greece (Papataxiarchis 1988). Men's claims to power, and the seeming acquiescence of women in such claims, can be viewed as a kind of "agreement" between the sexes, in which power is—to use Friedl's terms—traded for prestige (Rogers 1975).[22] These studies also suggest that such public activities represent men's marginal position vis-à-vis the larger society (reminding us that gender roles need to be considered in the context of class as well).

Beyond this, however, the study of gender offers a further challenge, a challenge to the categories themselves. Rather than assuming the dis-

---

[22] For a revised analysis, see Rogers's 1985 article. For a psychological perspective on this issue, see Gilmore (1985, 1987b).

tinction between public and private realms, and then trying to assess the relative influence of the sexes in each, anthropologists are increasingly coming to question the very concepts, as well as their isomorphism with gender roles (see Collier and Yanagisako 1987; Dubisch 1983, 1987; Herzfeld 1986; Hirschon 1983; Strathern 1988). Our past thinking on this matter has proved to be somewhat tautological, denying the public aspects of women's roles since by definition "public" means men. Thus men gathered together in the *kafenio* are "public," while women on a pilgrimage together or gathered in a church are not (Constantinides 1977; Dubisch 1987).

When we begin to move away from male-dominated discourse, we are confronted with an irony, since such a movement leads us to pay more attention to Greek *men's* domestic roles.[23] This is because once we cease to see men "as free from or as not determined by gender relations" (Flax 1987:629)—and cease to view their position in society as taken-for-granted, and unproblematic, with women as a "problem" or "special case"—we are led to reexamine certain aspects of masculinity and male roles. In fact this is a necessary consequence if we are to do more than simply "fill in the gaps" by adding women to our analysis. For example, many ethnographers have emphasized the significance of marriage for women, since it provides them with their most important social role as wives and mothers, and the means through which they fulfill their "destiny" (du Boulay 1986). Little attention, however, has been given to the role that marriage plays for men. And yet it is obvious that a Greek man cannot achieve full adult status until he is married.[24] In a sense, then, it is through his connection to a woman that a man takes his place in society. It is his "destiny" also to be married. And even though this "destiny" is not quite the same for a man as for a woman, the fact that the role of marriage for men is seldom stressed in the ethnographic literature on Greece suggests something about the way we look at systems of marriage and kinship. In fact, men are tied to the social system through women, as are women through men. It is in a sense by the joining of the "public" and the "domestic" that individuals—and society—become complete. Or, more accurately, "public" and "private" become not separate realms

[23] A feminist perspective does not necessarily in and of itself lead to this, however. As Flax points out, "To the extent that feminist discourse defines its problematic as 'woman,' it, too, ironically privileges the man as unproblematic" (Flax 1987:629).

[24] I encountered a number of examples of this during fieldwork: a middle-aged man much pitied because he had chosen to forsake marriage in order to care for his elderly parents, a retarded man who received the joking toast "to your wedding" (the joke being that since he was not really a fully adult man, he couldn't get married), teasing (but nonetheless serious) admonitions to young men about getting married. Even today, most young people set up independent households only upon marriage, and marriage remains a general expectation for both women and men.

isomorphic with male and female, but aspects of both men's and women's roles, structured in important ways by the activities of both.

The study of gender, then, does not (or at least should not) simply lead us to knowing more about women. By drawing anthropology away from male-centered discourse, examinations of gender can lead us to knowing more about men as well, and to a rethinking of some of our basic concepts such as gender, kinship, and religion. No longer should we speak of "women and religion" or "women's role in kinship systems," implicitly setting women in opposition to, or outside, these systems even as we purport to analyze their place within them. Rather, our notions of these systems should be based on women's activities and viewpoints as well as on men's, in recognition of the fact that men and women need to be seen both as equally basic and as equally problematic in our analysis.

Such rethinking, however, requires self-understanding. We need to be aware not only of the consequences of our own culturally determined gender identities (indeed of our very concept of "gender identity" itself),[25] but also of the biases inherent in our own scholarly traditions and of the historical and political contexts from which they spring. In addition, we need to confront our personal feelings about gender roles. Because gender roles are assigned to us from birth, and because they acquire an intrinsic quality, we have tended to perceive gender roles as "natural" and women as "especially" natural.[26] Precisely, then, because gender plays such a central role for those of us who study it—personally, socially, and ideologically—once we begin to wrestle with these issues, we find ourselves confronting some of the central problems of our discipline.

ACKNOWLEDGMENTS

I would like to thank Raymond Michalowski, Deanna Trakas, Akis Papataxiarchis, Mari Clark, and Michael Herzfeld for their very helpful comments on earlier drafts of this paper. I would also like to thank Akis Papataxiarchis for several stimulating conversations upon which this paper has drawn. Responsibility for the views expressed here is, of course, entirely my own. In addition, I would like to express my appreciation to the Foundation of the University of North Carolina at Charlotte and the Faculty Grants Committee and to the Fulbright Program for their sponsorship of my recent research in Greece.

[25] For a discussion of this, see Strathern (1988).

[26] I am using "we" here to refer to anthropologists in the Western, but particularly Anglo-American, context.

Chapter 2

COSMOS AND GENDER IN VILLAGE GREECE

Juliet du Boulay

INCREASING INTEREST in gender studies in Greece is stimulating research into aspects of the belief system which lie behind the traditional division of labor in the house and family. Recently, for instance, it has been argued that ideas of female physiology lie behind the customs governing the restraints put on women (Hirschon 1978). Theological ideas have been suggested as significant in that women, linked to the body of the Church (Rushton 1983), and to the Mother of God (du Boulay 1986), are ascribed an enormous redemptive potential which is part of their role as guardians of the spiritual life. Political aspects of gender are revealed in the argument that women's submission within the household is an image of the submission to the structures of the state which is demanded of everyone in the political and economic world, so that even while the house provides a refuge for its members from the public domain, it also provides a model of the obedience to hierarchy which makes them servants within that domain (Dimen 1986). And in the case of men, male identity among the Cretan shepherds has been analyzed as being the consequence of a rhetoric which defines the true man as being both the exemplar and the iconoclast of national virtues (Herzfeld 1986).

Inevitably, in this climate, and in the context of feminism, the question has arisen whether the submissive feminine role in certain Christian cultures is supported by elements of the cosmology. Thus in the wider field of feminist studies, attention has been drawn to the male gender terminology used for the Godhead in the Christian Church (Pagels 1979), and the phrase "male God" figures in a discussion of the hierarchy repressing girls in an English private school (Okely 1978).

In this paper, therefore, I attempt to address a few of the cosmological issues involved in Greek village ideas of gender. These are: how far Greek villagers conceive God and Christ in gender terms; whether they conceive the natural world (insofar as it is separable from God) in such terms; and what relation can be discerned between the divine and natural attributes revealed in the answer to the first two questions, and the construction of gender in social life. The emphasis in this latter section is particularly on death—a focus relating this analysis to recent work in Africa, Asia, and elsewhere, which has suggested that mourning not only reconstructs the cosmic order and reaffirms its authority, but does this through images of gender which associate women, the flesh, and pollution in opposition to that order (Bloch and Parry 1982). The cosmological focus of this paper necessitates at certain points reference to parallels with village thinking in Orthodox theology, and, without disturbing unduly the flow of the argument, I have sought to distinguish these points in the text, together with points where other interpretive comment is made.

The evidence given below comes from the village of Ambeli in North Euboea (du Boulay 1974) and was gathered during two periods of fieldwork, 1966–1968 and 1970–1973, although my last visit to the village was in 1980 and contact by letter and telephone has continued since. Changes in Ambeliot thinking recorded during the periods of fieldwork and afterward, are noted in the text, but since for the most part the village population is still made up of those who were householders during these periods of fieldwork—the younger people having moved away as they married—the rest of the text is written in the ethnographic present.[1]

THE VILLAGERS' PERCEPTION OF GOD

In Ambeli, the word *Theos* is the name for God most constantly on the lips of the villagers, especially in such formulaic expressions as "If God wills" (*ean thelei o Theos*), and "God first" (*prot' o Theos*, an expression which has the same meaning), which so often accompany the expression of desires and hopes about the future. These expressions emphasize

---

[1] The question has been raised (Davis 1987a:12–13) whether in the present climate of social change the use of the ethnographic present for fieldwork some years in the past is any longer appropriate. Problems and possible anachronisms are involved in the use of both the present tense and the aorist, for both carry unintended inferences—in the first case of stability, in the second case of definitive change—and these inferences of necessity fall outside the scope of the evidence contained in the fieldwork and cannot always be verified. In this paper I write about the same generations of people who even in the present day still form the majority of the village population, and the subject concerns not swiftly changing economic or political circumstances, but relatively fundamental categories of thought. Some change in these people's thinking on these subjects had certainly occurred before and during my fieldwork, and some will certainly have occurred in recent years, but the exact degree and nature of this kind of change is always ambiguous—as illustrated by the comment of an old woman to whom I once expressed surprise on hearing her say (contrary to her previous opinion) that men had landed on the moon: "With my lips I say it but I don't believe." The inner logic of the world in which she and others like her have lived their lives is the subject of this paper, and because this world, although increasingly fragmented and interspersed with parallel or contrary Westernizing notions, still in many respects lives on, the use of the ethnographic present is for the most part less misleading than the innovative use of the ethnographic past, with its implications of a world which has entirely gone. The basic use of the present also permits a wider range of past tenses to be used in marking successive changes.

God's active will—"God doesn't allow you to be lost" (*o Theos dhen se hanei*), and "He who goes with God makes progress" (*opoios paei me ton Theo proodhevei*); and this active will is felt not only in mercy but in judgment also: "God is punishing us" (*o Theos mas timoraei*) or "God is trying us" (*o Theos mas vasanizei*).

God is not, however, thought of only as a being who acts on the social world, helping or punishing; he is the creator of all things, and as such he "holds" (*echei*) the entire creation. The term "holds" in this context is untranslatable by any single English term, for it combines the senses of God "upholding," "shaping," "containing," or "constraining" everything that exists. Thus from the existence of the Devil "contained" by God (*ton echei o Theos*), and the predilection of men for fighting and killing one another—"That is how God shapes us" (*etsi mas echei o Theos*)—to the particular natures of different creatures and the characters of plants and herbs, all things are "from God" (*ap' ton Theo*). The nature of man's life on the land is divinely ordained—"This is how God shapes us, to struggle" (*etsi mas echei o Theos, na agonisoume*); the fate of the Christmas pig is from God—"Much food and few days, that's how God has shaped him"; and the properties of the smallest object, or the least substance or implement used in spells, are "upheld by God" (*ta echei o Theos*) who gives to the entire natural world its character and its being. Indeed God's energy invests this world in every way: thus instead of saying, "It is raining" (*vrechei*; or *richnei*, lit., "It is hurling down"), it is as natural for the villagers to remark, "God is raining" (*vrechei o Theos*); and in folktales the break of each new dawn is presented as an inevitable but miraculous phenomenon in the time-honored formula: "God gave the day" (*edhoke o Theos tin imera*).

The term *Theos*, however, is not the only one used to designate God, and two other commonly used expressions are the "All Powerful" (*Pandodhynamos*), and the "Higher Power" (*Anoteri Dhynami*). These are phrases familiar to every villager, but they are mysterious, and they are not charged with the definite, active attributes of the term *Theos*. Thus the All Powerful, or the Higher Power, tends to be referred to in contexts in which God is contemplated as the underlying creative source giving form and life to the "natural world" (*physis*). In order to argue the existence of God it was enough for the priest, a villager himself, to sweep his arm to indicate the ripened lentils, the white limestone mountaintops and the blue distances, and to say, "Here you see many living things" (*zondana pragmata*). And it is with this sense of the mysterious existence of life in the world that villagers will refer to the Higher Power. In this aspect, God is not seen in terms of specific actions or attributes, but is said simply to "exist," to "be" (*uparchei*). Thus while *Theos* is that aspect of the deity which governs the minutest detail of the natural world and of every man's life and character, the *Pandodhynamos* refers to that aspect of God so limitless and unfathomable that its only definition is that it "is," and empowers all things. And that such a distinction between the revealed action and the inner being of God is indeed being made by the villagers is demonstrated by the fact that among those, particularly from among returned migrants or those with higher education, who doubt the existence of God and of Christ, of the Mother of God and of the "other world" (*allos cosmos*), I never heard one who did not admit to some belief that of course "there exists a Higher Power" (*uparchei anoteri dhynami*).

There appear, then, to be various terms for God in use by the villagers, which emphasize both an active and immanent, and an essential and transcendent, nature. But none of these terms imply gender. However, God is of course also known as "Father," and this term needs to be considered carefully.

It is perhaps significant that, in my experience, the term *Father (Pateras)* is never used by the villagers to designate God except in the context of the Liturgy, and of the Lord's Prayer (*Pater Imon*). The recurring doxologies in the Liturgy each Sunday have as their refrain ". . . to Thee we ascribe glory, to the Father and to the Son and to the Holy Spirit, now and ever and to the ages of ages"; and the Creed, which comes immediately before the consecration of the holy gifts, narrates the same Trinitarian revelation. But I did not hear these terms used in the ordinary contexts of village life, but only the Pater Imon, the Our Father—a prayer which is thought of as a powerful apotropaic in situations of sudden, and especially spiritual, danger.

In the Liturgy the Our Father is given a place of great significance immediately after the consecration of the holy gifts—a moment so charged with sanctity that during those few moments many villagers prostrate themselves—and before communion. Up to this point God has only been addressed in terms such as "Lord" which emphasize his majesty, but at this decisive moment he is asked to "count us worthy with boldness, and unrebuked, to dare call upon thee, God of heaven, as our Father," after which the Lord's Prayer is said, and the priest's communion is taken—a moment which leads on to the communion of the people, although in the village the people in fact receive communion only very rarely. Thus the distant glory of the All Powerful is suddenly brought into the intimacy of fatherhood through the incorporation of the villagers with Christ in the consecration and partaking of the holy gifts. It is, therefore, in keeping with this particular liturgical significance that the Our Father has an especial quality in village life as a protection against evil. But here too it is not the engendered but the nurturant aspect of fatherhood which is invoked—God as the loving figure who will save his children from the snares of the Devil.

The names of God, then, seem in the village mind to be the attributes of a both immanent and transcendent power which is beyond gender but which, made familiar and intimate in the Liturgy, acquires the male name of "Father" in default of an alternative image which would better express the same mystical relationships. Rather than in terms of gender, the villagers refer primarily to God in terms either of his actions or of his mysterious being, and except in the minds of the few modernizing skeptics mentioned above, there is no real separation between the ways of naming God which these two understandings entail. The village insistence is, in fact, that God is "One," and this description given to me by more than one villager in conversation is repeated in the stanza, combining both types of name for God, which I heard repeatedly sung by a group of women from a neighboring village, as they were walking over the mountains bringing with them the relics of a local saint: "God is One, the great Power, the Lord have mercy upon us" (*Enas einai o Theos, o Megalo dhynamos, Kyrie eleison*).

If this can be said of God, however, what can be said of Christ who came to earth as a man, and who himself gave us the imagery of Father and Son?

THE VILLAGER'S PERCEPTION OF CHRIST

Christ as "Man"

The humanity of Christ is perceived by the villagers most strikingly in two events: his birth and his death. Christ's nativity is celebrated by the villagers in the Twelve Days of Christmas, which consist of two especial days of feasting, during which the pig is killed, followed by various saints' days and holy days until the Theophany, or Baptism of Christ, on January 6. However, the Christmas season brings for the villagers not only joy, but also a certain fear as they take precautions against the Christmas demons (*skallikantzouria*) who infest the village with their sinister presence and are thought to bring the whole world into danger. I have heard it said of this period that during it the Mother of God is a *lechona* (a woman still unpurified after giving birth); and it follows that during it, also, she and her child are at their most defenseless. This threat to the world thus corresponds, on a cosmic scale, to the hazards felt to surround human birth.

However, it is the events of Great Week (Holy Week), when the taking of Christ, his Crucifixion, and his Resurrection, are celebrated, in which the human nature of Christ is most deeply recognized by the villagers. This period, like Christmas, is canonically preceded by a fast of forty days, to which are added the days of Great Week, and these last days, at the very least, are kept by the villagers in all their severity. Throughout the Orthodox world the tension heightens on Great Thursday with the long Gospel readings of the Passion, and the climax of this service is reached when the great cross, normally kept in the sanctuary, is brought out and placed among the people, and, in Ambeli, hung with a white cloth at the moment of the Crucifixion itself. On Great Friday everyone in the village, until the service of the Epitaphios (the tomb of Christ) in the afternoon, maintains a total fast, except for perhaps a cup of coffee, dark and bitter and suitable for mourning, while early in the day the women and children scour the mountainsides for flowers to adorn the Epitaphios. Once completed, the Epitaphios is placed in the nave of the church, and the service of the descent from the cross and the laying of the body in the tomb is celebrated by laying the cloth, together with an icon of Christ, in the Epitaphios; while afterward, until the Burial Service in the evening, a watch is kept over the body of Christ, with the villagers—mainly women and children—talking, and singing the folk version of the lament of the Mother of God for her son.

Orthodoxy has a great power of symbolic representation, and the villagers are highly sensitive to the identification of the symbol with the archetype it represents. Talking of the service on Great Thursday, the priest said to me, "You wait for the moment when the Cross is brought out," and he bowed himself indicating the size of the cross and the majesty of the moment, "Your hair will stand on end!" Another man said of the Easter service, "When you go into church you feel emotion, you say, 'My God, my God,' and sometimes you might weep"; and when the villagers gather round the Epitaphios and kiss the icon lying there, it is clear that this for them is no mere sign, or mnemonic, it is Christ's dead body itself which is the object of their grief. In the great events of the Easter period the villagers are not spectators but actors in a drama, living witnesses of a burial at that moment taking place.

The reality of this death, then, and the grief felt by the villagers on Holy Friday, show clearly that they see Christ as a man; but it is equally clear that this manhood is seen not in relation to woman but in relation to that aspect of God which is invulnerable to earthly suffering, and that it is the humanity of Christ which the villagers contemplate as they come to venerate "the King of All" (ton panton vasilea), in the words of the folk lament, lying in the tomb. The Mother of God is indeed in this lament pitied as a mother grieving of the death of her "only son" (yio monogeni); but the villagers themselves do not grieve for Christ as andras—man as male—but as anthropos—human as mortal. And this gender-neutral term, which is clearly appropriate at his death, is characteristically used of Christ by the villagers in their daily lives, and reflects also the phrasing of the Nicene Creed according to which Christ "was incarnate (sarko-

thenda, lit., 'was made flesh') of the Holy Spirit and the Virgin Mary, and was made man (*enanthropisanda*)."

This humanity of Christ, however, poses the further question as to how far the villagers perceive him as human and how far as the Son of God, and what gender implications, if any, are to be found in this latter term.

Christ as the Son of God

Clear as they are about Christ being anthropos, the villagers are equally clear that he is Theos, and this understanding is so strong that in grappling with the mystery of the two natures of Christ the villagers are sometimes forced into uncompromising if not heretical positions. Once in a theological discussion in which I was being particularly obtuse, I was effectively silenced by the statement: "Christ wasn't anthropos, he was Theos"; and one of the villagers once expounded to me what was in fact the Docetic heresy: that Christ did not "in reality" (*sti pragmatikotita*) have a human form, but rather took on human form for the eyes of men. "Are we able to torment him?" it was asked, "He is almighty" (*boroume emeis na ton timorisoume? Avtos einai pandodhynamos*).

This understanding of Christ in his divine nature inspires in the villagers a tremendous reverence, which is especially clear in the recitation by an old man of the events at Pentecost, which, as he spoke, was accompanied by his wife who, like a Greek chorus, interpolated phrases into pauses in the narrative. "The disciples were gathered together in a hut." "In a hut . . . if God wills, the great All Powerful!" "The whole place quaked . . ." (*setai o topos*), said the old man. "The whole place quaked!" came the echo, in tones of awe, and, "Christ and the Mother of God!" (*Christemou kai Panaghiamou!*), "My little Christ!" (*Christoutsikos mou!*). In this story it is Christ who is seen as enlightening the disciples at Pentecost, rather than the Holy Spirit, and similarly Christ is the protagonist in the folktales which tell how he "decked out" or fashioned (*stolise*, lit., "adorned") various animals such as the pig and the cat, or modified them, as in the case of the buffalo. Christ thus inspires enormous awe at the same time as being addressed with extraordinary affection.

Christ, therefore, the known and loved person, is yet in some sense seen as being of the same nature as the creator, and this has to be assimilated to the understanding that "God is One"; and it is in the context of this difficult balance of perceptions that the term *Son of God* can be used. For example, in the story of the creation of light, God saw that man needed light, and so Christ, "because he was the Son of God (*Yios tou Theou*) and could do anything he wanted, created light." Christ is thus understood to be both separate, in a sense, from God—as doing his bidding—and to be "one" with God, as the creator of light; and it is this relationship which is expressed in the term *Son of God*. Otherwise the other solution is to make the terms *Christ* and *Theos* interchangeable, and this is demonstrated in the many folktales in which either name is given to the miraculous stranger who visits a house or a village disguised as a child, a beggar, or an old man.

In thinking of Christ as the Son of God, then, the villagers are expressing an idea analogous to the theological understanding of Christ the Logos, "the Word," which was "in the beginning" and brought the material world into being, and yet acts like themselves in obedience to the will of the Father. And it is clear that Christ as the Son represents, as the term *Theos* also represents, the active energy which manifests the will of the All Powerful, and that the gender connotations of the term are completely irrelevant.

If Christ as the Logos is beyond gender, however, there is another sense in which Christ is seen as immanent in the created world, but here involved in the minutiae of social interaction and individual decisions.

Christ in Social Life

This third aspect of Christ to which the villagers relate is that of the risen Christ present in every situation of every human life, in opposition to the Devil, with whom he is described as bargaining on familiar and even genial terms for the souls of men. Christ and the Devil are thus seen as fighting for the salvation or damnation of the human soul, Christ sitting on the right and the Devil on the left of every individual in every circumstance of life. In this perception, Christ is both savior—being infallibly victorious if he enters the contest—and judge—since he will not intervene unless called upon. But this aspect of Christ, although closely and intimately related to the details of human lives, and acting as source of moral authority for them, nevertheless appears to reflect again notions of Christ both as anthropos and as Theos, and to introduce no element of gender.

There is an area, however, in which some association of Christ with the male role in society can possibly be inferred, and this is in the relation of Christ with the house and family.

There is a saying in Ambeli to the effect that if women persist in doing handwork, particularly spinning and weaving, during holy periods, the bits of fluff that fall off their work get into the bread of the divine meal of Christ and his Mother, making it uneatable; for "just as we are eating down here, so Christ and the All Holy One are eating in heaven." This phrase, clearly associating Christ the man in a complementary relationship with his Mother, points to a parallelism between the meal of the Holy Family and that of the earthly family, and thus possibly to an association of the man of the household with Christ, and the woman with the Mother of God; but the mode of this association is tenuous and needs to be sketched in carefully.

It is in the case of woman that the relationship of the social with the divine role is most clearly made, and a detailed argument of the association of the woman with the Mother of God has been set out elsewhere (du Boulay 1986). It is perhaps significant, though, that the same sort of correspondence is not made in the case of men, and at no point did I ever hear it said, or implied, that men, as andres, were redeemed by Christ from the sin contracted by their first ancestor. The particular redemption of the Mother of God of women, as opposed to men, appears to be a process peculiar to women alone; while the redemption by Christ of Adam and Eve, who together represent the whole of the human race, is something which Christ does as anthropos, for anthropoi.

If Christ, however, is not cited specifically as the archetype for man as andras, the association of man with Adam is unequivocal. Mentioned in countless references to the story of the Fall, the fact that it was Eve who first listened to the Devil and then beguiled her husband is quoted as the charter for all the various aspects of masculine nature as intelligent or rational (logikos), "on the right," their work having "a blessing"—in a word, superior, as was forcefully expressed by a village man in the following conversation: "Men are superior." "Superior in what things?" "Superior in all things. Woman is cursed." The association, then, of man with Adam is as total as that of woman with Eve, and was encapsulated on one occasion by an old woman's saying emphatically: "Man, Adam; man, Adam" (andras, Adham; andras, Adham).

It is, then, the association of man with Adam, rather than with Christ, which gives man his personal position in the Greek family. But it must be remembered that Adam is revered over Eve precisely because of the two of them he was not the instigator but the victim of the first disobedience; hence, even in the fallen world, he is logikos and thus reflects more completely than she does the image of the Logos which created them. Adam is, in fallen nature, the more complete representation of Christ, appearing in the story of the Fall, as told in the village, as a curiously noble figure, quite unlike the willful and unstable figure of Eve.

It still remains, however, to be asked why, even granting the fact that man as Adam is closer to Christ than woman as Eve, the figure of Christ is nevertheless not invoked in relation to the man of the house, as is the figure of the Mother of God with woman. The answer lies, I believe, in the villagers' overwhelming sense of Christ not only as anthropos but also as God, which has been discussed already. According to Orthodox doctrine, while the Mother of God is venerated in Orthodoxy because she represents humanity sanctified by obedience to the will of God, Christ is worshiped as God becoming man for the salvation of the world. While the Mother of God, then, can be, as sanctified humanity, a vehicle for the cultural ideal of women (i.e., a practicable ideal realizable in behavioral terms), Christ as God and man cannot be that ideal for men in a cultural, but only in an iconographic, sense (i.e., in a sense which demands an inner transformation which is in this world always incomplete). And in this iconographic sense, Christ is the ideal for all mankind—for women as well as men. Thus while man as anthropos seeks to become one with God, as andras he cannot be said to be God. The villagers' refusal to identify men with Christ in the same way as they identify women with the Mother of God is thus entirely consistent with Orthodox theology.

It appears, then, that to see the man of the house as Christ is to mix categories between human and divine in a way which the villagers are reluctant to allow: they only accept that man is nearer to God (and thus to Christ), in fallen nature, and woman further away. Yet they accept also that woman is able by grace to draw closer to God and to be likened to the Mother of God who brings forth Christ in her family. In this family she both nurtures Christ as a child and becomes obedient to him as he attains manhood; and these two moments in the life cycle of the Holy Family are constantly reiterated in Orthodox iconography, typically appearing in the icons on either side of the Royal Doors which lead into the sanctuary, and which are the focus of the villagers' attention every Sunday. On the right, Christ the man, at the height of his powers, looks outward blessing the people; on the left, the Mother of God carries the infant Christ in her arms. The analogy is tacit but suggestive: as a woman becomes like the Mother of God, so both the child and the man in her family can become to her like Christ; and as the mother of God and Christ are eating in heaven, so a woman and her family eat on earth.

The implications of this imagery for the relations between men and women are both striking and extremely subtle. In fallen nature man and woman are Adam and Eve; but by woman's grace, the child and man can be bound together in a holy family where they become Christ, and the woman the Mother of God. It is not the man alone who is Christ; it is the child and the man, both nurtured and obeyed, united in a family, and freed from the ambiguities of sexuality, temptation, and the struggle for power which haunt Adam and Eve.

It can be said, therefore, that from the time that Christ became a child and a man in a human family, the human family as a whole has been in a manner taken up into the divine world. This dispensation is opposed to that which follows the Fall, where Adam, nearer to God and superior to woman by nature, rightly rules over Eve—a hierarchy of worth and a subordination in power which, in comparison with the biblical narrative, the village version—together with various folk elaborations—markedly accentuates. The old dispensation, in village thinking, unequivocally asserts masculine authority. The new, however, is a complex balance—one in which woman is the center of a divine harmony, her children depending on her in their time of weakness, she depending on her man in his time of strength. Between these two dispensations the villagers remain suspended, forever falling back into the old, forever recapturing the new. And the transformation of gender relations which lies at the heart of this experience derives very clearly from their picture of the incarnation of Christ. This is indeed the only way in which gender enters the divine world; and the other apparent gender terminology which villagers use in their talk of God—God as Father, Christ as God's Son, Christ as a man—seems to be without gender implications at all.

THE NATURAL WORLD

The Moon

Of the various aspects of the natural world which were still, by the time of my fieldwork, being given a gender in village thinking, the sun and the moon appear prototypical; and it is perhaps the moon which, of all the forces operating on the villagers' lives, has (or had, at least until the moon landings in the early 1970s) retained the most coherent mythology. Before this time, which amongst other things was the time when electricity was brought to the village, the nights were lit, except for the dim glow of lamp-lit windows and the odd torch beam as someone made his or her way home in the darkness, only by the moonlight and starlight; and the waxing and waning moon, its position in the sky, its relation to the sun, its companionable presence "following one to the spring and back again," was a continuing and indispensable part of the villagers' consciousness. And even now the presence of this changing light in the sky is still, to many, a beautiful and living phenomenon, and a miraculous dispensation in particular to all, man and beast, who have to survive in the wild, the full moon being given "so that the shepherd and the traveler should have light by night," and the dark nights "so that the hunted creatures should have rest," "so that the fishes should shoal."

To these perceptions of the moon, however, another has to be added—one certainly in the late sixties still believed by some, though perhaps finally extinguished now—and this is the idea that "the moon is a cow" (*agheladha* or *voi*). This belief was quite literal. The moon was a cow which could, by "words" (*loyia*) or sorcery, be brought down to earth, where it could be milked and the milk used for magical potions, especially for love. "It is not a good thing to bring the moon down to earth,"

I was told seriously; but it could be done, and one of the signs that some-one had done this was when it was big and red and low on the horizon. It was said to bellow (*velazei* or *rokazei*) when it wished to go back again into the sky, and although it needed words to bring it down it could go back of its own free will.

It is the nature of the moon as variable, constantly changing through-out the month, which dominates the villagers' understanding of it, and this varying nature is expressed in the idea of the moon as "giving birth" (*gennaei*) and is associated in the villagers' minds with a powerful meta-physical cycle. In the season of the waxing moon—the days "of the filling of the moon" (*tous geomous tou fengariou*)—so long as the moon is still "like a sickle" (*tripani*) the times are not good, but when it begins to get round "like a loaf" (*karveli*), that is to say four or five days after the new moon, the auspicious part of the cycle takes hold, and these are the days in which to inaugurate any important piece of work. A process of match-making, for instance, a journey to achieve important business, or the work of planting and sowing, have all to be inaugurated during these days, although they may be continued after the full moon without dan-ger. The grafting of plants has to be carried out only over the days of the full moon itself (*panselinos* or *nea fengari*), and the celebration of wed-dings also.

The period after the full moon, referred to as the days of "the losing of the moon" (*sti hasi tou fengariou*), is the time when the moon, as it is said, "begins to twist" (*pernei na stripsei*) or to "go back" (*pernei piso*), and these terms in many other contexts denote a reversal of the proper order of things, a sense of impending doom. Thus the "turning back" of the moon indicates the first signs of weakening, the leaning of this great influence away from its perfect balance, and the beginning of the reign of the baleful forces which gather increasing strength throughout the last two quarters until the final phase of the "disappearance of the moon" (*hasofengaria*).

These days of the waning moon are thought to be appropriate for the collection of certain plants for cures, in those cases in which the weak-ening of the moon is associated with the weakening of the illness. The brooding of eggs under a hen, a process which takes twenty-two days, is also something not to be done "over one month" or "over one moon" (*monominitika* or *monofengaritika*), so that the turning of the old moon into the new is conceived as being essential to this new life. However, notwithstanding these customs, the period as a whole is conceived as in-creasingly inauspicious, and there is one moment in the cycle of the moon when this influence becomes not merely inauspicious but actively diabolical. This is the moment when the moon actually "turns round" (*gyrizei*), for it is said that sorcery, carried out at precisely this moment, is infallibly effective; and I was told, by someone who claimed to have done it, that if at this instant someone drops water into a glass, "Frrrr! It is thrown around in confusion (*anakatevetai*)" before their eyes. Sorcery is thought of by the villagers as "demonic activity" (*dhaimoniki energeia*), and the ascendancy of sorcerers at that time, in contravention to the normal doctrine of the unqualified power of God, indicates a potential for evil in this particular phase of the moon whose explanation lies in an entirely different understanding of the moon from that to which the modern world has become accustomed.

It was the moon landings which acted as a catalyst for clarifying my understanding of the way in which the villagers had traditionally perceived the moon. The veracity of the American claims to have landed on the moon had been for weeks the subject of furious debate in the cafés and the houses, and impassioned resistance was put up, based to a large extent on the villagers' profound skepticism of the motives of those in power. A simple denial of the idea was thus expressed in arguments relating to the power of American propaganda and the ease with which photographs could be faked. However, none of this explained the basis for the villagers' disbelief, nor the reasons for the intensity with which it was held, until at one gathering it was suddenly asked rhetorically: "When the moon is lost in the daytime" (*hanetai tin imera*), "where are the men?" and "Where are they, also, when the moon is lost (hasofengaria)?" No one had any answer to this, and the inference was a revelation—during these times there was no moon there to be stood upon by anyone. And later on, as we sat beside her fireplace, a woman drew in the ashes, with a poker, little diagrams of the "turning round" of the moon. Little by little the full moon grows smaller and smaller, until finally it diminishes to a minute speck—illustrated by a tiny tick, a "little line" (*grammitza*)—too small to be seen, but there, she said, all the same. Then, at a precise moment which comes and goes in a flash, the tiny curl of the old moon "turns round" (gyrizei) in an instant and becomes the minute crescent of the new. And it is this moment, when this catastrophic reversal is taking place, in this briefest flash of time when the old cycle is vanquished and the new not yet begun, that creation is in chaos, the dark forces momentarily victorious and everything reduced to a primordial state of flux before the everlasting stability of the regenerative cycle once again informs the natural order; and it is in keeping with this understanding that it is at this moment that the demonic forces gain the ascendancy.

The moon literally disappears from the sky, then, when it is not seen in the daytime—an idea also expressed by the phrase "It goes to its Mother" (*paei sti Manna*)—and it physically grows and diminishes throughout its monthly cycle. The moon is thus revealed as a living process of birth, generation, and renewal, constantly dying away into its final phase, constantly renewing itself through its own spontaneous life principle. It has already been mentioned that the moon "gives birth," an image whose obvious femininity is reinforced when it is remembered that in the village a fertile mind is thought of as "feminine" (*thyliko myalo*), because it "gives birth" to ideas, or breeds. Thus an intelligible meaning is given to the belief with which this discussion began, that "the moon is a cow," for this image, life-bearing and milk-giving, is one which expresses potently this experience of a primordial feminine power, the archetype of motherhood, a regenerative principle so intense that it, literally, gives birth to itself.

The traditional view of the moon, then, is as a cosmic force concerned with the generative cycles of the temporal world and the continual ebb and flow of the life force within it. Primarily to do with matter, the elements most closely related to the customary observances connected with the moon are earth and water, the dark womb of creation, the seedbed and the plant graft; while the sphere of influence governed by the moon is that concerned with the recurrent themes of health, sickness, and regeneration in the physical world—the perpetual, minute but all-important processes of germination, growth, decay, and rebirth, with darkness, fertility, and breeding.[2] The moon, then, seen as a great feminine force reigning in God's heaven, is so powerfully imbued with femininity, so intrinsically connected with earthly growth, that it can find embodiment in the living animal world and grasp the imagination of generations of villagers as "a cow."

The Sun

The sun has in this analysis deliberately been placed after the moon, not because it holds a less important place in the villagers' cosmology, but because its association with gender, although unequivocal, is less immediately experienced than that of the moon.

The gender-based association of the sun with the moon is clear in village thought. They are thought of as "brother and sister" (*adherfia*); the moon "follows" the sun, that is to say that when it is full it rises where the sun rises, and when it is new it appears in the evening sky above the sunset; it is also, however, "opposite" (*anditheto*) for the same reason—the full moon rises as the sun is setting; and to this one man added that the moon was high in the winter when the sun was low, and low in the summer when the sun was high. There are also respects in which the sun

---

[2] There are some interesting parallels between beliefs about the moon held by the villagers of Ambeli and those of the Portuguese peasants of the Alto Minho. See Pina-Cabral (1986:121–124).

is defined not just in relation to the moon, but to the cosmos as a whole. It is Lord (*Kyrios*), superior (*anoteros*), and "on the right" (*dhexia*), and these attributes it holds over all things because "it burns" (*kaiei*), is untouchable, and dominates all things. It is a classification which, in certain contexts, includes the moon as its complementary opposite, but it is one also which holds good whatever the context, as is demonstrated in a discussion in which I was trying to elucidate the nature of the sun's right-handedness, to see if it had any basis in the way the natural phenomenon was observed. Eventually my interlocutor, having had enough of this, put an end to the conversation: "The sun is right-handed, and that's all there is to it" (*o ilios einai dhexia, paei*). In a similar way, also, the sun, no matter where its current position in the sky, is identified with the East, so that the phrases "toward the sun" (*pros ton ilio*) and "toward the East" are synonymous.

The sun is thus categorically Lord, superior, on the right-hand side, and associated with the East—the sacrally significant quarter—and these classifications, even though they define absolute rather than relative attributes, nevertheless tacitly place the moon, insofar as it is the sun's complementary opposite, on the inferior, left-handed and relatively inauspicious side of creation. Thus the customs which in the village are associated with the sun also relate to a set of phenomena very different from those which relate to the moon, and these latter customs have to do particularly with human birth and death. Before 1964, when women used to give birth in the village rather than in the local clinic, it was the custom for both mother and child to remain unwashed until the third day after the birth, during which time the three Fates were said to sit over the child "fating" it (*moiranane*) or laying down its future. However, on the third day, very early in the morning, the midwife would come, would wash both mother and child who until then had lain uncleansed of the blood of childbirth, and dress them in clean clothes. She would then wash all the clothes; and after this had been done, she would go to the threshold of the house and call the mother to come with her child to the doorway. Here she would tell the mother to spit three times "toward the sun" (or "toward the East"), and three times into her own bosom. Spitting three times is a symbolic rejection of evil which occurs in many occasions of village life when there is danger of the evil eye, and it is also found in the baptismal rite of the Orthodox Church symbolizing the casting out of the Devil. Thus this ritual, establishing the purity of mother and child as they were led by the midwife from the world of birth and the dominion of the Fates, into the society of the village and the light of day, established the sun as the awesome power which would not tolerate pollution and whose presence had to be invoked at the gateway of life.

As at birth, so at death also the power of the sun is invoked. It is said that if a person in mortal agony is unable to die, he should be turned "toward the sun" to permit the advent of death; and I was told of an instance in 1952 when this was done, so that a young boy who had been fatally hurt in an accident "shouldn't suffer any longer," and immediately afterward, he died. And this ascendancy of the sun does not end with the moment of death, for at the wake the dead person has invariably to be laid out "facing the sun," that is to say, with his feet pointing toward the East; the coffin at the burial service, and indeed the orientation of the church itself, is toward the East; and finally the grave has to be dug and the person buried, "facing the sun."

The sun, then, invoked at birth and at death, appears to be the principle which governs the fundamental categories of human existence and the movement between them; and this same perception according to which the sun is associated with events of permanence and finality used to occur again in practices relating to the building of a house. During this event a bunch of flowers and a silver coin were buried "on the right-hand side of the house," a side which was also described as "facing the sun." The house in Ambeli used to be passed down through the male line, built once only in a series of generations and made to shelter and nourish a putatively unending line of descendants. Built, so a lament from the area goes, "broad for the dance, and wide for the promenade" (i.e., of the married couple), and with windows through which the "nightingales of spring (i.e., the children) may come and go,"[3] the house was a symbol of permanence, and it was the sun which was the auspicious power which would be invoked at its inauguration.

These practices are particularly revealing about the sun's fundamental attributes. However, there is a sense in which the sun's nature is expressed less in absolute than in relative terms: although the sun is "Lord," both the sun and the moon govern cycles of life and death, and are differentiated in this sense only by the sun's being the more powerful, and controlling a longer cycle of time. The sun governs the year, as the moon the month. And like the moon, also, the sun has its dangerous moment of weakness, in this case over the Christmas period, and like the moon the sun has a potential both for creation and destruction.

The year's climax, the harvest, is the reference point of certain customs designed to ensure an equilibrium between these extremes. On May 1 a red rug is hung out of an eastern window at dawn, remaining there until sunset, "so that the wheat should ripen for bread" (*yia na psomosei to sitari*). Another custom, however, again relating to the wheat, empha-

---

[3] *'Na 'nai plati yia to horo, fardhi yia to suriyiani/Kai ap' tin dhexia sou tin meria na afisei parathuri/na mpainovgainoun ta poulia, tis anoixeis ta aidhonia'*. This lament was obtained from Ambeli between 1970 and 1972.

sizes the danger of the sun's heat. This custom stipulates that on Sundays and saints' days, as well as every Wednesday and Friday, "people don't do any washing" (*dhen plenoun*). It is plunging things into boiling water which is thought to be particularly dangerous, and the reason given by the villagers is revealing: "We say it is so that the wheat should not be burned up" (*yia na min kaei to sitari*). In contradistinction, then, to the custom on May 1 which is designed to ensure the life-giving warmth of the sun's rays to the growing crops, that relating to the Wednesday and Friday washing of the clothes asserts the equal and opposite principle that the power of the sun, lacking due proportion, burns up the crops, becoming instead an agent of death.

The sun, then, is associated with long cycles of growth, and with ideas of masculinity, authority, superiority, right-handedness, finality, stability, and permanence. The moon, paired as the feminine counterpart of the sun and automatically placed in the subordinate and complementary position, is associated with short cycles of growth, and with ideas of relativity, transience, mutability, and process. Thus while the sun inaugurates birth and death as categoric changes, and relates to those aspects of the life cycle which are momentous and cataclysmic, the moon relates to those processual aspects of birth and death which are part of the unending regenerative cycles of the natural order and which, although constantly in motion, nevertheless assure within the material world the fundamental continuity of village life.

THE SOCIAL WORLD

In the foregoing section relating to the natural world, there appear to be clear genders ascribed to the sun and the moon, and the spheres of influence thought to pertain to either have a reciprocal symmetry. Meanwhile, in the first section relating to the divine world, real gender implications seem to be found only in the sanctification of the human family by the birth of Christ from the Mother of God. This final section moves on to examine how these cosmological ideas connect with the gender roles in the social world.

There are two principal ways in which this occurs. First, the figure of the Mother of God is crucial to the position of women in the family. This has been discussed elsewhere (du Boulay 1986) and will be omitted here. Second, the complementarities of stability and process seem to be crucial to the role of men and women, particularly at the crises of birth, marriage, and death. Here I summarize the evidence on the first two topics, referring to published evidence where available, and I retain the main body of the analysis for a discussion of the ceremonies of death.

Birth

Before 1964, when women used to give birth at home, it was women alone who occupied the liminal position between two worlds. Midwives (*mami*, pl. *mamidhes*) were always women, and figured importantly, as indicated above, as negotiators not only of the physical transition from the world before birth to that after it, but also of the initial transition from the secluded area of the house to that of the sunlight and the world outside. And in this context it is significant that the Fates (*Moires*), who were seen as holding the essential ground in the critical three days while the most dangerous part of the transition was being negotiated, were also feminine and were known not only as Fates but as "old women" (*gries*). The father did not really figure in this process; and though if he happened to be in the house he would if necessary hold his wife during the birth, his presence at such a time was fortuitous and not customary. Otherwise he would go about his daily work, or sit in the café celebrating (or, in the case of yet another daughter, lamenting) with his friends.

The theme of blood pollution[4] dominated this period, at its most in-

---

[4] *Pollution* is perhaps too broad a term to use, without explanation, for the range of meanings involved in this concept in Greece. The word closest to "polluted" in the village is *margarizmenos*, meaning merely "dirty" or "unclean," and this is applied chiefly to scavenging animals such as dogs and hens. The noun, *margarsies*, is similarly used for bits and pieces of filth, such as hens' droppings. There is, however, in the Greek experience of birth, menstruation, and death, an idea of ritual uncleanness which is nearer to Mary Douglas's concept of a dangerous intermixing of categories (Douglas 1966). It is a concept which is realized, however, not by specific vocabulary, but by a series of prohibitions and the ideas of causation which lie behind them.

Crucial to this awareness of impurity and danger is the spilling of blood. Women's blood shed in menstruation and childbirth is taken as evidence of the Fall (see n. 6), and it seems that this should not be juxtaposed with the sacrificial shedding of Christ's blood (women during their periods must not venerate an icon nor light a candle—ideally speaking, during their periods they should not enter the church at all—so it goes without saying that such women may not take communion. No women before the menopause may go behind the sanctuary). Nor should women's blood be juxtaposed with the bloodless dead (the memorial food for the dead must be taken with a spoon, and the bones of the dead at an exhumation must not be handled by a menstruating woman). While the explanation for the prohibition on venerating an icon normally runs, simply, "It is not effective" (*dhen pianei*), a positive danger is seen to reside in the breaking of the prohibition at death, threatening, in the opinion of some, the dead with a perpetual sojourn underground. Similarly, the explanation given by an old woman for her house's nearly burning down on a saint's day was that her daughter-in-law had not yet washed her clothes after her period. In the case of a lechona too, some danger to others is involved, for she must not enter the houses of any of the other villagers for fear of articles in them suddenly breaking. Chiefly, though, it is for the lechona herself, together with her child, that danger is involved—a danger seen unspecifically as demonic attack, and guarded against through the avoidance of the lechona's crossing over ravines (typically the home of demons), through constant censing of the house, and through care in keeping the doors closed at night.

tense during the first three days after the birth, but continuing for the full forty days during which the mother was a lechona; and as well as the washing of the mother and the baby on the third day, mentioned above, various additional steps were taken to protect the two during this dangerous period, and to negotiate their full entry into society when it came to an end. Thus immediately after the birth someone from the house would fetch water from the spring, which, having been taken to the priest and blessed, would be brought back to the house and sprinkled first over the mother and child, and then around the house. During the forty days the house would be frequently censed, and the doors once shut at night would not be opened until the dawn. The child would be kept inside, and though the mother was permitted to go about the village, she did not enter other people's houses, nor, significantly, draw wine.[5] Finally the end of this period would be marked by the blessing of the mother and child by the priest at the church door—a service of purification which freed the woman from the association with the Fall with which both the blood of menstruation and of childbirth is associated.[6]

It seems, then, that the women were the principal participants in the continuing negotiation of a birth, and the people on whom the dangers and responsibilities of the transitions were focused, while the actual moments at which the transitions—from one world to another, one state to another—were confirmed, were moments at which the male, in the figure of the priest, was invoked.

Marriage

From the moment of the birth of a daughter, thoughts about marriage are involved, for daughters mean dowries and trousseaux, and these take many years to gather together[7] (du Boulay 1983; Salamone and Stanton 1986). Men were traditionally "in the house," a phrase meaning that marriage in Ambeli, before the emigration of young couples to the towns which took hold in the 1960s, was usually virilocal, at least in its early

---

The word *pollution* here, then, covers a range of physical states from that of vulnerability to one of active danger both to self and to others.

[5] Wine is thought of in the village as the blood of Christ, as bread is his body, and oil his tears.

[6] A village woman, commenting on her period, said to me "What is this? What is this? Eves, that's what we are, Eves" (*ti einai avta; Eves eimaste, Eves*). Sexual intercourse is also thought to be "a bad thing" (*palaiodhouleia*) because of the villagers' stress on sexual awareness as being involved in the Fall; and the clearly sexual manifestation of the menstrual cycle is thus tainted with the first sin.

[7] I have retained the present tense for this passage, because although a law making the dowry illegal was enacted in the recent past, further evidence is needed before it can be certain that the villagers have complied with it.

stages; and thus the dowry became in itself a symbol, not only of marriage, but also of the essentially transitory position of the woman in her natal home, representing, from the moment of her birth, the fact that she would one day be leaving it. It could be said, then, that the transition of marriage occupied, for a daughter, the whole of her life until her wedding day—at which point the rules of residence used to confirm the character of mutability given to a woman as she herself became the mobile element, moving from her natal home to the set pole of her husband's house and family (du Boulay 1982, 1984). This movement of women to their husbands' houses was, however, governed not only by the rule proscribing marriage with "kin" (up to and including second cousins), but also by the additional rule of *katameria* (du Boulay 1984), which gave to it a unidirectional and symbolically "right-handed" character by which "return" marriages were prohibited for a number of generations. The movement of women in marriage through the community was not random, but ordered.

While the women, however, are thus prepared for marriage from the day of their birth, the men's preparation for their adult life is not directed exclusively toward marriage, but is a normal part of the combined effort of the household as a whole toward prosperity. In contradistinction, therefore, to the long initiation of the women into the marital state, the men's concern with the process of marriage can really be said to last only from the initiation of the marriage negotiations (significantly conducted and ratified by the men) to the marriage service itself.

These gender roles traditionally relating to birth and marriage can be seen to correspond in certain respects to some of the cosmological ideas which have already been discussed. Stability and decisive moments of change are characteristic of men as they are of the sun; process and change as a continuous movement are characteristic of women, as they are of the moon. At the same time another cosmological principle, that of the Fall, is related to the blood pollution of women generally and of the mother at birth in particular. These correspondences are continued or inverted in society's response to a death.

Death

From the moment of death[8] till the body is "raised" to go to the church and the grave, women are preeminent. The task of washing and laying out the body is performed by women; it is they who have to see that the acts of ritual purification—such as changing all the clothes worn at the

[8] A substantial treatment of mourning rituals in Greece in Potamia in northern Greece is given by Danforth and Tsiaras (1982), which shows a great similarity with many of the features in Ambeli discussed below.

time of the death—are duly carried out by the members of the household in which the person has died; it is the women who work through the long hours of the night preparing the bread and the food which is to feed the entire village on the following day, and providing those at the wake with tiny cups of black coffee; crucially, it is women who sing the laments at the wake, and they on whom the duty of holding the memorial services, and of observing the long task of mourning, is laid. The men of Ambeli are present at the wake, and their presence is important in the community's traumatic encounter with death, as I hope to show; but their formal tasks are limited to relatively simple acts concerned with making the coffin, carrying the body, in procession, to the church and thence to the graveyard, digging the grave, and completing the burial.

It is at the critical moment when the body leaves the house that the male presence first comes to the fore, in the form, once again, of the priest. Arriving at the house of the dead when the body is to be taken for burial, the priest, with a chanter, enters the room where the wake has been held and prays briefly over the body. After this, four men "raise" (sikonoun) the body, and it is carried in procession to the church, preceded by five acolytes who are themselves followed by the priest. The coffin is laid facing the East, and toward the end of the service the priest places the icon of the Resurrection on the right breast of the body, and, men first, the congregation come forward to make their "last farewell" (teleftaios aspasmos), crossing themselves, kissing the icon, and making a token gesture of veneration toward the head or the hands.

At graveside the coffin is lowered into the grave, prayers are again said over the dead, and the final actions of the priest are to take the sanctuary lamp which has been burning before the icon of the Mother of God,[9] extinguish the flame, and empty the oil and water from it onto the face of the dead; to take a piece of tile—representing the earth and water symbolic of the life of man—and place it over the mouth; and to take on a spade some earth, which someone then sprinkles with water, and, intoning "For earth thou art and unto the earth shalt thou return," throw it into the coffin. Finally the lid is placed on the coffin, and all the community throw a stone or a clod of earth into the grave and watch the burial completed by two or three men, before they turn back to the village and, men first and women after, are given a meal by the bereaved household to which, as it is put, they have been invited by the dead person (e.g., Barba Thanasis se echei trapezi, "Uncle Thanasi invites you to a meal"). The priest is present at this occasion also, initiating the

---

[9] In cases where a chapel of the saint whose name the dead person bears is in or near the village, it is the oil and water from this sanctuary lamp which is thrown on the face of the dead.

meal by blessing a plate of hot *kollyva*, or food for the dead,[10] and singing the short service of the *Trisaghio*, the Thrice Holy.

It is clear, then, that the priest—present at the critical moments of the final departure of the dead person from his house, at the burial service, at the burial itself, and at the first return of the mourners, bereaved now of the body, to the house which they had left in its company—is essential for the safe transition not only of the dead from this world into the other, but also of the living back again from the grave into society. It is only, however, these momentous transitions which have by this stage been accomplished; and there now follows a long period, chiefly the concern of the women of the household, during which the two reciprocal processes of transition—of the dead into the other world and of the living back into life—are finally confirmed.

At this point in the rituals of death the men have completed the parts formally allotted to them, and from now on, although they carry still the burden of their grief, they do not lament openly, and they are merely expected to wear black arm bands, to participate in the various ritual acts in which the house as a whole is involved, and to observe a decent decorum in their normal behavior. Similarly the memorial rituals also involve the priest at specific moments. But for the women, the level of involvement is very different.

For women, the observance of full mourning consists in the wearing of black, including black stockings in summer as well as winter, and a black headscarf pulled well forward over the hair and brow, together with abstention from any kind of celebration, including dancing and singing, the wearing of jewelry, the giving of sweets (*glyka*) inside the house, and the celebration of name days. The house reflects a similar change: the wall hangings and the cloth under the icons are dyed black, a black cloth is hung just inside the door, a broad black diagonal mourning band is pinned on the outside, and the door itself and shutters are painted a dark color. In cases of deep mourning the practice can become more extreme—for seven years in the late sixties a young widow kept her interior walls painted dark blue—an extreme contrast to the usual whitewash—and in the late forties a village family, on the death of a son in the civil war, painted all the interior walls black and dyed every carpet black as well.

---

[10] Kollyva is only ever made for funerals or memorial services, and consists normally of a large plate of boiled wheat which is sweetened and mixed with toasted flour, raisins, and sometimes pomegranate seeds. The top is smoothed over with a thick layer of icing sugar, and the initials of the dead, or the initials I C N A (*Iisous Christos Nikaei*, Jesus Christ Conquers) marked out with silver balls. It is only at the funeral meal that the kollyva is presented while it is still hot, and in this case it is plain, although sweetened, and lacks the decorative finish.

Although men are necessarily implicated in these arrangements, it is on the women that these constraints chiefly fall, particularly as a woman recently bereaved is not expected to leave the house for any other than essential tasks, and it is from them that is expected the conspicuous demonstration of genuine grief. Similarly it is to women, and especially to widows, that a strict prohibition on going to church is applied—since it involves "joy" (*hara*) and "people" (*kosmos*). This prohibition endures for the first forty days at least after a death in the house, and in the case of the death of a husband the widow is expected to refrain from going to the Liturgy for two or three years, although she may come in quietly, light a candle, and leave, or be present at the blessing of the memorial food at the end of the Liturgy. It is also the women who are responsible, not only for the twelve lesser memorials (*psycholeitourgies*) but also for the five great memorial services (*makaries*, or *kephaliaka mnimosina*) at which, in earlier times, the whole village as well as all visitors used each to be given a quantity of various sorts of breads, in addition to the remembrance food, and a cooked meal of beans and rice.

A significant element in the way these memorials used to be organized before my time in the village was that three "(virgin) girls" (*koritzia*) who had to be, it was emphasized, "mature" or "grown" (*megala*), were "chosen" by the relatives of the dead to go round the village on the Saturday evening, each carrying, respectively, some wine, a bowl of boiled wheat, and a basket full of little loaves called "pieces" or "soul-loaves" (*kommatia* or *psychonia*), the last two of which they had prepared themselves. At each house they would leave a "piece" for every person normally living in the house, and offer the wheat and the wine. This procession used always to go around the village in a right-handed (counterclockwise) direction, taking in all the houses in one great circle "like the dance" (*san horos*), as it was said; and this procession was—like the movement of the women in marriage which has already been mentioned and of which it is clearly an echo—on no account to turn back. Thus if the girls ran out of anything before they had finished their distribution, the woman of the house at which they had stopped would go back to the original house for more.

Finally, in addition to the uniquely feminine character of the organization of the wake and of the memorials, it is women who are uniquely involved in the singing of the laments for the dead, both at the wake and for months, sometimes years, afterward. It is in these laments, and in the improvised verses or single lines called out by the mourners round the body, that the initial significance of the mourning dress and customs becomes apparent, for they voice the terrible grief not only of the bereaved, but also of the dead, who lies under the black earth, bereft of light and air, with earth for a blanket, a stone for a pillow, and worms for company.

Strongly reminiscent of the ancient Hellenic tradition of the afterlife, the world which the mourners imaginatively inhabit along with their recently dead is one characterized by deprivation—the antithesis of this life, with no dancing nor singing nor company, no blood, no recognition, no kin (du Boulay 1982, 1984). And this same understanding becomes apparent from the villagers as they talk about the dead, so that dominating even their own grief is the overwhelming pathos of those who have been torn from the light and thrust into the moldering darkness of the grave. "*He doesn't see*" (*avtos dhen 'lep'*) is the comment continually heard on such occasions, which contrasts specifically with the more favored situation, however full of grief it may be, of those who still walk the earth.

Mourning, then, is for the dead, not the living, and the black of mourning is the analogy of the darkness of the grave, not a mere representation of personal grief—a supposition which is confirmed by lines such as the following, "You have dressed me in black, black earth" (*me dithikes sta mavra, mavri yeis*), which occur so frequently in the laments; and is confirmed also by the custom, for all but widows, for the mourning period to end, and for the mourning dress to be put off, after the final memorial service at the *xechoma* or exhumation of the bones, at which the bones are, as it is said, brought up "into the air." Mourners enclose themselves in black, then, for as long as their dead are enclosed in earth—a custom which expresses the reality of the grave before it expresses the reality of sorrow, and yet which links the two in a single experience.

This release of the mourners from black at the same time as the bones are released from the earth indicates that it is with the dead rather than with death itself that the mourner is identified; and this is borne out by various customs which show the mourner's concern to distance herself from the association with Charos, or Death, which the wearing of black tends to invoke. In earlier times it was the custom for the mourners not to change to black immediately following a death (as they do now), but on the third, fifth, or seventh day afterward. The explanation for this ran: "It may have been because people didn't have a black scarf ready . . . ," and then, with more certainty, ". . . but it was especially so that Charos should distance himself" (*epitidhes yia na anallargei o Charos*). And similarly, even in the period of my residence in the village, the total black of the modern mourning dress was in some instances relieved by a tiny block of stitching in red silk, or by a single red thread, "So that Charos should keep away" (*yia na apofevgei o Charos*). But perhaps most interesting of all these instances is the custom, for forty days after a death, of the close relatives of the dead refraining from eating meat or fish, because, as it was often said to me, "It seems as if you are eating the dead" (*einai san tros to nekro*). The earth, also, is said to "eat" the dead, and in the refusal of the mourners to touch flesh of any description during the period immediately following a death is seen the extent of their resistance to too complete an identification with the grave.

This fact is of significance in understanding the role of the mourner, for participation with the dead is the opposite of participation in death: the dead are devoured, but death itself is the devourer. Thus dressed in black, deprived of joy, motivated by grief and compassion, and carrying out the meticulous customs laid down by tradition for the salvation of the soul, the mourner is a penitential figure, and her activity is not to identify with death but to overcome it in the name of the dead; and this she does by means of a doctrine which is central to the whole process of mourning—that concerning the dissolution of sins.

There is a folk belief which pictures the soul on arrival at the other world having to pass through a sieve: the sinful soul cannot pass, but the pure soul flows through and reaches everlasting life. This image of the gross soul, opaque and full of sins, is a fundamental one in rural Greek symbolism, and finds its most complete expression in the insistence that the body should "dissolve" (*na liossei*) in the earth, and that the bones, when they are finally exhumed after three or five years, should be clean and yellow "like candle wax." An undecayed body or unclean bones are thought to indicate "sins" (*hamarties*),[11] and it is for this reason that while younger people are often exhumed during the third year after their death, an older person, having accumulated more sins and thus taking longer to dissolve, is left for five.

The intervals at which the great memorials are held symbolize certain important stages in the progress of the soul after death and in Ambeli occur at the third day after the death (*trimero*), the ninth (*enneamero*), the fortieth (*sarandamero*), and again on the anniversary of the death, while the final great memorial service is held at the exhumation. In Orthodox theology, this timing of the third-, the ninth-, and the fortieth-day memorials is explicable by reference to the tradition of the vision of Saint Makarios (Hapgood 1975), in which the saint is shown how for the first three days the soul remains in contact with the earth; then, until the ninth day, it is given a vision of the joys of paradise; and finally, from the ninth till the fortieth day, it is shown the torments of hell. At each of these dates it is taken briefly before God by its guardian angel, until on the fortieth day it is once more brought before God and sent "to its place" (*sti thesi tis*). However, there is an interesting folk parallel to this which I did not discover in Ambeli but which Alexiou gives in an example of a

---

[11] See also the relationship of this idea with Orthodox thinking, in Danforth and Tsiaras (1982:49–52). In Nisos, a Cycladic island, unclean bones at the exhumation are a sign of an unquiet soul due to causes such as quarrels among surviving relatives (Kenna 1976a).

lament from Epirus (Alexiou 1974). In this example the dead gives to the living instructions about what they are to do at the exhumation, adding:

> On the third day I begin to moulder, on the ninth I smell,
> And from the fortieth my limbs fall one by one.[12]

When one remembers that in folk belief the dissolution of the body in the natural world implies that in the spiritual world the soul has been cleansed of sin, it is clear that the reference in the lament to the progress of dissolution on the third, ninth, and fortieth days is on its own level an analogy of the vision of Saint Makarios, which portrays, in similar stages, the increasingly enlightened soul as it passes toward its final judgment. And it is because of this connection of thought that, while it is specified in Ambeli that the wheat in which the candles at the wake are stuck must be "impure" (akatharto), that is to say, still mixed with tiny stones and little seeds from the fields, that which is used for the first great memorial, and thereafter, has to be "sorted over" (to dhialexoun) three times. The process of dissolution, from its inception at the third day, remains tied throughout the mourning period to the purgation of sin, and these beliefs are linked in the successive celebrations of the great memorials.

While, however, the conception of the sins clustered round the soul finds an apt image in the flesh which clings to the bones, and the purgation of sins is echoed in the process of physical decay, the memorial services do much more than merely mark the passage of these processes—they reveal the means by which the processes are enabled, and this consists of forgiveness, both social and divine.

This is particularly strongly marked during the period immediately after the death, when the dead person's name tends always to be uttered together with the adjective "forgiven" (synghoremenos). After the burial, as they turn from the graveside, people going to the memorial meal will say to one another, "Let us go and forgive" (pame na synghoresoume); the words invariably uttered by anyone receiving the memorial food are, "May God forgive him/her" (Theos synghores' ton/tin). This prayer is accompanied by the belief that the eating of the memorial food by those on earth brings consolation to the dead person, who is consequently feasting in the other world, and I remember at one memorial celebration the sister of the dead woman saying: "What joy Katerini will have today!" It is thought too that the steam from the plate of hot boiled wheat at the Trisaghion reaches and nourishes the dead with its aroma. However, there is more involved in the memorial practices than this, for it is believed also that the candles lit and the memorial food given in the name

---

[12] Alexiou 1974:48. " 'Stis treis pira kai arachniasa, eis tis ennia myrizo/kai ap'tis saranda kai ystera, armous armous horizo.' Giankas 885.4–9."

of the dead bring them not only comfort but, if they are in torment, some degree of release also. I was told by several people that a person in the flames of hell will, each time such a gift is made in his name, be drawn just a little bit out of the pitch (*katram*) in which he suffers. And it is firmly asserted that it is possible by means of the memorials to bring someone out of hell into paradise, the argument running that God would say of them, "Look how they are loved, how good they were."

In this nexus of customs, then, which accompany a death, themes of the tragic situation of the dead, the dissolution of the body, the forgiveness of the community, and the purgation of sins are all welded together into a single action, the memorial service, and expressed largely in a single figure, that of the mourner. Standing over against the community in her lack of "joy," her black clothes, her seclusion, she also stands over against the dead, who now is nourished only by the steam from the memorial wheat, whose eyes are darkened, and whose mouth is stopped with earth. And it is an indication of her position that the "joy" from which she is specifically excluded is something which she gives, not only to the dead, but also to the living, who receive the bread and the memorial meals, and especially to the children, whose "joy" on eating the memorial food is often commented on by the villagers.

The function of the mourner, then, is, crucially, to live not for herself but for others. Her business is not to receive joy, and nor is it, on the occasion of the great memorials, even to receive thanks or the normal salutation "Good night" when people leave her house, for on both occasions the formula is the familiar words, "May God forgive him." It is, then, by symbolically resigning her claim on life that the mourner becomes transparent, as it were, to communications from either world to the other and, neither wholly of one world nor of the other, is able to act as a medium between them, bringing food to the living in the name of the dead, and forgiveness to the dead in the name of the living.

Significantly, this process ends only when the dissolution of the body is complete, and the bones brought up into the light and air. With this, the association of the person with the darkness of the earth, and thus in some respects with hell, is ended, and the soul has definitively gone "elsewhere" into an "other world" which is beyond the reach of the human imagination or of human care. And it is only at that point that, ideally, the close female relatives of the dead, their task finally completed, may return to normal life. All but widows put off their mourning dress at this time, and even widows, though still dressed in black, may relax, just a little, their demeanor—may wear their headscarf farther off their face, leave off their stockings in the hot weather, and perhaps begin to consider remarriage.

The role of women, then, at death, is twofold. On the one hand, the mourner simultaneously guides the body through the long period of its dissolution and cares for the soul until its final liberation into the other world. Woman is seen here in a self-denying and intercessory role which is the more striking when it is realized that the mourner's exclusion from the "joy" of the liturgy—though a folk custom too extreme for the Church—has an analogy in one of the ascetic practices of the Church during Great Lent, when the penitential character of the time denies to the faithful the celebration of the Eucharist except on Saturdays and Sundays. And this role has on its own level parallels with the figure of the Mother of God, whom the villagers regard as their chief intercessor with Christ, and to whom they primarily appeal. On the other hand, this ascetic mourner used to have as her helpers the mature virgin girls who, moving "like the dance" through the village with their memorial gifts of wheat and bread and wine, represented not only forgiveness for the dead, but also the healing promise of marriage alliances and the birth of children among the living. This composite role, then, in its long duration, its concern with infinitesimal and continuous change, and in its echoes of the movement of women in marriage, is thus consistent with the ideas of process and mutability which have appeared through this exposition.

If this is the role of the women, however, that of the men has still to be understood. It has been noted that the role of the men at death seems, in distancing them from society's encounter with grief and loss, to make them passive participants in a drama managed, and suffered, almost entirely by women. Nevertheless, seen in the light of the ideas of permanence and stability which have already, in different contexts, been associated with masculinity, this supposition is overturned—for, in this perspective, the men are held back from demonstrations of sorrow and despair precisely in order to balance the feminine role which is to be so unreservedly involved in them. In this way, situated structurally as the stable elements in a ritual which requires their women to move from normal life to the very margins of existence, the men stand solidly in the light of day, representing the acceptance of death, the necessity of everyday realities, and the continuity of the social world, counterbalancing the liminal and numinous experience of their women, and pulling them back from the dangers of too prolonged a contemplation of disintegration within the tomb.

The contrasting themes, then, of stability and process, which are associated with masculinity and femininity in the customs and beliefs associated with the sun and the moon, appear again in the gender roles relating traditionally to men and women, and illuminate the social construction of the sexes which lies behind them. It is notable that the similarity between the social and cosmological classifications does not extend beyond this common sharing in gender characteristics—while men seem to share in the same properties as the sun, and women those of the moon, I found nothing to indicate that men are associated specifically with the sun, or women with the moon. Rather there appears in Ambeli to exist a general understanding of what is involved in being male or female, so that, while the cosmology and the society do not seem to be directly related with each other, both are informed by a similar and constant conception of gender.

CONCLUSION

It appears from the evidence which has been quoted concerning death, marriage, birth, and the natural and divine worlds, that gender is related to the cosmos in three different discourses, or levels of thinking, and that it depends on the specific context as to which of these is brought to the fore at any particular moment. These discourses may be described as the Old Testament discourse of Adam and Eve, the New Testament discourse of the Mother of God, and the nonbiblical, pre-Christian or "Hellenic"[13] discourse of the sun and the moon. These discourses hold in themselves a number of contrasts, of which the most striking concern, firstly, the relations between men and women, and, secondly, the relation of women with the world of the flesh.

Firstly, in the Old Testament and the Hellenic discourses, men are superior, and this is reflected both in relations within the house, and in the shadowy identification of the male role in society with the characterization of the sun—both being concerned with significant events in the life cycle and thus becoming associated with ideas of stability and permanence. By contrast, however, in the New Testament discourse women can attain to a kind of superiority of honor in which, retaining still their subordinate and processual role, they can by virtue of their approximation to the Mother of God, epitomize the divinization of humanity and attain a unique status within the house.

Secondly, the New Testament discourse treats woman as having an enormous capacity for spiritual mediation between the divine world and

[13] In what follows I refer, for brevity, to the nonbiblical strain in village thinking as "Hellenic." This nomenclature is not intended to prejudge issues about the exact extent of the ancient Greek contribution to contemporary village culture (for a discussion of these debates in folklore studies, see Herzfeld 1982); it serves merely to indicate that a strain of "natural" or "agricultural" religion is involved here of which ancient Greek folk religion is a significant example, and which may owe something to this antecedent. See, e.g., beliefs about the dead, and about Artemis (among other things a moon goddess) and Apollo (among other things a sun god) in Nilsson (1961:115f. and 15f., respectively).

the world of the flesh. Thus the Mother of God, the means whereby Christ became man, becomes the intercessory figure relating the human world to God; and in a similar way women, mediating between the living and the dead, become curiously asexual figures in their abstention from the eating of flesh, their seclusion, and in their required denial of "joy." And this denied sexuality used to be paired, although contrasted, with the virgin sexuality of the girls who, called in to take the memorial food "right-handed" round the community, embodied ideas of purity, forgiveness, and reconciliation through marriage among the earthly community.

Neither in the case of the mourner, therefore, nor in that of the grown girls who used to be so essential a part of the mourning rituals, is feminine identity seen as polluted; and this contrasts with the Old Testament discourse in which women are seen as inherently negative and evil, their sexuality associated with infant death,[14] blood pollution, and the sin of Eve.[15]

These conclusions in the case of Christian Greece invite comparison with the societies in Asia and Africa alluded to in my introduction. For although the role of Greek women at death bears striking resemblances to that of women in these societies, there are striking differences also, particularly as regards, firstly, the relation of the mourner with the pollution of death, and secondly, the social function of mourning as a means of reconstructing an ideal society which is hard to realize in the flesh.

In Ambeli, as with the societies described by Bloch and Parry, the mourner is clearly associated with the decomposition of the body, but this association is one in which she is involved, not in partaking in the pollution of the flesh, but in an ascetic withdrawal from it. Thus the phrase—quoted by the villagers—associating woman with both Eve and the Mother of God, "From one woman came sin, and from another woman came salvation" (apo gynaika egine hamartia kai apo gynaika egine sotiria), gains an extra dimension, for while woman as Eve was the agent through whom sin and death entered the world, woman as the mourner has, like the Mother of God, a compassionate and intercessory role which plays a part in the defeat of death and the freeing of the soul into the other world. However, this denial of feminine sexuality is only one facet of the way in which society traditionally answered death, for at the same time as the mourner was enacting most dramatically her ascetic role, the "grown virgin girls" used to be chosen to link house to house in a great chain of reconciliation, and to express, in opposition to the asso-

---

[14] A folk addition to the story of the Fall recounts how Eve, commanded by God to have only three children, said, "What? Go to my husband only three times?" So God replied, "Have as many children as you like, only half will be mine and half yours"; and that, the storyteller commented, was when death entered the world.

[15] See n. 6.

ciation of the mourner with the dead body in the grave, and with the dissolution of sins and the progress of the soul into the "other world," the renewal of society among the living in the regeneration of the earthly kindred—a different picture entirely from Bloch and Parry's description of the reconstruction, by the societies they discuss, of the idealized kin group in the world beyond the grave.[16] Thus, although half of this picture only now remains, the rituals of death in Ambeli used to negotiate the reconstitution of the social order by means of the idea of regeneration through marriage alliances and the birth of children, and, through ideas of forgiveness and remission of sins, to assert the final and utter freedom of the soul from this world and all the categories it holds.

At different levels, then, of discourse in Greek village cosmology, women both redeem the flesh in childbearing and mediate ascetically between the material and the immaterial worlds; and at different levels they may be both cursed by the sin of Eve and, with the Mother of God, be "more honorable than the cherubim." But the limits of gender vocabulary in this cosmology must also be emphasized. It is interesting that the gender aspects of social life, while they have important antecedents in all three discourses embedded in Greek village cosmology, appear to owe nothing at all to the way in which the Godhead is conceived. Although the terms *Father* and *Son* might lead us to expect a patriarchal archetype to be present in the villagers' thinking on the Godhead, there is no evidence to suggest that they attribute a theological significance to the gender aspect of this terminology, and it seems that it is the parent/ child aspect which dominates their thinking in their relation with the All

[16] The "other world" of rural Greek culture is a complex picture in which theological and folk understanding of the "judgment," "hell," and "paradise" of the Christian tradition, as well as the Hellenic world of the dead, both play a part; but in no case—although passing reference may be made to kin relations in the folk versions—is there any consistent reference to kinship. Rather relationships in the "other world" beyond the exhumation are left strictly undefined, and the Hellenic world of the dead, which is overwhelmingly present in the villagers' consciousness in the period immediately following a death, is contrasted specifically with blood, personal loyalties, and kinship of human society (du Boulay 1982 and 1984).

The reasons for this difference between the significance of the death rituals in Greece and those of the societies cited in Bloch and Parry's study, are beyond the scope of this paper; but it may be that they are to be found in the universality of the Christian religion. The internal metaphysic, as well as the history, of such a religion must clearly be radically different from a religion operating in a locally bounded cultural sphere, and it is perhaps for this reason that the case of the Hindu death rituals is a difficult one for Bloch and Parry's thesis. And similarly, although the role of women at death in rural Greece bears so marked a resemblance to the evidence cited by Bloch and Parry, this view of women is not homogeneous, but incorporates a long and varied history which puts these perceptions into dialogue with other levels of discourse which, according to the context, invert and transform their meaning.

Powerful. Similarly Christ, the Son of God, while historically a man, has his principal significance in the fact that he became anthropos and suffered death on behalf of all humanity. To the villager all these understandings about the Godhead say little about gender, but tell rather of the mystery of the Incarnation and of the incorporation of the human into the divine.

ACKNOWLEDGMENTS

I am extremely grateful to Peter Loizos for his great encouragement and help to me in writing this paper, and for a perceptive reading of the first draft. I would like also to thank Philip Sherrard for his valuable comments on the text, and John Davis for an interesting discussion about the use of the ethnographic present. Finally, I am indebted to the S.S.R.C. who funded the research from 1970 to 1973.

Chapter 3

SILENCE, SUBMISSION, AND SUBVERSION: TOWARD A POETICS OF WOMANHOOD

Michael Herzfeld

Submission as Subversion

In the ethnographic literature on Greece, women are usually either submissively silent or dangerously garrulous. These ideal types, symbolized and personified in the characters of the virginal Mary and the wanton Eve (e.g., du Boulay 1986), agree on what women are *not*: controllers of their own discourse. Women who cleverly "answer back" may sometimes be respected,[1] while women who appropriately perform funeral laments may arouse sensitive men's admiration (Caraveli 1986:179). By and large, however, women appear as incomplete humans because of their stereotyped inability to speak rationally. Their besetting inarticulacy is only a virtue inasmuch as it covers, controls, and suppresses an equally innate and far more dangerous urge to gossip. And silence and gossip—like holiness and pollution (Douglas 1966)—represent the twin aspects of what lies outside formal social structures defined and controlled by men. The *Panayia* and the Devil represent complementarily opposed alternatives to a male world.

Greek women may also use inarticulacy, like hospitality, as a defensive and inwardly ironic barrier to keep domineering intruders in their place, much as other socially disenfranchised groups do elsewhere (e.g., Anderson 1983:135; Heath 1983; Steiner 1975:33). Since explicitness necessarily involves the use of words, deciphering a display of submissiveness can never offer the satisfaction of certain interpretation. But this very indeterminacy may also be part of what renders silence or inaction effective. For example, Greek women sometimes call themselves "illiterate" (*aghrammates*). A Cretan woman running a newsstand often used this to justify getting the customer to figure out the change, while an elderly widow in a Rhodian village claimed it as the reason for not knowing what was happening during the 1974 Cyprus crisis.[2] Certainly, we may understand

---

[1] For examples of this, see my discussion of *mandinadha* (couplet) singing contests, in which a woman will occasionally compete directly with a man (Herzfeld 1985a:142–146).

[2] She commented that women don't understand "the radios that talk." During the Turkish invasion of Cyprus in 1974, while I was conducting fieldwork on Rhodes ("Pefko" vil-

such illiteracy as relative: Greek women were more illiterate than Greek men, but less so than any Turk. But such remarks *may* also comment ironically on the male control of public discourse. As another Rhodian village woman pointed out, in a quarrel "people will always justify the man," but "both should be judged [fairly]"; on the other hand, "that's how we found things." This combination of awareness and resignation suggests that claims of "illiteracy," as a means of contrasting women's domesticity with men's public expertise, can conceal a less than admiring view of men. "Letters" are all very well; but, if only men know them, are they worth taking seriously? Such stances may—but do not necessarily—rework outward, dominant meanings. Whether they do depends, presumably, on contextual aspects such as the actors' existing social relations, sensitivities, and attitudes.

Some stock expressions play on disenfranchisement (see also Chock 1987). A Greek woman can quite seriously maintain to outsiders that her sex is inferior to the male while internally mocking the men of her kingroup and community for insisting on exactly the same claim. Gender stereotypes are rhetorical strategies that only make sense in terms of social practice. We can thereby dispense with the false contradiction between the virginal and diabolical images of woman in a trivially *structural* sense and penetrate to the dialectical interplay between them. A woman—mirroring a reciprocal ambiguity in male attitudes—may castigate men in general or use the generic follies of men to berate her husband or son; but she will stand strongly beside him in the face of a threat from other men. People may seriously mean what they say about being *categorically* inferior or deficient when talking to outsiders; but these same utterances may *also* be directed ironically *at* the group, in which case they convey virtually the opposite implications to its members. Village women who describe themselves as illiterate are exhibiting normative submissiveness before outsiders. *If* they are also implicitly making fun of the poorly educated local men's pretensions to high literacy, their very indirection shields them from refutation: either way, the men can hardly complain.

RHETORIC AGAINST WORDS

Social performance may not always be aggressive, dramatic, thrusting, a use of words to wound. On the contrary, one can perform—through exaggeration—a submission that ridicules all who rush to accept it. The discursive use of stereotypes creates rich ambiguities, embedded in con-

---

lage), there was a good deal of local tension, as Rhodes is close to Turkey and constantly under threat.

flicts between different levels of loyalty. The analytical term *poetics* serves us better here than the related but more restricted *performance* to describe the interactional strategies involved. A social poetics not only more comprehensively addresses the ideological and historical processes affecting cultural form than does *performance*, but it also brings casual social interaction into comparative juxtaposition with more obviously "framed" (Goffman 1974) or ritual modes. A social poetics calls for the recognition of three essential ingredients: the active *creation* (poiēsis) of meaning; the presence of more than one level of social context; and the expressive deformation of a conventional form within negotiable limits. The last of these conditions removes social aesthetics from the synchronism of pure ideology, treating it as both cause and effect in cultural change.[3]

Olivia Harris (1985), commenting on my use of social poetics to analyze male interaction (Herzfeld 1985a), usefully asks whether, even in this extended sense, *poetics* could apply to women. She notes the importance of swaggering self-display among Cretan men and asks contrastively whether an approach so directly geared to an aggressive sociality can reveal the masked values of women. But women's self-restraint and their frequent displays of submission to male dominance do conform to the model in that women *creatively deform* their submission. They perform their lack of performance, as it were. In so doing, they may also implicitly deflect the appearance of submission to their own ends.

A social poetics need not be concerned only with the conspicuous consumption of rhetoric. The focus on social *action* apparently suggests a stereotype that we still residually seem to share with Cretan shepherds. We recognize aggressive performances as performances because they *do* something, and the dominant ideology seems to define women (and weak men) as those who do very little at all. But doing little can also be a dramatic performance: the criterion is whether people notice it. Thus, the difficulty of articulating a poetics of Greek womanhood reflects, not so much any lack of poeticity in Greek women, but, rather, the assumption that poeticity lies only in the bombastic and the verbal.[4] Absences are harder to interpret than presences. Friedl (1986[1967]:45–46), for example, notes that in Vasilika ritual transvestism at carnival was almost

---

[3] This is the key feature of Jakobson's definition of the "poetic function" (1960:356). Confining its application to purely linguistic phenomena deprives it of the major part of its utility (see also Herzfeld 1985a:10–19).

[4] In Miller (1986), the one essay that suggests a partial departure from the exclusively linguistic and literary use of *poetics* is Showalter's, on "piecing" as an active metaphor in American women's literary production. I use *poetics* here for the study and analysis of the phenomenon under discussion, while *poeticity* stands for the poetic *quality* of discourse (verbal or other).

exclusively male-to-female. The women's poetic may indeed have consisted in the extent to which they did *not* participate; but, since such a stance would register only as an absence, it could hardly satisfy an androcentric canon of proof that demands presence as its main criterion.

The androcentric stereotype of Greek men as "intelligent" (*eksipni*) and women as "cunning" (*ponires*) provides some support for this criticism of received ideas. The essence of *poniria* is that a person who plays the fool, or who seems stupid, may—by a kind of strategic inversion—prove the dupe to be even more of a fool. A Lebanese Muslim village provides a structural parallel. A habitual liar was able to show that a visiting holy man was an even greater liar by offering fake declarations of religiosity that the visitor failed to see through (Gilsenan 1976:206–210). In much the same way, if less dramatically, Greek village women may not only get great practical advantage from the pose of dumb subservience but may actually be enjoying a collective joke at the expense of the dominant sex. This does not appreciably better their condition—on the contrary, it confirms male prejudice—but it does afford a significantly different perspective on the exercise of domestic and communal authority. We must first examine the techniques whereby female silence and garrulousness are constructed. We shall then see that—just as the dual Panayia-Devil image of women is not really a contradiction in social terms—the contrast between silence and garrulousness is actually a dialectical complementarity. It allows *poniria* to comment ironically on self-serving male ideas about intelligence without subverting the community's common interests in the face of the wider world.

SILENT VOICES

Greek androcentrism—and its reproduction as verbocentrism—appear as a complex linguistic symbolism. On Crete, grammatical contrasts between the active and passive voices can index the unequal character of the relationships between men and women, while the objects of male contest are commonly feminized through the creative deformation of grammatical norms (Herzfeld 1985a:157–160, 215–217; 1985b). There are also adjectives for gender-related sets of ideas; "manly" (*andrika*) things are usually positive, whereas "women's" (*yinekia*) affairs are spoken of (by men) with contempt. The cognate abstract nouns reinforce the point. They include unambiguous terms for masculinity or maleness (*andrismos, andria,* and other etymological cognates of *andras,* "man"); while femaleness, despite the artificial *yinekiotita* (from *yineka,* "woman"), has no equivalent term in everyday discourse. There thus is a curiously appropriate irony in Friedl's observation that in certain forms of power—none of them, be it noted, embodied in an explicit terminology of social institutions—"Greek village women are past *masters*" (1986[1967]:52; my emphasis). In the Greek context, it is significantly easier to verbalize manhood than womanhood.

How, then, do we avoid searching only for *verbalized* notions of femaleness and its production (and reproduction; see Dimen 1986), and how do we seek meaning in what from a male perspective is "inarticulate" and "female"? Caraveli (1982), in discussing the many nonlexical ornaments on Greek village song, points out that these contain rich meanings that cannot be reduced to verbal formulae; she might have added that rural women's speech is also much ornamented with exclamations of pain, compassion, empathy, enthusiasm—emotions that corresponding men's spoken style usually disciplines with verbal explicitness. There are also female discourses that shy away from verbality altogether (e.g., Messick 1987). These are, in E. Ardener's (1975) sense, "muted" ideologies. "Muted" does not necessarily mean "verbally silent," since mutedness may take the form of a masking of alternative ideologies with the external signs of androcentric values (i.e., speech). Muting may be semantic rather than lexical. In Basso's (1979) Apache ethnography, for example, an expressive device that reinforces core values within the community becomes, when deployed in dealings with the politically dominant Anglo culture, a potentially subversive mode.

There remains, however, the practical difficulty that we, like many of our informants, generally look to language as the key to all other codes, and this underscores the ultimate opacity and hence the political limitations of most nonverbal messages. Basso's (1970) analysis of Apache silence partially proceeds from the verbal behavior that elicits it. Messick's exploration of North African women's weaving depends on the *terminology*—the verbal classification—associated with the physical acts of weaving that, in his interpretation, "silently" comment on women's life and values. Messick also extrapolates his evidence from historical sources and so sidesteps the sort of contextual approach to the problem that I am attempting here; the particular *agents* of subversion and their motives simply do not enter into his analysis, so that it is not clear that anything actually gets subverted except in thought. Weaving images are expressive of female responses, but do they actually achieve very much in practical terms? While the Homeric Penelope's constant weaving by day and unweaving by night "entices and allures and indeed entraps" the suitors, she still has to pass the chastity test set for her by her husband Odysseus on his long-delayed return (Felson-Rubin 1987:73–77). At best these are "blank banners" (Ardener 1971:xlii–xlvi)—a protest too inchoate to do more than set the stage for future action. "[P]erhaps . . . when in the early 1960s my Bryn Mawr classmates and I knitted as well as noted in lecture after lecture on the male literary classics, we were protesting

against patriarchal culture in a secret women's language we used even if
we did not fully understand it" (Showalter 1986:225).

   In Greece, males may define the public sense of "order," setting up a
less patterned and therefore less immediately identifiable female domain
of "practice" by contrast (Caraveli 1986). It is especially hard for the anthropologist to achieve critical distance when, as often happens, the identification of local cultural rules—representing strategies at once officializing and androcentric—translates into a quest for universal principles
(Bourdieu 1977; Herzfeld 1987; see also Dubisch 1986b:40n.13). The dependent condition of nation-states like Greece, conceived in the heyday
of European bourgeois nationalism, adds further reinforcement to androcentrism: the unyielding identification of "male" with "rule-governed"
ensures that the reproduction of explicit social norms—even when their
direct transmission is through women (see Handman 1983)—will conform
to an essentially male etiquette. Silence, loneliness, "shame"—these are
not simply the values of "Greek women" writ large; female seclusion
springs from the same roots as some of the core components of bourgeois
respectability (see Mosse 1985) and is thus problematical for a discipline
that is still struggling to break free of some of the same assumptions (see
also Bottomley 1986; Dimen 1986:61). How, then, does one begin to
elicit the subversive strategies of female silence? How does one *interpret*
without reducing to mere words, and so transcend the effects of history
shared in common by anthropology and the people anthropologists
study?

   Even the most modest attempt requires a clear distinction between
elicitation (the verbal "way in") and interpretation. Messick's discussion
of North African weaving, for example, works from the elicitation of concepts such as male and female shuttle to the relationship between the
warp-in-preparation and the warp-in-use (immature son vs. mature son).
Messick, however, then goes on to demonstrate how these terms are
used. In other words, by essentially discarding a referential theory of
meaning in favor of a use (or "action") theory, he is able (albeit somewhat
speculatively) to escape the illusion of pure language and so to suggest a
subversive (or at least subdominant) level of discourse.

   The distinction between reference and use is a complementary opposition that closely parallels Caraveli's order-practice contrast. Everyday
usage subverts legal, or legalistic, definitions; actor-speakers use ambiguity to provide both expressive richness (see Fernandez 1986) and, with
it, the means of redeploying official (or "structural") language to more
contextual and negotiable ends. This is the reverse of what Bourdieu
(1977:37–40) has dubbed "officializing strategies." In the strategies of
women's silence, absences suggest noninvolvement where male presences perform identities. Absence and presence represent two kinds of

power that cannot exist independently of each other, but of which, in a verbocentric world where all is presence, absence takes on the outwardly lower symbolic value.

ETHNOGRAPHIC ILLUSTRATION: STEALING A PIG

The recovery of the meanings conveyed by absence—these are Ardener's (1971) "blank banners," a phrase that also recalls his "muted" models (1975)—is highly problematical. Can we distill dissident perspectives from normative data? We would have to move between at least two social levels of the tension between collective self-display and collective self-knowledge.[5] Few Greek women will readily undermine the standing of their fathers, husbands, brothers, and sons in the world of male-defined competition. Equally, however, they understand, and disapprove of, many of the strategies that men use to maintain their positions.

In my ethnographic study of a Cretan mountain village, I focused on the reciprocal, competitive animal-theft in which the stronger of the shepherds engaged, and on the ways in which they represented these exploits narratively. Even the men themselves recognize how much their female kin disapprove of these actions; they may even concede that at one level the women are morally right. For example, one ex-shepherd proudly told me that his mother had "never wanted to *see* stolen meat" and that she would throw it into the street if she discovered it in the house. Another man, while praising his female kin for helping to conceal stolen meat, indicated that both they and his elderly father had privately disapproved of his actions. In the context of male competition, women do indeed act as virtual appendages to male performance. In the more intimate context of the home, however, they often roundly condemn it. Men are uncomfortably aware of that practical ambivalence.

One thief's sister, fourteen years old at the time, flung herself at a policeman who was about to discover the stolen meat her brother had concealed among the underclothes and sheets in her dower-chest. This symbolic defense of her chastity shows how the concept of social worth (*filotimo*) operates as a *collective* and *male-determined* value, but says nothing of what that value meant to *her*. It indicates a deployment of that value in defense of the collective family interest: the girl would hardly have benefited from the incarceration of the family's most agile breadwinner. It tells us (and told the police) absolutely nothing, however, of how the family women regarded being put in that situation to begin with. Women do not categorically praise animal-theft, and whenever men

[5] The expansion of *disemia* (Herzfeld 1987:95–122) from the purely linguistic domain of *diglossia* exactly parallels what I have argued for poetics (see nn. 3 and 4, above).

mention female reactions, it is as negative ones. Family solidarity is more a matter of public face than of internal actuality. The tension between these aspects offers extensive play for female irony against male control.

It is very unusual for women to raid. I have heard of one Cretan shepherdess who grew up in an otherwise male sibling group that was orphaned early and who herself became an active animal-thief. She adopted male dress—as, indeed, in a mainland folksong, does a female guerrilla or kleft in the Greek struggle for independence (Politis 1973:122–123).[6] The Cretan case suggests that such exceptional tales may have some basis in historical experience. The song is also closely related to the ironic idiom under discussion here. The young woman looks like a true kleft; but her eventual unmasking suggests otherwise. Similarly, in Crete, where men's thefts symbolize male contest over essentially feminine or female objects, women normatively do not steal animals; exceptions are, indeed, exceptional.

My access to animal-theft was through narratives. When I asked whether women ever discussed animal-theft, one woman replied with a stylized expression of disbelief and rejection (ba!). She then, under my continuing pressure to respond, categorically pronounced, "Women never get involved in such things!" Verbal narration of male combat is directly opposed to the usual representation of women as peacemakers and unifiers.[7] Thus, even though women allegedly gossip while men deliberate, the point here is that women do not always or necessarily talk; when they bear silent witness, invoke the name of Deity, or physically interpose their bodies between angry men, they appear in their Panayialike role rather than as diabolical schemers. Men's words, on the other hand, are always socially divisive; men's original sin may stem from the temptation of Eve, but the men themselves are the bearers of harmful speech, conflated with disruptive events in a single term (istories, "stories").

The only Glendiot tale in which I heard of women stealing an animal serves to highlight women's views on the entire, institutionalized practice. Asked whether she had ever raided for animals, one of the protagonists (the other was her mother) first let her male cousin begin the tale;

---

[6] Kleftic, klefts: the term kleftis, "thief," came to be applied to the mountain-dwelling guerrillas who were particularly associated with the struggle against the Turks, but whom Hobsbawm (1959) has claimed as "social bandits." Their apotheosis entailed considerable historical reconstruction.

[7] Women often break up male quarrels, through either bodily intervention or apparently uncontrolled cursing from the sidelines. In a category of satirical verses representing disputes over the distribution of the meat of a dead donkey or other domestic beast, they are usually represented as attempting to soothe male tempers by accusing them of committing sin (amartia) through their quarrels. Note that these verses are composed by men.

then, as she bustled about her coffee shop, she kept correcting his weak memory. Everything about the tale reversed the normative pattern: the selection of a pig (a domestic animal, and as such a nominally "unworthy" if occasionally encountered object of *male* raiding), the endocommunal character of the theft (subverting the normative use of raiding to create alliances between the inhabitants of *different* villages),⁸ the fact that the exploit took place in broad daylight (supposedly only men dare to circulate during the night), the narrative style itself (a subordinate commentary on the "main" tale that nonetheless highlighted the male narrator's incompetence). These elements were sufficient to ridicule male norms of raiding and narrative alike; and the cousin showed through his hesitant speech and evasion of detail that he felt this keenly. Yet because a man *might* steal a pig, and *might* do it in broad daylight, and because men *have* been known to raid covillagers on occasion, a slight flicker of doubt remains; and this made it all the harder for the cousin to reproach this woman directly.

Women's categorical denial of involvement recognizes a definitively masculine domain. On the other hand, one could read it as, simultaneously, an equally comprehensive criticism of men. That a woman might, atypically and in adolescence, herself have taken part in a raid merely shifts the irony. In this verbal representation of normative practice distorted, the woman kept correcting a somewhat embarrassed male, exhibiting no small contempt for male incompetence in general. She began interrupting right from the beginning; her cousin's discomfited response—"Leave it alone, let me tell it. Well, she *does* know it, so to speak"—confirmed rather than blocked the implied criticism. As she spoke in a high-pitched "explaining" tone in contrast with the masculine affectation of a deep growl, her cousin kept muttering, "Yes . . . yes . . . yes . . ."—drumming, as it were, with his verbal fingertips. Her interruptions became increasingly shrill, notably when she reminded her cousin that they had also recognized some social obligations in the home community: "We gave a *ghoulidhi*"⁹ to one of their fellow-villagers. Here she was ironically claiming to have performed a conventionally male act of generosity. Her cousin appeared ever more awkward as she, by repeatedly taking over the story, made fun of male self-projection. The story was of a kind that the cousin might ordinarily have expected to

⁸ The characteristic pattern of a raiding cycle is for the initiator to find himself the victim of a counterraid; after several such exchanges, interested third parties attempt to bring the protagonists together by creating, through them, ties of baptismal sponsorship (*sindeknia*) between their patrigroups, in the hope that this bond will prevent further outbreaks of hostility and may even furnish the basis of a practical alliance.

⁹ *Ghoulidhi*: the quarter-animal that, especially, the representatives of the bride's and groom's patrigroups bring in a basket, one per household, as a wedding gift (*kanisci*).

laugh off as trivial. Indeed, in reply to a question, he pointedly deduced from the fact that it was "a small animal" that "it must have been around '33"—in other words, a safely long time ago, when they were too young to steal large animals.

Note the indirectness of his remonstrances. As a cousin rather than a husband, and as a guest on her and her husband's territory, he could only express his unease in a "muted" fashion—a truly ironic inversion of gender relations. When I asked whether the victims had ever found them out—a normal phase in the cycle of reciprocal animal-raiding among male shepherds—he responded with the disbelieving "ba," only to be immediately set right by the woman. Finally, when I wanted to know *how* the victims had ever found out, and while the woman gleefully recounted the pattern of questioning that characterizes men's searches for stolen livestock, her cousin tried to damp down the whole description by asserting, "They *felt* it [to niothane]. Did you understand?[10] They felt it!" Roles were reversed: the man defensively attributed to the (male) victims the *embodied* response that is supposedly more appropriate to women and opposed to the men's verbalized, investigative reasoning; the woman continued to speak (though always in the same high-pitched voice) as though she had taken part in an ordinary raiding cycle between equally powerful (male) shepherds. She thereby both paid tribute to the social institutions of reciprocity and at the same time represented the raid itself as an easy adventure in which men take more pride than they have a right to take.

SEXUALITY AND THE CONCEALMENT OF SELF

Another Glendiot woman gives us a dramatically different illustration of resistance to male discourse. Here, the issue is that of male control over female sexuality. This woman had been widowed young (she was under thirty at the time) when her husband was killed in a road accident.[11] Her husband's brothers kept a close watch on her; they immediately announced that she was pregnant at the time of her husband's death, to deflect possible later suspicions about the child's paternity. The widow's

---

[10] *Katalavate?* ("Did you understand?") is the polite plural; coming as it did from a man with whom I was on generally amiable terms, this formal and nondialect (cf. Cretan *ekateśes*) usage is a mark of his discomfort.

[11] Her husband died when, asked by his uncle (MB) to give the latter's disabled truck a tractor-tow downhill to Iraklio, he had fallen asleep at the wheel and driven off the road. The uncle survived. Some of the deceased's agnates tried to exploit the uncle's "responsibility" for the accident for their own political ends. The incident is discussed in greater detail in Herzfeld (1985a:84–91).

public demeanor exhibited deep mourning, symbolized by voluminous black weeds that covered her entirely except for her eyes and nose. As the weeks went by, however, and as tensions aroused by her husband's death subsided, she began to revert to a more normal mode of clothing, though always maintaining the obligatory, lifelong black of widowhood.

Initially, she appeared to accept the control exercised by her brothers-in-law. In practice, there was very little she could do about it, as her house was located in a patrigroup residential cluster and her movements restricted to her own home, the cemetery, and the (very visible) main road between these two points. As she calmed down, however, she also began to show resentment of their surveillance and of their insistence that she exhibit hostility toward the kinsman whom they held responsible for their brother's death. She was especially annoyed that, while this man's political patrons helped her financially until her brothers-in-law forced her to return the money, their own political patrons promised equivalent help but failed to keep their word.

Her gradual assertion of independent feeling, expressed privately in terms of this conflict, could not become even that articulate in a more public arena. She continued to wear only black, to confine her movements to the environs of her house and the cemetery, and to break out upon occasion into fits of loud keening for the deceased. But her submission was no longer so dramatic, nor were her views kept so silent among people she trusted. She had begun to articulate her complaint, and to discard the more burdensome appurtenances of mourning-as-submission that had hitherto been her only source of protest against anything. As Caraveli (1986) has pointed out, mourning is not simply a plaint against death. It is also an expression of defiance against the circumstances that force women to find their sole escape from the travails of their social woes, and the sole means of transcending their dependent condition, in the execution of rituals for the dead; the hostility of the often misogynistic church to these practices, as well perhaps as their persistence in strongly anticlerical communities like Glendi, seems to confirm their significance as an idiom of protest (see also Alexiou 1987). The Glendiot widow began by expressing in the dramatic deployment of formal mourning the bondage that she later came to resist, however partially and carefully, in speech. Here again, outward conformity and submission—an intensely dramatic display of solidarity with the sorrowing agnatic group of which she was, after all, a member[12]—masked an inward resistance that could only be specified, if at all, by verbal means.

[12] A woman joins her husband's patrigroup at marriage; she acquires her husband's surname and an andronym, and is treated as the bride of the patrigroup in village usage.

SEXUAL FIDELITY

In Pefko, on Rhodes,[13] a coffee shop owner insisted that, while women should always remain faithful to their husbands, men should be free to conduct extramarital affairs. This is an attitude widely reported in the ethnographic literature (see especially du Boulay 1974:125–126). Moreover, the speaker's wife smilingly insisted that she was quite happy for her husband, a good breadwinner, to have some extra sex on the side— indeed, she expected and demanded it!

The weight of ethnographic parallels might suggest a literal reading. In practice, however, there was little the woman could actually have done to stop her husband from having affairs. Men often go to Rhodes Town on business, where they find prostitutes (and, allegedly, tourist women) for their pleasure; women rarely travel outside the village. The wife may simply have been accepting the inevitable; her motives remained masked. On the other hand, by telling me, a stranger, that she accepted her husband's infidelity, she effectively confronted me with the family's solidarity. The affirmation of a male-dominated social ideology does not necessarily, at all levels, mean what it appears to mean. Her smiling acquiescence appropriately challenged my inquisitiveness in a society where, people claim, one can never know what goes on in another person's mind (du Boulay 1974:84; Herzfeld 1985a:239–240).

Domestic behavior can invert public appearances. Another Pefkiot, a drunkard, though hardworking enough when sober and quite well-to-do as a result, was married to the cheerful sister of the deeply respected village priest. At home, he would often declare women inferior; his wife never let those comments go by without a riposte, usually through acid observations about who was doing the real work in the family, and sometimes—especially if he was drinking too heavily—by slapping his face. Her forthrightness never appeared to embarrass him before me, perhaps because this was a Pefkiot family with which I enjoyed some intimacy. The husband justified his notorious drinking on the grounds that wine guarantees the birth of sons; this wine, his own (as is usual), was a source of pride. The fact that he drank might have conduced to greater violence on *his* part (cf. Handman 1983) rather than hers; in fact, this couple seemed to enjoy an affectionate relationship marked by slapstick rather than real physical aggression. Within the home, she simply rejected self-serving male generalities in favor of forthright badinage. As the priest's sister, she introduced an element of power on her own side; she never alluded to this, however, perhaps because it was already implicit in her

---

[13] Pefko is a small (pop. approx. 160) agricultural village on Rhodes, where I conducted fieldwork in 1973–1974.

husband's apparently defensive—and certainly persistent—declarations of agnosticism.

In this partial inverse of the previous example, the wife does not concede to her husband the right to do as he pleases. Instead, she defends her own rights and views. In a situation where the outside observer has been admitted as a family intimate—a stage reached when the wife agreed to sit down at table with her husband and me instead of meekly serving us—self-assertion replaces submission. True, the violence is presented as a jest. But her emphasis on this humorous aspect, I suspect, is one clear residue of the socially perceived need to disguise notions of female power and even (moral) superiority before outsiders, even trusted ones. Perhaps, indeed, this concession to conventional concerns actually allowed the wife to express her dissatisfaction more fully than she would have done had they been alone together. In this combination of privacy and audience, her response to her husband's performance of male superiority could be more explicit and less dependent upon the secretive play of irony without running the risk of real violence.

URBAN CRETE: PARALLELS AND VARIATIONS

In the Cretan coastal town of Rethemnos, where women often seem more willing (and have more opportunities) to criticize men, a more indirect discourse nevertheless still also subsists. Women of the Veneto-Turkish Old Town spend a great deal of their time in the late afternoons and evenings (except when it is cold or wet) sitting in the narrow roadways where traffic is light and children and pets play freely and noisily. While men may join them more openly and frequently than in a village like Glendi, this is still clearly a women's domain, an extension into restricted public space of the domestic sphere.

These women often sit on chairs turned a little sideways but mostly toward the open doors of their houses, with their feet planted on the doorstep and their backs to the road. They pass the time knitting, chatting, and keeping an eye on the children; but, unlike their rural counterparts, they seem disinclined to watch the road directly or to remain within. When asked about this, both men and women acknowledge that while they recognize the trait, they neither normally remark upon it nor can explain its frequent appearance. Men, in fact, more readily account for it than do women; the latter usually claim that they simply cannot explain it, while men remark variously that it is a comfortable posture for female work such as knitting and sewing, that it avoids exposing female thighs to the road, or that it allows women to keep a watchful eye on their proper—that is, domestic—domain. Note that all these "articulate" explanations are conceived in terms of the androcentric view of how women should spend their lives. The women who sit thus—often deeply engaged in lengthy, if outwardly somewhat desultory, conversations from doorstep to doorstep—seem quite uninterested in "explanation." Theirs is a *bodily* declaration (cf. Bourdieu 1977:93–94; Cowan 1988; Jackson 1983), not easily reducible to words, but expressive of the ambiguity of the married woman's guardianship of the boundaries between inner domesticity and outward sociability (on this role, see especially Hirschon 1981, 1985). Men apparently never adopt the inward-facing pose.

"Sitting" is a common expression of power and possession in Greece.[14] In this sense, women as housewives representatively express their families' social and economic autonomy (cf. Salamone and Stanton 1986); they are also, however, *inverting* the balance of domestic power since "sitting" is commonly conceptualized as a male prerogative in, for example, the context of the all-male coffeehouse idiom of sociability. Women here claim power through the use of a "domestic" object, the chair (see Hirschon 1985), which extends the physical boundaries of the domestic domain. Its use both performs and reproduces subversive truths about social relationships: women lay claim to power of their own, pushing their way into a more or less public space that only serves to increase the risk of moral exposure. As du Boulay (1986:162–163) reminds us, to be a housewife (*nikokira*) is divinely ordained: what she fails to mention, perhaps because of her preoccupation with denying the existence of a female "subculture," is that the very concept is redolent with power and indeed (Bennett 1989) may carry connotations of class differentiation. The women who sit outside their houses in this characteristic way may be guarding against the exposure of their own sexuality—a theme sufficiently well documented in the ethnography of rural Greece to need no further elaboration here (see especially Campbell 1964:287). Women, appearing *to the men* to be guarding their sexuality in an entirely proper way, are also silently bearing witness to the paradox inherent in the very concept of the household: that the housewife has authority in this interior domain, which acquires meaning through its defensive and contrastive juxtaposition with the public world.

Silence both expresses and represses. A nonlocal woman, an extremely articulate militant feminist who had dedicated enormous energy to various radical political causes in Athens before coming to live in the provincial setting of Rethemnos, encountered a peculiarly vivid form of nonverbal rejection and then proceeded to elicit, through her own understanding of the situation, an interpretation that was vastly more subversive of male values than the *form* of the event would have sug-

---

[14] On sitting as a symbol of possession and power, see Herzfeld (1985a:154).

gested.[15] "Khara" arrived in Rethemnos with a male companion. Unmarried as a matter of principle, so Khara assured me, they proceeded to make a home together in the heart of the Old City. The man worked at home or on various jobs; Khara went out to work every day, returning in the evenings to an increasingly hostile reception as she walked along the long, narrow street in which hoarse whispers and harsh glances seemed to ricochet at her off the walls. As the days lengthened into weeks and the whispering intensified, other little incidents began to press in upon her: garbage thrown into her house, a set of women's knickers suspended from the doorknob (another use of a symbolism already encountered in the animal-thief's sister's dower-chest), a pair of men's shoes pointing in toward the house with the accompanying jibe: "You've got a visitor, Miss!"

One day a relatively friendly neighborhood woman she met in the local grocery shop asked her why she spent so little time with the other women there. At this, Khara's irritation boiled over. Demanding to know how she could possibly be expected to seek out the company of her persecutors, she then discovered, as others joined in, that the local women's hostility did not derive from a straightforward objection to her living in sin, but from the fear that this behavior—which signaled "student" and "tourist" to them—meant that she was also liable to seduce their husbands and sons. This was not a positive endorsement of the dominant ideology of sexual continence but, to the contrary, expressed the fear that her presence might give their husbands a sexual freedom categorically denied the women themselves and thus eventually destroy their sole economic support. From that day on, the neighbors have treated Khara with elaborate friendliness, if not—she suspects—with full sincerity or trust.

A highly articulate woman thus galvanized her verbally cautious and sexually suppressed neighbors into articulating their resentment. Granted, her interpretation may have been guided by her own ideological concerns; but it did elicit a positive response—an immediate change in her relations with the neighborhood women. This in itself suggests that she was right. In effect, she provided the means of transforming a nonverbal and outward-directed expression of mute hostility into verbally explicit female solidarity. In this example, no less than in the rural cases examined above, we encounter acts that *appear* to endorse an androcentric ideology while casting a critical perspective on the way in which men behave. What appears to the outsider's eye as an uncritical acceptance of hegemony becomes, from an internal perspective, the expression of defiance.

[15] Cowan (1988:97–100), in a sensitive account of local reactions to her presence as an ethnographer, explores some similar perplexities.

SOME CONCLUDING OBSERVATIONS: SILENCE, SUBVERSION, AND ARTICULATION

All these cases document a true hegemony. While women have the means of expressing their resentment of male control and pretensions, they must always do so by ostensibly endorsing what ideologically they subvert. In the public sphere, women submit to male control of material resources, decisions regarding their children's future, and the family's public image. Their subversion is notional, an "englobing" (Ardener 1975) of male authority and action.[16] Because men are the idealized masters of language, women's protests are by contrast seen to possess little reality. They are effective only within the community of women—except, of course, when an articulate woman such as Khara appears on the scene and gives them an explicit counterdiscourse. Even then, however, great changes are unlikely, as Khara herself thought. How many of Khara's neighbors used the revelations that her situation had disengaged in order to confront their husbands?

Nonetheless, the contradiction between the externally held, male-defined consensus and the silent observation of its inequalities does imply some intellectual independence. Through irony, women can acknowledge the besetting paradoxes of their condition. Irony plays socially upon the tension between an outer-directed ideology of consensus and the inward-directed experience of social division. The tension between inward and outward perspectives operates at every level of social grouping. Irony depends on the subversion of a shared cultural *form*—the outward idiom—in conjunction with a strong differentiation of *meaning* within. Words, as merely external display, are more appropriate to the externally focused male ideology. Silences and gestures mark alternative meanings that may contradict the literal and the obvious.

Greek verbal irony, commonly used to explore the tensions between an idealized cultural self and experienced realities, provides a suggestive model for interpreting silence as well. Chock's recent (1987) study of Greek-Americans emphasizes such conventional uses of irony as the claim that a non-Greek wife has assimilated Greek culture "better" than the Greeks themselves; in Greece itself, local people will sometimes tell foreigners, "You speak Greek better than we do." The structure of this irony is identical with that of the male villager who assured me that "men are worse gossips than women," and to that of the claim that the exceptional woman animal-thief was "better" at raiding than any man.

These uses of spoken irony all come from speakers who contextually occupy the dominant position: men, members of a family into which the

---

[16] For a related point, see Bruner and Kelso (1980:250).

hapless bride has married, the Greek "speaking down" to a foreigner. Although women often use verbal irony, especially when mocking their menfolk's pretensions of bravery, their silence can be especially effective. Ethnographic accounts and male-promulgated norms to the contrary, women often do indulge in bawdy badinage when they are among friends and intimates (see Clark 1982; Dubisch 1986b; Kennedy 1986). In a solidary closing of the ranks, rowdy verbal acts disappear behind a submissive, respectful silence that merely masks the internal mockery.

Women are not necessarily at all silent among themselves, however, and here I have to confront my own limitations as a male ethnographer with only partial access to these intimacies. Khara, who read an earlier version of this essay and expressed surprise that a male researcher could get even as far as I did, pointed out that I had nevertheless taken "the most difficult route." This is because I worked at understanding the silences that I encountered rather than the talk that I did not. Khara wrote, "On the few occasions that I attended such [informal] gatherings [of women] in Crete and elsewhere, I was astonished at the transformation of the women. Although they customarily continue some dumb[17] task—crochet, embroidery, lacework, etc.—they use discourse [logho(s)] in an unexpected way." A foreign woman had expressed surprise at the range of Rethemniot women's discussions: they voiced "social criticism, a critique of men that was often of great severity, exposure of all their problems including even sexual ones, with great ease." If I understand her point correctly, I might have recognized a greater role for speech in female discourse had I myself been fully privy to women's gatherings. This fits with Khara's own interpretation of the events in which she was embroiled; she was able to try out her insights and attitudes verbally in a way that her neighbors might never have tolerated in a man. The privacy of female gatherings in Rethemnos's Old Town permits the explicit articulation of ideas that, in public and male-dominated contexts, more usually find expression in indirect modes; women thus still appear on the surface to accept the dominant values (see also Cowan 1988:19–20). And this, ultimately, is the local women's dilemma. Unless and until they are enabled to verbalize their resentment in a public context, whatever subversion they bring to their discourse will, in the public world, have the force of the proverbial tree falling in an uninhabited forest.

While the "blank banners" of inarticulate protest may have little effect on the language-centered, legalistic, combative world of men, they are no less important for all that. Gesture, for example, may both symbolize

---

[17] "Dumb" (vouvi) is not *necessarily* a derogatory term here; it corresponds to the "silence" of these quintessentially female activities—note again the weaving/sewing/knitting theme. The term's ambiguity here both reproduces and expresses the ambiguity of the women's position and of Khara's reaction, at once admiring and frustrated.

and effect the ideological subversion both of language and of the values that language makes explicit. A covert gesture—a conspiratorial wink that conscripts a friend into a raid, for example—flouts convention and thereby achieves intimacy. In Crete, such a gesture is, significantly, called a *noima* (lit., "meaning"): once again, *meaning* is opposed to *verbality*, even in male contexts.[18] Sexual indiscretions—things that should be "covered up"[19]—are often initiated with a look, a glance, a gesture. This does not mean that words have no place. But "giving one's word [loghos]" is a binding, official act, particularly associated with male concerns;[20] a significant gesture—a wink accompanying a solemn "word of honor"—can undercut it. We should not forget in this context that effective cunning and deceit are important aspects of the female stereotype.

When Greek women exhibit silence and submission, they outwardly perform their female identity in a male-dominated world; when they talk, they are women alone. Since we cannot penetrate individual thoughts, we can learn most from examining how this self-presentation varies and how women evaluate each other's performances. Addressing Harris's concern about the appropriateness of a poetic model, we should note any situations in which women clearly play up their submissive role. Exaggeration is the essence of a poetics that addresses the social manipulation of cultural form. Khara's neighbors in effect both valorized the ideal of sexual continence, symbolized by the paradoxical display of an intimate garment, and protested against the one-sided freedom of men to abandon it. A woman's pig-theft is both a reproduction of socially approved male behavior and a sarcastic deformation of the raiding code. The woman who assures the outsider that her husband is welcome to his extramarital adventures may thereby be according him a value lower than he demands for her. In a poetics of the womanhood for which the Greek language has no name, irony operates from behind a mask of noncommunication and anonymity. Submission may be subversive; but, to become effective action, it requires the verbal articulation of resistance. Women who are constantly and curtly told by their husbands and fathers, "*Mi milas* [do not speak!]"—do not express an opinion—would have to be determined indeed to bring about a radical change in their social lives.[21]

[18] This conflation of all kinds of meaning as meaning-as-usage is characteristic of the local concept of *simasia*.

[19] "God wants people to cover things up" is a stock phrase reported by du Boulay (1974:82).

[20] The "word," which local men consider especially typical of Crete, is given most dramatically in matters concerning animal-theft. When sworn over a reputedly miraculous icon, it is invested with supernatural sanctions against perjury. The Word of God furnishes the archetype, so that perjury is a particularly heinous form of blasphemy as well as a cowardly act—a defiant confession usually goes down very well, by contrast—for which the perjurer forfeits any claim to true manhood.

[21] Men invoke the dual identity of women as both more religious (positive) and, ipso

ACKNOWLEDGMENTS

In revising this paper, I have derived great benefit from the critical insights of many friends. I would especially like to thank Jane K. Cowan, Jill Dubisch, Nancy Felson-Rubin, Renée Hirschon, Peter Loizos, Akis Papataxiarchis, Gail Rosecrance, Eric Schwimmer, Cathy Winkler. I also benefited greatly from the opportunity of presenting an earlier version in the Department of Anthropology, New School for Social Research (1988). Despite the rich polyphony of voices in the field and elsewhere, some strong agreements also emerged, and I have tried to show my appreciation by responding here in my own way to both the particular and the collective reactions.

The research on which this paper is based was partially supported by a Summer Grant from the American Council of Learned Societies in 1981; a Fellowship for Study and Research from the National Endowment for the Humanities for research in Rethemnos in 1986–1987; and grants-in-aid from the Office of Research and Graduate Development, the Russian and East European Institute, and the West European National Resource Center, Indiana University. I am grateful for this extensive help over the years. The opinions expressed here are my own and do not in any way reflect those of the granting institutions.

---

facto, more credulous (negative). Religion is based on faith, and Orthodox Christians are adjured to "believe and not investigate." Clearly, if women are constantly and actively silenced by men, their religiosity can become both a spiritual refuge *and* a passive mode of opposing the skeptical and combative ideology of manhood; Glendiot mothers and wives who oppose animal-theft, for example, appeal to an essentially Christian moral code. By allowing themselves this refuge, however, women thereby also reinforce the stereotype of women as credulous.

Chapter 4

THE RESOLUTION OF CONFLICT THROUGH SONG IN GREEK RITUAL THERAPY

LORING M. DANFORTH

THE ANASTENARIA is a ritual involving trance and possession that is performed in several villages and towns in Greek Macedonia. It is a ritual system of psychotherapy that is often effective in treating illnesses which in Western psychiatric terms would be considered psychogenic in nature. In this paper I will suggest an explanation for the therapeutic effectiveness of the Anastenaria that focuses on the manner in which it resolves, both at a symbolic and at a social level, the conflicts that often underlie these illnesses. I will examine one particular set of social relationships that is often characterized by a great deal of conflict and tension, and show how this conflict is symbolically expressed and resolved in one of the songs that accompany the dance of the possessed Anastenarides. Then I will show how involvement in the Anastenaria can often restructure a patient's social reality in such a way as to resolve the conflicts responsible for the illness and bring about a cure.

The Anastenaria was performed in northeastern Thrace near the Black Sea until the conclusion of the Balkan Wars in 1913. Among the many Greeks who were forced to flee the area a year later were the Kostilides, residents of Kosti, the most important town where the Anastenaria had been performed. The largest group of refugees from Kosti eventually settled in the western part of Greek Macedonia in the village of Ayia Eleni, where the Anastenaria continues to be performed.[1]

Although the Anastenaria is denounced by representatives of the Greek Orthodox Church as a sacrilegious survival of pre-Christian idolatrous rites, it exists within the religious and cosmological context of the Greek Orthodox Church and draws heavily on Orthodox symbolism, beliefs, and ritual practices. On certain important feast days in the Orthodox calendar, the Anastenarides of Ayia Eleni and nearby towns, perhaps ten or fifteen women and three or four men, gather at the *konaki*, the

---

[1] The village of Ayia Eleni, which in 1986 had a population of approximately seven hundred, is composed of several distinct ethnic groups, the most important of which are the Kostilides and the indigenous Macedonians. Ayia Eleni is a fairly wealthy village that lies within the irrigation network of the Strymon River.

shrine where the Anastenarian icons of Saints Constantine and Helen are kept. These icons are believed to possess the power to perform miracles, as are the large red kerchiefs, known as *simadia*, which are kept with the icons.

The culmination of the yearly ritual cycle of the Anastenaria is the festival of Saints Constantine and Helen which is celebrated by the Greek Orthodox Church on May 21. The Anastenarides gather at the konaki early on the eve of May 21. Shortly thereafter the music of a three-stringed Thracian lyre and a large drum begins, and the Anastenarides enter a state of trance and begin to dance. The Anastenarides believe that when they begin to dance Saint Constantine "seizes" or "calls" them, and that, as long as they dance, Saint Constantine is both in control of and responsible for all their actions. The Anastenarides dance for twenty or thirty minutes. Then after a short break, they dance again. This process continues until the ritual gathering breaks up around midnight.

On the morning of May 21, the Anastenarides sacrifice a black lamb to Saint Constantine. Afterward they dance in the konaki until evening, when they are notified that the large fire which had been lit several hours earlier in an open area near the edge of the village has burned down to form a huge mass of glowing red coals. Then they process barefoot from the konaki to the site of the fire, where several thousand people have gathered to witness the spectacular firewalk.

As the Anastenarides approach the fire, several men spread out the mound of coals with long wooden poles until it forms a large oval bed. Then the Anastenarides, each holding an icon or a simadi of Saints Constantine and Helen, enter the fire, running and dancing back and forth across the coals, stirring up showers of sparks and glowing embers with their feet. They continue dancing until the fire is completely extinguished, and nothing remains but a bed of harmless gray ash. Then they return to the konaki where a meal is served to all present. The Anastenarides believe that they alone are able to perform the firewalk unharmed because they are protected by the supernatural power of Saint Constantine.[2]

As a system of ritual psychotherapy, the Anastenaria is concerned with the diagnosis and treatment of a wide variety of illnesses. A sick person is likely to consult the Anastenarides, rather than a university-trained physician or a local folk-healer, if he or she exhibits any of the following symptoms: unusual, obsessive, or deviant behavior particularly of a religious nature or involving fire; persistent dreams or visions concerning the Anastenaria; periods of unconsciousness, paralysis, or involuntary and

---

[2] The most useful descriptive accounts of the Anastenaria are the following: Romaios (1944–1945), Megas (1961), and Kakouri (1963).

uncontrolled activity; or states of depression or anxiety characterized by general malaise and an inability to eat, sleep, or work. An initial diagnosis that a person is suffering from an illness associated with the Anastenaria is strengthened if he is a descendant of an Anastenaris, if he is known to have ridiculed the Anastenaria, or if the onset of his symptoms happened to coincide with an important ritual gathering of the Anastenarides.

When such a diagnosis is made, it is said that the individual "is suffering from the saint" (ipoferi ap ton ayio) or that he "is suffering from those things" (ipoferi ap afta ta pramata). The patient or a member of his family then invites the Anastenarides to gather at his house. After the patient has discussed the onset of his illness and his present condition, an Anastenarissa may suddenly begin to rock back and forth in her seat and clap violently several times, or jump to her feet and dance for a few seconds. She will then shout out a command to the patient that is believed to be an expression of the will of Saint Constantine. At such times the Anastenarissa is said to speak "with the power of the saint" (me ti dinami tou ayiou).

The utterance of the Anastenarissa is invariably an order to correct some "ritual fault" committed by the patient or a member of his family. For example, the patient may be told that in order to regain his health he must repaint his family icon, sacrifice a lamb to Saint Constantine, or serve the saint by regularly attending the ritual gatherings of the Anastenarides. The saint is believed to have caused the patient's suffering in order to force him to act to correct his fault or to serve the saint in the desired manner. When the patient carries out the instructions of the Anastenarides, or when he merely agrees to carry them out, he often experiences an improvement in his condition, which is attributed to the beneficent power of Saint Constantine, who has forgiven the patient for the commission of his ritual fault. Regardless of the specific recommendations of the Anastenarides, a patient who believes that he has been cured by Saint Constantine usually feels obligated to attend the ritual gatherings of the Anastenarides. Quite often he is subsequently "seized" or "called" by the saint, begins to dance, and becomes an Anastenaris himself.

This process is illustrated by the following account of how a woman I will call Maria became involved with the Anastenaria.

Maria had known nothing about the Anastenaria until she married a man whose brother was an Anastenaris. When her husband told her that his brother danced on fire, she said he must be crazy. Her husband warned her not to talk like that. Shortly after her wedding she saw the Anastenaria for the first time and was very frightened.

As a young bride and mother Maria was sick a great deal. A young Anastenarissa in the village told her not to worry and not to consult a doctor. She was not sick; she was suffering from Anastenaria and would one day become an Anastenarissa herself. During this time she had dreams in which she saw the Anastenarides dancing with the icons of Saints Constantine and Helen.

Maria did not get along well with her mother-in-law, who lived with Maria and her husband. According to Maria, her mother-in-law had an evil soul and was very selfish and demanding. Maria felt that her own behavior had been characterized by patience and compassion. She told me that she had given in to her mother-in-law for so long that she had become nervous and high-strung. According to other village women, Maria gossiped and argued a great deal and was easily upset. They say that mainly because of the anxiety and tension generated by her conflicts with her mother-in-law, Maria suffered a "nervous breakdown" (nevriko klonismo) several years after her marriage.

Maria's mother-in-law told me that Maria did not treat her well. When Maria's husband was not home in the evening, Maria did not invite her to meals but let her eat bread and cheese by herself in the back room of the house, where she lived. Maria's mother-in-law also complained that Maria and her son did not give her enough money to live on. She took care of the family cows, but her son and her daughter-in-law sold them and kept all the money. They left her to live on her widow's pension.

At the festival of Saints Constantine and Helen, several years after her marriage, Maria sat in the konaki crying and trembling. She twisted and turned in her seat but did not dance. Throughout the next year she often dreamed that she was dancing in the fire. After this dream she always woke up very excited and dripping with sweat. She would then get up and light some incense, as she had been told to do by an Anastenarissa.

The next year, several weeks before the festival of Saints Constantine and Helen, Maria fell ill and lost weight. She thought about the Anastenaria without wanting to. She knew she would dance, but was afraid of the fire. On the first day of the festival she sat writhing and twisting in her seat until she was helped to dance by other Anastenarides. Later she danced in the fire with no difficulties at all. She felt that she had become an Anastenarissa relatively easily and had not suffered greatly because her husband had been good to her and had supported her.

Rituals involving trance and possession like the Anastenaria are performed in many societies throughout the world. It is generally agreed that such rituals are often therapeutically effective in the treatment of illnesses of a psychogenic nature, those which may be caused at least in part by persistent anxieties and tensions that result from situations involving psychological and sociocultural conflict. Explanations for the therapeutic effectiveness of these rituals have stressed a variety of factors, many of which play an important part in Western systems of psychotherapy. For example, it has been argued that such rituals are therapeutically effective because they provide the patient with group support, with a conceptual framework with which to interpret his illness, and with an opportunity for the cathartic expression of socially unacceptable behavior.[3]

While all these factors play a part in the therapeutic process of the Anastenaria, I feel that a much deeper understanding of the Anastenaria as a therapeutic system can be gained by examining the manner in which the Anastenaria furnishes the suffering individual with a set of symbols—symbols with which he is able not only to articulate or express the particular conflicts responsible for his illness, but to resolve them as well.

As Claude Lévi-Strauss has stated in his article "The Effectiveness of Symbols," ritual systems of psychotherapy provide the patient with "a language by means of which unexpressed and otherwise inexpressible psychic states can be immediately expressed" (1963:193). According to Lévi-Strauss, during the therapeutic process the patient "receives from the outside a social myth which does not correspond to [the patient's] former personal state" (195). As the patient becomes involved in the therapeutic process, his social reality is made to conform to this social myth, which, unlike the patient's former personal state, is free from conflict.

Not only are the conflicts responsible for the patient's illness expressed and resolved at a symbolic level, but a structurally parallel resolution of conflict often takes place at the social level as well. Thus the patient's social reality may be transformed or restructured in such a way as to conform to the conflict-free social myth provided by the symbolic structure of the rite. When the social conflicts and tensions responsible for the patient's illness are actually resolved as he becomes involved in the ritual system of psychotherapy, he is often cured.

I would now like to illustrate this therapeutic process with data from the Anastenaria. After examining one constellation of social relations often characterized by a great deal of conflict, I will show how this conflict is symbolically expressed and resolved in one of the songs that accompany the dancing of the possessed Anastenarides and in the beliefs concerning the relationship between the possessed Anastenarides and Saint Constantine. Then I will demonstrate how the reduction of conflict in the patient's important social relationships, which is brought about by his participation in the Anastenaria, often contributes to an improvement in his condition.

The particular set of social relationships I propose to examine here con-

---

[3] My thinking on ritual therapy generally has been influenced by the work of Crapanzano (1973), Moerman (1979), and Kleinman (1980).

sists of the relationships between husband and wife, mother and son, and mother-in-law and daughter-in-law. As a result of the virilocal residence pattern of the Kostilides, the mother-in-law, the daughter-in-law, and the son or husband often live together in one house. If the family is relatively poor, this living arrangement may be permanent. If they are more wealthy, it may last several years, until the young man is able to build his own house. However, this new house will often be only a few yards away from his parents' house, in which case this triangular set of social relationships continues to be an important one.

The relationship between mother-in-law and daughter-in-law is generally characterized by a great deal of conflict. The figure of the evil mother-in-law is a common one in Greek folklore.[4] In one folk song a daughter-in-law leaves her husband's household and returns to that of her parents because of the unreasonable amount of work demanded of her by her mother-in-law. In another a "wicked mother-in-law" kills her daughter-in-law by poisoning her food.

As might be expected, conflict between women in this difficult relationship often arises over the proper performance of household jobs, over the raising of children, and over the management of household finances. The position of a daughter-in-law is strictly subordinate to that of her mother-in-law since she is the younger of the two and a newcomer to the household. If a daughter-in-law does not obey her mother-in-law, conflict arises and the daughter-in-law is usually held responsible. People say: "The mother-in-law is in charge. The mother-in-law holds the reins." (*I pethera kani koumando. I pethera kratai to halinari.*)

Young married women I spoke with stressed the difficulties they encountered in their relationships with their mothers-in-law. They were not independent, they could show no initiative, and they were not respected. One woman told me that at times she felt like a prisoner in her own home and that her mother-in-law did not think she was worth anything. As a result she lost all self-respect. She could not complain to her husband because he would only tell her to be quiet. "Occasionally," she added, "these difficulties can become so severe that you go crazy." Daughters-in-law often say that they feel anxious about whether their performance as a housewife lives up to the expectations of their mothers-in-law. They are afraid that if they are found wanting, their mothers-in-law will gossip about their inadequacies with other village women.

A further component of this relationship is the sense of embarrassment or shame (*dropi*) that daughters-in-law say they feel in front of their mothers-in-law. The paralyzing effect that this sense of shame can have

---

[4] See Alexiou (1983).

on a daughter-in-law is indicated by the following comment of a young married woman.

> When I first got married, it was really hard. I always hesitated and felt ashamed. I was ashamed to buy clothes for myself. My mother-in-law would say, "Why does our daughter-in-law spend so much money?" I was ashamed to ask for anything. I eat slowly, and my mother-in-law eats quickly. So I went hungry many times because I was too ashamed to ask them to wait for me.

Furthermore, a daughter-in-law is an outsider, a *xeni*, in her family of marriage. She and her mother-in-law live together in the same household as a mother and daughter do, but their relationship can never be that of mother and daughter. As an often quoted proverb suggests, "A daughter-in-law can never become a daughter" (*I nifi kori de yinete*).

The implication is that if the blood ties of mother and daughter existed between the two, then the difficulties between them would be manageable. The position of a daughter-in-law is rendered even more difficult by the fact that she has only recently undergone what is often a very traumatic separation from her family of origin, as evidenced by remarkable similarities between wedding songs and funeral laments in rural Greece. The peripheral or marginal quality of the position of women in a village where residence after marriage is virilocal is indicated by expressions such as the following: "A woman has no village" (*I yineka horio den ehi*) and "a daughter is just a guest" (*I kori ine mousafirisa*).

The focus of the conflict between mother-in-law and daughter-in-law is usually the son or husband, for he has authority over both of them by virtue of the fact that he is a man. Kostilides say that ideally a man should make sure that his mother treats his wife fairly and that his wife in turn takes care of his mother when she grows old. If a man must take sides, however, it is agreed that ultimately his sympathies must lie with his wife since, after all, he must live the rest of his life with her, while his mother will die. Yet Kostilides also recognize that it is often very difficult for a man to criticize or discipline his mother, especially during the first years of his marriage, a time when his wife is in greatest need of his support. With both women trying to win the favor of the man through whom they are related, the balance of power in this conflict-laden relationship often depends on which woman is able to gain his support.

When a man fails to support his wife in her dealings with her mother-in-law, she is completely isolated and experiences a great deal of tension and conflict in her relationships with the other members of the family. A young woman in this position may become depressed, anxious, and unable to eat, sleep, or work. She may then be diagnosed as "suffering from the Anastenaria," become an Anastenarissa herself, and eventually be cured.

The conflict between mother-in-law and daughter-in-law is symbolically expressed and resolved in the most important of the songs that accompany the dance of the possessed Anastenarides. The song is usually referred to as *Mikrokostantinos*—"Little Kostantinos" or "Young Kostantinos." A brief summary of this song's plot runs as follows: Young Kostantinos goes off to war and leaves his wife at home with his mother. He instructs his mother to take good care of his wife, but, as soon as he leaves, his mother cuts off her daughter-in-law's hair, dresses her as a shepherd, and sends her off to the mountains with a flock of diseased sheep. Kostantinos's mother tells her daughter-in-law not to return to the plains until her flock has increased a hundredfold. Kostantinos's wife then goes up into the mountains "loaded down with tears." There she prays for help to Christ and the Virgin Mary. Soon her prayers are answered, her flocks multiply miraculously, and she descends to the plains where she meets her husband Kostantinos returning from battle. When Kostantinos learns what has happened, he goes home and kills his mother. (A complete text of the song appears at the end of this essay.)

In his book *Folk Poetry of Modern Greece* (1980), Roderick Beaton analyzes in some depth the Mikrokostantinos song. In what is otherwise an excellent book, Beaton makes several inaccurate statements about this song:

> It will be immediately apparent that none of the details of the ceremonies at the Anastenaria correspond to details in the narrative. The only exception is the name of the hero in the song, which is also that of the principal saint honored in the ritual. But the Kostantinos of the song is not specifically equated with the saint, nor is there any mention of the other saint celebrated—St. Helen, the mother of Constantine the Great. The behavior of Kostantinos' mother in the song, and his treatment of her at the end, surely preclude any identification between her and St. Helen. . . .
>
> As regards the equation of Kostantinos with the Christian saint, it seems to me that his final action in the song, that of murdering his mother, absolutely disqualifies him from this role (20).

As an anthropologist I strongly disagree with these claims. In the remainder of this paper, I will argue that this song is intimately connected with the Anastenaria and that it plays a central role in its therapeutic process.

Although Beaton claims that the Kostantinos of the song is not and cannot be equated with the Christian saint of the same name, this is exactly what all the Anastenarides and all the Kostilides I spoke with do. Invariably they say, "Mikrokostantinos, Kostantinos the young, is the saint when he was young." With regard to Beaton's claim that there is no mention in the song of Saint Helen, the mother of Saint Constantine, I would point out that many Anastenarides believe that Saint Helen is the wife, not the mother, of Saint Constantine. These two insights, readily obtainable through anthropological fieldwork among the Anastenarides, indicate that in the context of the Anastenaria, in the culturally constructed reality of the Anastenarides, the Mikrokostantinos song is a song about Saint Constantine when he was young, his wife (usually identified as Saint Helen), and their conflict with Kostantinos's mother. With this in mind we are now in a position to consider the song more closely.

The first few lines of the song suggest a concern for the individual life cycle and the problems of generational passage associated with it. Kostantinos's youth is emphasized, as is his dependence on his mother. His early engagement points to the impending break in his relationship with his mother, while his departure for war constitutes a crucial separation from his wife. The anxiety generated by this separation is indicated by comments Kostantinos's wife makes in other versions of this song after Kostantinos tries to comfort her in lines 8 and 9. When Kostantinos's wife asks: "Where are you leaving me?" he replies: "I leave you first to God and then to the saints. I leave you last of all to my sweet mother." In other versions of the song, Kostantinos's wife then says: "What will God do with me? What will the saints do with me? What will your mother do with me while you are away?" (*Ti na me kani o theos? Ti na me kanoun i Ayii? / Ti na me kani i manna sou horis tin afendia sou?*).

Kostantinos's wife is worried about what will happen to her during her husband's absence, since she has no security and no social identity, other than that which she derives from her relationship with her husband.

In spite of Kostantinos's instructions to his mother to treat her daughter-in-law as she would her own child, the mother treats her daughter-in-law very cruelly. By cutting her hair like a man's, dressing her like a shepherd, and sending her up to the mountains, Kostantinos's mother deprives her daughter-in-law of her sexual and social identity. The opposition between mountains and plains, which figures prominently in this song, represents the opposition between the world of nature, on one hand, and the social or cultural world, on the other. In other versions of this song, the daughter-in-law is dressed up as a monk, a powerful symbol of someone who is "outside" society and who will not leave any offspring. The rejection by Kostantinos's mother of her daughter-in-law is an egregious failure to maintain proper family ties. One woman I spoke with about this song said that Kostantinos's mother did this because she was an evil woman and because she hated her daughter-in-law.

Kostantinos's wife is given a small number of mangy and rabid animals and told not to return from the mountains to the plains unless they multiply a hundred- or a thousandfold. She is also told not to water the animals at the Jordan River, because "there are snakes and vipers there that will come out and eat [her]" (*yat' ehi fidhia ki ohendres, tha xevoun na se fane*). In one version of the song, Kostantinos's wife is told that if she goes to the Jordan River she will find "snakes and vipers and pregnant wolves" (*ehi fidhia ki ohendres ke likous gastromenous*).

Kostantinos's wife goes off forlornly to the mountains where she prays for help to Christ and the Virgin Mary. Her prayers are answered when her flock multiplies miraculously. She takes her sheep "with their collars of gold" and her dogs "with their ribbons of silver" down to the plains to the Jordan River, where she meets her husband. The miracle that takes place here is one of fertility. Through divine intervention Kostantinos's wife's animals are made healthy and fertile, and they multiply. It is this miracle of fertility that is responsible for the reentry of Kostantinos's wife into society and for her reunion with her husband. Why does Kostantinos's mother warn her daughter-in-law not to take her flock to the Jordan River? Perhaps she knows that her son will pass by there and wants to make sure that her daughter-in-law does not meet him. But what is the significance of her assertion that her daughter-in-law should not go to Jordan River because it has snakes and vipers and pregnant wolves? These images suggest male sexuality, fertility, and impregnation. It is as if Kostantinos's mother is warning her daughter-in-law that if she goes to the Jordan River she will become pregnant. In fact, young children in rural Greece are sometimes told that babies come from rivers, in much the same way that young children in the United States might be told that babies are brought by storks. Commenting on this part of the song, one Anastenarissa said to me: "God protected Kostantinos's wife. Instead of finding snakes, she found her husband Kostantinos." A more psychoanalytically inclined commentator might say she found both.

The reunion of Kostantinos and his wife represents the restoration of the proper relationship between husband and wife. That this restoration should be associated with images of sexuality, fertility, and reproduction is not surprising. Just as in the song the miracle of fertility and birth is a precondition for the return of Kostantinos's wife to the social world, so in everyday social life it is a precondition for a woman's more complete acceptance into her husband's family.

Following this recognition scene, Kostantinos returns home and asks his mother about his wife. Kostantinos's mother tells him that his wife has died. When Kostantinos asks, in line 57, "Where, mother, is her grave that I can go and weep?" his mother replies, "Her grave is overgrown and cannot be recognized" (*Poune, mana m', to mnima dis na pago na tin klapso? / To mnima dis hortariase ke gnorismo den ehi*). This neglect of her daughter-in-law's grave is another example of Kostantinos's mother's complete failure to fulfill her social obligations to her daughter-in-law. It serves to emphasize in a particularly horrible way Kostantinos's mother's total rejection of her daughter-in-law. Kostantinos then punishes his mother for her mistreatment of his wife by stabbing her and taking her to a mill where he will presumably grind up her body as a warning to other women.

In this song, then, the conflict between mother-in-law and daughter-in-law is resolved in favor of the daughter-in-law when she receives divine assistance and the support of her husband Kostantinos. Discussions with many young Anastenarides like Maria, whose involvement with the Anastenaria was described earlier, suggest that they identify closely with the wife of Kostantinos. Thus the very conflict that has contributed to the illness of many Anastenarides is symbolically expressed and resolved in one of the songs sung during their ritual gatherings.

In addition, both factors in the resolution of this conflict in favor of the daughter-in-law (divine assistance and the support of the husband Kostantinos) characterize the relationship between the possessed Anastenarides and Saint Constantine. In the context of ritual possession, the source of the divine assistance that the Anastenarides receive is Saint Constantine himself. It is from him that the Anastenarides receive the supernatural power which enables them to perform the firewalk unharmed. They also receive from him the supernatural knowledge that enables them to predict the future and to diagnose the illnesses of others. Most important, however, it is the beneficent power of Saint Constantine that brings about the cure of their own illness.

The parallel between the plot of the Mikrokostantinos song and the relationship that develops between the possessed Anastenarides and Saint Constantine is further emphasized by the fact that the possessed Anastenarides, who identify with the wife of Kostantinos in the song, are symbolically married to Saint Constantine when they become members of the cult group and each time they are possessed by him and dance. The symbolic expression of the relationship between possessing saint and possessed worshiper as one of marriage is quite common and is found in rituals involving trance and possession throughout the world.

In the case of the Anastenaria, this relationship of marriage is expressed most clearly through the exchange of the large red kerchiefs, or simadia, that occupy such an important position in the symbolic system of the Anastenaria. These kerchiefs are given by the faithful to Saint Constantine as offerings and are kept with the Anastenarian icons in the konaki. In this way they are believed to acquire the supernatural power of Saint Constantine and therefore to be effective in curing illnesses caused by the saint. When a person falls ill and is believed to be "suffering from the Anastenaria," he receives a kerchief from the chief Anastenaris, which he may keep for forty days. Similarly, when a person is possessed by Saint Constantine for the first time, a kerchief is placed on his shoulder or around his neck to indicate that he has now been "offered" to the saint, that he now "belongs" to the saint. From then on, every time he dances, he receives from the chief Anastenaris a kerchief, which he holds for the duration of his dance. These kerchiefs, therefore, symbolize the relationship between Saint Constantine and the possessed Anastenarides, and the exchange of supernatural power that is such an important feature of this relationship. These same red kerchiefs were traditionally exchanged at engagement ceremonies by the bride and groom. In this context these kerchiefs were also referred to as simadia, meaning "marks" or "signs." These kerchiefs symbolized the bond uniting husband and wife, as in the context of the Anastenaria they symbolize the bond between Saint Constantine and the possessed Anastenarissa.

It is clear that, during the course of the ritual therapy of the Anastenaria, the conflict between a young woman and her mother-in-law is expressed and resolved at a symbolic level in the songs which accompany the dance of the possessed Anastenarides. In addition, as each young woman is incorporated into the cult group, becomes an Anastenarissa, and is cured, she receives divine assistance that consists of the supernatural support and protection of Saint Constantine, her spirit husband.

As a woman becomes involved with the Anastenaria, a structurally parallel resolution of this same conflict, the very conflict that was at least partially responsible for her illness, takes place at the social level as well. A woman's participation in the Anastenaria may actually restructure her family relationships in such a way as to resolve the conflicts present in her relationship with her mother-in-law. By becoming an Anastenarissa, a woman gains the support of her husband, since he is forced to commit himself publicly to helping her regain her health.

A woman who is diagnosed as suffering from the Anastenaria is encouraged to attend the ritual gatherings of the Anastenarides. If she begins to show signs of being possessed, she must become an Anastenarissa and dance in order to be cured. Since this is an extremely public act, a woman needs the permission of her husband in order to become an Anastenarissa. If he grants his permission, she may dance in public, perform the firewalk, and be cured.

If, however, a man refuses to give his wife permission to dance, she is unable to become an Anastenarissa. If she is allowed to attend the ritual gatherings, she will writhe and twist in her seat. If she is not allowed to be present at the konaki, she will suffer wherever she is. This suffering is interpreted as a form of punishment that Saint Constantine imposes on those who do not carry out his will. Most important, however, if a woman is not allowed to dance, she will not be cured but will remain ill indefinitely.

There are many reasons why a man might not allow his wife to become an Anastenarissa. He may not believe in the Anastenaria, or he simply may believe that her illness could be better treated by medical doctors. On the other hand, he may want to avoid the notoriety that surrounds a woman who becomes an Anastenarissa. If his wife continues to suffer, however, he may give in and allow her to become an Anastenarissa. He must then attend a ritual gathering of the Anastenaria with his wife and formally give his permission for her to dance by saying, "May she be well and may she dance" (As yini kala ki as horepsi). He must also be willing to contribute his time and money to whatever ritual activities and offerings the saint may demand. For example, he may have to agree to sacrifice a lamb to Saint Constantine, to finance the repainting of an icon, or to entertain the Anastenarides at his house during the celebrations of the Anastenaria. In short, he must commit himself publicly to his wife's cure and support her in her attempt to regain her health.

Thus a woman's participation in the Anastenaria may actually change the social relationships within her family of marriage. By changing her relationship with her husband, her participation in the rite changes the balance of power within her family in such a way as to resolve the conflict between her and her mother-in-law. Just as in the Mikrokostantinos song the wife of Kostantinos receives her husband's assistance, and just as the possessed Anastenarissa receives supernatural power from her spirit husband Saint Constantine, so a woman is able to enlist the support of her husband when she becomes involved with the Anastenaria. Through the symbolic resolution of conflict, together with a structurally parallel resolution of conflict at the social level, the Anastenaria often proves therapeutically effective in the treatment of a wide variety of illnesses.

Ὁ Μικροκωσταντίνος

Ὁ Κωσταδῖνος ὁ μικρὸς κι ὁ μικροΚωσταδῖνος
μικρὸ δὸν εἶχ᾽ ἡ μάννα δου, μικρὸ δ᾽ ἀρραβωνιάζ ει,
μικρὸ δὸν ἧρτε μήνυμα νὰ πάῃ στὸ σεφέρι.
Νύχτα σελλώνει τ᾽ ἄλογο, νύχτα τὸ καλλιγώνει.
Βάν᾽ ἀσημένια πέταλα μαλαματένιες λόθρες.   5
Καὶ ἡ καλὴ δὸν ἔλεγε ἀπὸ τὸ παραθύρι.
- Ἐσύ διαβαίνεις, Κωσταντῆ, καὶ μένα ποῦ μὲ ᾽φήνεις;
- Φήνω σε πρῶτα στὸ Θεὸ κ᾽ ὑστερινὰ στοὺς ἄγιους,
᾽φήνω σε κι ὁλούστερα στὴν ἐγλυκειά μου μάννα.
- Μάννα μου, μάννα μου καλή, μάννα μου ζαχαρένια,   10
ὅπὼς ἐμένα εἶχες παιδί, νὰ ᾽χῃς καὶ δὴ καλή μου,
νά ᾽χῃς καὶ δὴ γεναῖκα μου, τὴν ἀγαπητική μου.
Πήδηξε, καβαλλίκεψε σὰν τὸ γοργὸ πουλάκι.
Ὥστε νὰ πῇ σᾶς ᾽φήνω γειά, σαράντα μίλλια πῆρε
κι ὥστε νὰ ποῦνε στὸ καλό, ἄλλα σαραντατρία.   15

'Ακόμα κρότος του βαστᾷ κ' ἡ πιλογιὰ κρατιοῦντο
κι αὐτὴ ἡ σκύλα ἡ γάνομη, ἡ γόβρέσσας θυγατέρα
ἀπὸ τὸ χέρ' τὴν ἄρπαξε, στὸ μπερμπεριὸ τὴν πάει.
Πὰ στὸ σκαμνὶ δὴ ράθισε κι ἀντρίκεια δὴ ξιουρίζει,
μιὰ ρούκλα δὴν ἐφόρεσε καὶ βέργα δήνε δίνει.   20
Τὴ δίνει δέκα πρόβατα καὶ κεῖνα ψωργιασμένα,
τὴ δίν' καὶ τριὰ σκυλιὰ καὶ κεῖνα λυσσασμένα.
Τὴν παραγγέλνει στὰ γερά, γερά τὴν χωρατεύει.
- Θὰ πάῃς πάνω στὰ βουνὰ καὶ στὰ ψηλὰ κορφᾶτα,
πὄχουν τὰ κρύα τὰ νερά, τὶς δροσερούς τοὺς γήσκιους   25
κι ἂ δὲ δὰ κάνῃς ἑκατὸ κι ἂ δὲ δὰ κάνῃς χίλια
καὶ τὰ σκυλιὰ βδομηνταδυὸ στὸ γάμπο μὴ γατέβῃς.
Σὲ οὔλους πόρους πᾶνε τα, σὲ οὔλους πότισέ τα
καὶ στὸ Γιορδάνη ποταμὸ μὴ bᾶς καὶ τὰ ποτίσῃς,
γιατ' ἔχει φίδια κι ὄχεντρες, θὰ ξέβουν νὰ σὲ φᾶνε.   30
- Ἔλα, Χριστὲ καὶ Παναγιὰ μὲ τὸ Μονογενῆ σου.
Πὰ στὰ βουνὰ ποὺ βρίσκουμαι νὰ φτάνῃ ἡ εὐκή σου.
Πῆρε καὶ πῆγε στὰ βουνὰ τὰ δάκρυα φορτωμένη.
'Αρνάδα ἀρνάδα γέννησε, ἀρνάδα πέντε δέκα,
γίνηκαν χίλια πρόβατα καὶ γίδια πεντακόσια   35
καὶ τὰ σκυλιὰ βδομηνταδυό, στὶς κάμπους ἐκατέβη
καὶ στὸ Γιορδάνη ποταμὸ πάει καὶ τὰ σταλίζει.
Κι ὁ Κωσταντῖνος ἤρχουντο ἀπὸ τοῦ σεφεριοῦ dου.
Κοιτάζ' αὐτὰ τὰ πρόβατα, μαλαμοβραχιολᾶτα,
κοιτάζει καὶ τὰ σκυλιὰ ἀσημορερδανᾶτα.   40
- Καλημερά σου, λυγερή. - Καλῶς τὸν Κωσταντῖνο.
- Τινοὺς εἶναι τὰ πρόβατα, μαλαμοβραχιολᾶτα,
τινοὺς εἶναι καὶ τὰ σκυλιά, ἀσημορερδανᾶτα;
- Τοῦ Κωσταντίνου τοῦ μικροῦ, τοῦ μικροκωσταντίνου,
ὅπου μικρὸς παντρεύτηκε, μικρὸς γυναῖκα πῆρε,   45
μικρὸ δὸν ἦρτε μήνυμα νὰ πάῃ στὸ σεφέρι,
τὴ μάννα dου παρέγγειλε, τὴν καρδιακιά του μάννα
καὶ στὸ σκαμνὶ μὲ ἔκατσε κι ἀντρίκεια μὲ ξιουρίσε,
μ' ἔδωσε δέκα πρόβατα νὰ πὰ νὰ τὰ φυλάγω.
(Ὕστερα αὐτὸς τὴν πῆρε, τὴν ἔβαλε στὸ ἄλογο, γνωρίστηκαν   50
κεῖ πέρα τὴν πῆγε στὸ σπίτι.)
Στὸ ἄλογο τὴν κάθισε, στὸ σπίτι τήνε πάγει.
Κάτου τὴν ἄφησε κι αὐτὸς πάγει ἀπάνου.
Βρίσκει τὴ μάννα του, κρατοῦσε στὴν ἀγκαλιά της ρόκα.
- Μάννα μ' ποῦναι ἡ γυναῖκα μου, ποῦναι καὶ ἡ καλή μου;   55
- Γυναῖκα σου ἀπόθανε, γυναῖκα σου ἐθάφτη.
- Πόναι, μαννά μ' τὸ μνῆμα δης νὰ πάγω νὰ τὴν κλάψω;

- Τὸ μνῆμα dης χορτάριασε καὶ γνωρισμὸ δὲν ἔχει.
Στὴ μέση τὴν ἔσκισε, στὸ μύλο τὴν πηγαίνει.

(Megas, 1961, pp. 488–90)

LITTLE KOSTANDINOS[5]

Kostandinos the Little, Little Kostandinos
was little in his mother's arms, and little when she betrothed him,
and little when a summons came to him to go to war.
By night he saddled his horse, by night he shod it.
He put on silver horseshoes and nails of gold.   5
And his beloved called to him from the window,
"You are going, Kostandis, and to whom do you leave me?"
"I leave you first to God and then to the saints,
I leave you last of all to my sweet mother.
Mother, good mother, mother sweet as sugar,   10
as you looked after me as a child, look after my beloved,
look after my wife, my loved one."
He leapt into the saddle, and rode off like a swift bird.
No sooner had he said goodbye than forty miles went past,
no sooner had they said farewell, than another forty-three.   15
The sound of hooves could still be heard, his voice was still in the air
when that impious bitch, the child of a Jewess,
seized [his wife] by the hand and took her to the barber,
made her sit upon a stool and cut her hair like a man's,
dressed her in a shepherd's cloak and gave her a staff.   20
She gave her ten sheep and those were mangy,
she gave her three dogs and those were rabid.
She commanded her loudly, and loudly mocked her.
"You shall go up to the mountains and to the high peaks,
where the streams are cold and the shadows cool   25
and if you don't make them a hundred, and if you don't make them a
    thousand
and the dogs seventy-two, don't come down to the plain.
Take them to all the fords, at each one water them,
but to the River Jordan do not go to water them,
because there are snakes and vipers there, they'll come out and   30
    eat you."
"Come Christ, come Holy Mother with your Begotten Son.
Even in the mountains where I'll be, may your blessing reach me."

[5] R. M. Beaton's translation and the Greek original of the song are reprinted, by permission of the translator and the publisher, from R. M. Beaton, *Folk Poetry of Modern Greece* (Cambridge: Cambridge University Press, 1980).

She set out and went to the mountains weighed down with tears.
Lamb gave birth to lamb, lambs in fives and tens,
they became a thousand sheep and five hundred goats   35
and the dogs seventy-two; she came down to the plains
and by the River Jordan went to rest them.
And Kostandinos came by, returning from the war.
He looked at those sheep with their collars of gold,
and he looked at the dogs, with their ribbons of silver.   40
"Good morning, pretty girl." "You're welcome, Kostandinos."
"Who owns the sheep, with their collars of gold,
and who owns the dogs, with their ribbons of silver?"
"Kostandinos the Little, Little Kostandinos,
who was little when he married, little when he took a wife,   45
and little when a summons came to him to go to war;
he left orders with his mother, his own heart's mother
but she made me sit upon a stool and cut my hair like a man's,
she gave me ten sheep to go and watch over."
[The singer glosses part of the story in prose:] Then he took   50
her, set her on his horse, they recognized one another there
and he took her home.
He put her on his horse and took her home.
He left her below and himself went up [to the house].
He found his mother, with a distaff in her arms.
"Mother, where is my wife, and where is my beloved?"   55
"Your wife is dead, your wife is buried."
"Where, mother, is her grave that I can go and weep?"
"Her grave is overgrown and can't be recognized."
He stabbed her through the middle and took her to the mill.

ACKNOWLEDGMENTS

The fieldwork upon which this paper is based was carried out among the Anastenarides of Ayia Eleni in the *nomos* of Serres in Greek Macedonia between September 1975 and September 1976. It was supported by grants from the National Science Foundation (SOC 74-23895) and the Wenner-Gren Foundation for Anthropological Research (#3089). The substance of this paper has appeared in Danforth 1989:109–118 (*Firewalking and Religious Healing: The Anastenaria of Greece and the American Firewalking Movement*. Copyright © 1989 by Princeton University Press), which provides a more detailed discussion of the Anastenaria as a ritual system of psychotherapy.

Chapter 5

THE LIMITS OF KINSHIP

ROGER JUST

THIS PAPER addresses one of the most conventional subjects within social anthropology and particularly the anthropology of southern Europe: namely, the role of kinship and family in a relatively isolated village community. Moreover, given the title of this volume, it is perhaps wise to state from the outset that my concern will be with kinship itself rather than gender. Admittedly the two are closely interwoven, and it is usually within a familial context that gender roles are most apparent to the anthropologist. Nevertheless, just as the social manifestations of gender are neither exhausted by nor limited to the field of kinship, so kinship, especially at the structural level, displays features that invite analysis separate from the issue of gender (if only to pave the way for its consideration).

If I may start with an autobiographical note: When, in 1977, I began field work in Spartohori, one of three villages on the tiny island of Meganisi (administratively attached to the Ionian island of Lefkada), I had little enthusiasm for the study of kinship and family. Doubtless prejudice played a greater part than reason, but inasmuch as my reluctance had basis, it involved the following (not entirely consistent) reflections. First, in the 1970s there was a widespread feeling that kinship, for so long anthropology's sacred cow, might well be ready for poleaxing and that its centrality was perhaps no more than the fetishized product of the discipline's own history. Second, even supposing the importance of kinship studies could be defended, the very structure of Mediterranean (and European) kinship—or perhaps one should say its lack of structure—seemed to preclude the sort of interest aroused by the study of the formal intricacies of more "exotic" systems. Last, and for me most cogent, had not the whole subject of Greek kinship been more than ably dealt with by those who had gone before? The prospect of making any significant addition to the work of Peristiany, Campbell, du Boulay, and others seemed depressingly remote. In sum, I thought it advisable to leave kinship and family alone and, as contemporary wisdom then enjoined, to explore the more "relevant" issues of politics, economics, and, of course, class.

It did not, however, take long to discover that my mentors' interests had not been misplaced. It was impossible to understand anything about the village without first understanding something about kinship. The values of kinship seemed to permeate almost every aspect of village life—from where one shopped to whom one voted for, from the forms of local economic cooperation to the adventures of overseas migration. Moreover, it was impossible to avoid the rhetoric of kinship: "My uncle in Lefkada who will help you"; "My brother-in-law, the best man in the village." Certainly if there were any one thing around which an ethnography of the village could be centered, any one thing that would provide a constant point of reference, a continual series of links between one aspect of village life and another, then it was the Spartohoriots' concern with kinship and family.

I still believe this. But by the time I left Spartohori in 1980 I felt that an important modification had to be made. It was true that one had to understand something about kinship and family to understand the way the Spartohoriots construed their social world, but if I have carefully used such phrases as "the *values* of kinship and family" and "the Spartohoriots' *concern* with kinship and family," it is because the role that kinship and family played was not an entirely objective one. Within the household itself, as has often been observed, the bonds of kinship and family did appear to impose a categorical set of rights, obligations, and duties on household members;[1] once outside the household, however, though kinship and family could be (and were) used to explain almost every social connection, in fact they determined very little. Rather, kinship and family provided a set of values on the basis of which people's actions could be judged and, importantly, social relationships entered into; but kinship and family could not predict what the quality of those relationships would be, nor could they even specify with which individuals they would be formed. Outside the household the real bases for cooperation, loyalty, amity, and trust lay elsewhere. Kinship was their cover.

Such is the gist of my argument. It is not an original one. Within a Greek context, it has been foreshadowed by Campbell, du Boulay, Friedl, and Loizos.[2] Moreover, as an observation on the workings of Eu-

---

[1] See, for example, Peristiany (1965c:179–180); Campbell (1964:36–38 and 185–203); du Boulay (1974:17–19 and 121–141; 1976:391–393). In the case of the Sarakatsani (Campbell 1964), one has to speak of the elementary family rather than the "household," since the Sarakatsani were transhumant pastoralists without permanent dwellings.

[2] See Campbell (1964:106–109), du Boulay (1974:150–155) and Friedl (1962:73–74). It was, however, a remark by Loizos (1975), who contrasts kin relationships in the settled village of "Kalo" with those obtaining among the transhumant Sarakatsani, that prompted the line of investigation pursued in this paper: "Kin and affines are not dispersed, but concentrated within the village, so they are less a scarce resource to be cherished, than a fact

ropean kinship, it was made some twenty years ago in Firth, Hubert, and Forge's study of London.[3] But though the rest of this paper will amount to little more than a step-by-step substantiation of these introductory remarks, a part of my aim will also be to draw attention to demographic factors (whose interplay with kinship cannot be ignored) and to certain specific features of Spartohoriot kinship (which are not necessarily generalizable for Greece as a whole).

Kinship and Cooperation

Late September to early November is the wine-making season. Nowadays no one in Spartohori grows grapes in quantity, but a number of people (not least some of those who live most of the year in Athens) continue to make wine, buying and transporting grapes from Lefkada. I happened to be in one of the village's olive oil mills when about 2,500 kilos of grapes were receiving their second pressing in the mill's hydraulic press (which should have produced about 1,500 liters of wine). Five men were directly involved in the enterprise. I knew them well enough, but I asked the son of one of the mill's joint owners for whom so much wine was intended. Irritated by what he thought a silly question, the young man replied that *naturally* the wine was for "all the brothers and all their *gambroi* [sisters's husbands] and *kouniadoi* [wives' brothers] and their *petheroi* [fathers-in-law] and all the rest."

If my informant's answer was less than precise, this was because he was stating what he took to be the obvious—that the wine was for its makers and all their *relatives*. In fact the five men present consisted of three brothers, the husband of one of their sisters, and the father of one of their wives. As it happened, this father-in-law was also a part owner of the mill that was being used (and the first cousin of my young informant's father). But, as my informant indicated, the wine was intended for more than these. Another brother, in Athens at the time, would be taking a share, and another share was to go to another of the brothers' relatives who lived sometimes in the village, sometimes in Athens. He was their "double" relative, the *badzanakis* (wife's sister's husband) of one of the brothers and at the same time the affinal uncle (wife's father's brother) of one of the other brothers. Other recipients were to be the brothers' own father (in whose village house the wine would be stored) and some of their kouniadoi (wives' brothers) and gambroi (sisters' husbands). The full range of the participants was elicited because one of the brothers over-

---

of life, to be judged on merits and usefulness" (1975:63). The argument also owes much to Davis's review of Mediterranean kinship (1977:197–222).

    [3] See Firth, Hubert, and Forge (1969), and particularly chap. 4, "Kinship Ideology" (87–118).

heard my inquiry and was quick to add that the *spitia* (households) were many—lest I should have thought the amount of wine excessive, for the brothers were all wealthy men who had joined the ranks of the Athenian bourgeoisie and who would have been loath to have been considered too fond of village wine. Finally, the caïque that had been used to transport the grapes from Lefkada belonged to one of the brothers' patrilateral first cousins—though this particular cousin was not a member of the wine-making group, but rather employed by them (a point to which I shall return).

In sum, then: three brothers, one sister's husband, and one father-in-law were actually present for the wine making; then, as silent partners, a wife's sister's husband cum wife's father's brother, some of the husbands of some of the sisters, some of the brothers of some of the wives, and, of course, the brothers' own father. Finally, to transport the grapes, a patrilateral first cousin. All in all, a good enough illustration of one of the commonplaces of Mediterranean anthropology—the cooperation of the bilateral kindred.[4]

Further examples of this commonplace were not difficult to find. Fishing provides a convenient context, for on Meganisi it has been a traditional pursuit and ranges from a pastime that supplements the household food supply to a profession that, though it is seldom anyone's exclusive occupation, may provide the major part of their income. But whether the fishing is more or less amateur or more or less professional, the *parea*, the "company," that fishes together is almost exclusively recruited from kin.

Many of Spartohori's older residents would fish for a couple of hours a day in the immediate coastal waters. Whenever their sailor sons were home, however, and especially if the shoals of *palamidia* (horse mackerel) were running, they would be joined by the younger generation, and small crews consisting of some combination of fathers, sons, fathers-in-law, sons-in-law, brothers, and brothers-in-law would be formed, the catch to be split among their respective households. The cost of professional fishing equipment is, however, high, and among those who fished for a living more formal financial partnerships were not rare. Thus one man would own a caïque, another its engine, and another the nets (with the division of the catch then being based on capital contribution as well as labor).[5] But even though each partner owned outright his particular

---

[4] See, for example, Campbell (1964:88–94); du Boulay (1974:155 and 158–159); Loizos (1975:68 and 74–76). Cf. Davis (1977:220–223).

[5] The division of the catch was based on the following formula: one for the boat, one for the engine, one for the nets, and one for each person's labor, with the proviso that should the catch be too small to divide, then it went to whoever had been taken on simply as a "worker"—i.e., whoever had been hired by the owners of the capital equipment.

item of equipment and could thus withdraw if the partnership soured, such partnerships were still formed almost exclusively among kin[6]— brothers, brothers-in-law, and cousins.

It could of course be argued that such "economic cooperation" amounts to no more than the good-natured sharing of time and resources among those who have always lived together in easy intimacy. And so it does. But the role of kinship is highlighted by the part it can also play in actually initiating cooperation. I noted one day that two brothers who regularly fished together in a rather old caïque were fishing in a new and well-equipped one, and in the company of a young man, Lakis, whom I had not seen fishing before. The next day the brothers were again fishing in the new caïque, but with Lakis's father who, to the best of my knowledge, had never been a fisherman. The events behind the formation of this new parea were as follows. The two brothers had a sister whose husband, a fisherman, had recently and unexpectedly died, leaving her a widow with an only daughter of sixteen years or so. In order to provide a man for the house, a marriage had been quickly arranged between this daughter and Lakis, himself only twenty years old. Since Lakis's bride-to-be was an only child, an "heiress," Lakis's dowry was to be the entirety of his deceased father-in-law's estate, including his caïque. Since Lakis, however, knew nothing about fishing, the caïque effectively reverted to his newly acquired affinal uncles who had need of better equipment and who at the same time could instruct Lakis in the use of his acquisition. Moreover, since Lakis still had his military service to do, and since the new family would need an income, in his absence the uncles were going into partnership with Lakis's father. The family rearrangements caused by death and by marriage thus immediately resulted in a new fishing parea and a new financial partnership.

It should also be remembered, however, that the ties of affection and intimacy that made it seem "natural" for a couple of brothers to go off fishing together are of substantially the same order as those which result, for example, in a family-owned shipping company. Indeed, to revert to the wine makers, their joint village "holiday" activities were paralleled by their business enterprise in Piraeus, for the brothers were all part owners of a shipping company, and they had originally been in partnership with another set of brothers, their matrilateral first cousins. Moreover, their above-mentioned badzanakis and several of their gambroi and kouniadoi were officers or captains on their ships. A continuity exists between casual familial cooperation and formally constituted business enterprises precisely because no threshhold is perceived over which one

---

[6] Throughout this article I have not made the standard anthropological distinction between "kin" and "affines" for reasons that, I trust, will become readily apparent.

passes into an impersonal world of commerce where the affections of family and kinship are to be subordinated, or where it is to be presumed that impersonal constraints will take their place in guaranteeing trust and fair dealing.

This attitude was nicely revealed when it was rumored that a company in Lefkada was considering establishing a ferryboat link to Meganisi, which would, of course, run the local ferry caïques out of business. It was loudly proclaimed in the coffee shops that the Spartohoriots were fools and that those who owned (or who had owned) ferry caïques ought to have pooled their resources years ago, established a company, and purchased a ferryboat of their own. "Ah, forget it," laughed Christos, who had once owned a ferry caïque, "It wouldn't have worked anyway. How many times have I quarreled with Iannis? We could never run a company together." It was immediately protested that Christos now owned a new fishing caïque in partnership with his wife's brother, Pavlos. "Certainly," replied Christos, "but Pavlos and I are *family.*"

In fact there is more to this story, for Christos and Pavlos's partnership—or rather the partnership between their families—extended beyond their joint ownership of a fishing caïque and involved another matter in which cooperation between kin is also clearly manifest: emigration. Christos and Pavlos had bought their new caïque after Christos's return from nearly six years in the United States, where he had worked as a barman in order to support his son who was studying for a degree in business management. Indeed Christos had "emigrated" in advance of his son in order to qualify for residency, which in turn would qualify his son for a subsidized education at a state college. Christos's emigration had been sponsored by none other than Pavlos's brother (i.e., the other brother of Christos's wife), who had settled permanently in America many years before. One kouniados was thus Christos's business partner in the village; the other had been his sponsor (and employer) in the United States.

Such assistance by way of sponsorship to America, Canada, South Africa, and Australia is commonplace between relatives and may last over generations, since the Spartohoriots still practice a form of temporary migration for the sole purpose of accumulating capital with which to return to Greece. Within this strategy, those relatives who are permanently settled overseas provide the necessary staging posts. In the case of Christos and his wife's brothers, however, this assistance too was only part of their history of familial cooperation. As well as being part owner of a fishing caïque, Christos's brother-in-law, Pavlos, also owned a *kaphenio* that he had inherited from his father. Pavlos's father had died young (after returning from a period of temporary migration to the United States), and

Pavlos and his siblings had thus been left "orphans."[7] It was Christos's old father, Akis, who had looked after the orphans and who, for fifteen years (1949–1964), had run the coffee shop on Pavlos's behalf—perhaps because he too, a generation earlier, had been left an orphan after his own father had died in the United States, or perhaps just because he and Pavlos's father had been friends. At all events, this kindness was followed by the marriage of Akis's only son, Christos, to Pavlos's orphan sister.

The sort of cooperation between relatives I have been discussing is not, of course, limited to such major questions as family companies, capital investment, or overseas migration. Nor, equally, is it limited to the activities of men (though as a single male my entry into and knowledge of women's activities was necessarily restricted). The groups of women who take turns to light their brush-fired ovens for the weekly bread baking are almost invariably sisters or sisters-in-law, or perhaps first cousins. The domestic cooperation that for many of them was mandatory when they were members of the same household continues in later life when marriage has parted them and they are established in their own households. Similarly, in the public world of men, the groups who regularly drink together, though not exclusively composed of kin, will be found to have a solid core of related members. Patronage of a particular coffee shop is itself allied to kinship. My host always claimed that his kouniados was "helping" him by drinking regularly in his bar, for his brother-in-law was a highly respected man, and wherever his brother-in-law drank, there, according to my host, the "best men" gathered, thus improving not only the quantity but also the quality of his trade. Such kinship-based patronage extended even to the clientele of the several general stores. Nothing other than a commercial price was ever asked for or received—nevertheless, the mere fact that relatives shopped at their relative's store was construed as "help" and was seen as a minor but continual confirmation of the spirit of cooperation that ideally informed all dealings between kin.

Cooperation between kin is, then, a social reality. The ideals of kinship—of trust, good will, fair dealing, and the preferential extension and receipt of favors—do translate themselves into practice. They must, however, be confronted with another social reality: the structure and extensiveness of kinship itself.

The Meaning of Family

The commonest way of expressing kinship in Spartohori is simply to make reference to the concept of *oikoyeneia*, of "family." Three closely

---

[7] It is perhaps worth noting that the word *orphan* was regularly used of people who had lost their father even if their mother was still alive.

related points should be noted. First, that oikoyeneia is an ill-defined and fluid concept. Second, that oikoyeneia in Spartohori is capable of being construed very extensively. Third, that oikoyeneia in Spartohori is bilateral to an extreme.

Let me take the last two points first. The term *soi* is heard in Spartohori. Unlike its usage amongst Campbell's Sarakatsani, however, it does *not* equate with the bilateral kindred. The soi is agnatically defined. One's mother's brother or one's spouse's brother or even one's spouse are emphatically "family," but they are not soi. On the other hand, unlike its appearance among Herzfeld's Cretan Glendiots, the agnatically defined soi has no corporate existence.[8] Indeed, it plays no part in social life at all. Two people who share a common surname but who do not know the precise nature of their relationship (if any) will be inclined to say that perhaps they are soi. In all significant contexts, however, what is important is not the soi, but the "family"—and that is completely bilateral.

In common with "standard" Greek usage (if such a thing exists), there is not only a complete terminological assimilation of kinship terms between patrilateral and matrilateral relatives, but also, with the exception of certain specific affinal terms,[9] an almost complete assimilation between the terms for relatives on the husband's side and for relatives on the wife's side, and again for the spouses of all these relatives. The simplest way of conveying this is to point out that there are not, as anthropological orthodoxy would have it, four genealogical specifications for first cousins

[8] The classic article on Greek kinship is, of course, by Campbell (1963 and cf. 1964:36–58) and relates to the Sarakatsani. In Sarakatsan usage the soi refers to the bilateral kindred—just as it does among the inhabitants of "Ambeli" in Euboia (du Boulay 1974:144ff.). In Spartohori, however, there was no doubt that the soi was agnatically defined. Among definitions of the soi offered by Spartohoriots were that it consisted of all those who carried the same surname, or that it consisted of all those who bore the same patrilineally inherited nickname or *paratzoukli*. (Both these definitions were, on reflection, then rejected by informants on the grounds that the former was too inclusive and the latter often too exclusive.) The Spartohoriot usage of *soi* is certainly not unique. See, for example, Peristiany (1965c:179) and Herzfeld's discussion of the question (1985a:282–283). Herzfeld (1985a:52) translates the term *soi* as used in "Glendi" (Crete) as "patrigroup"—though, as he explains, under certain circumstances it can refer to the bilateral kindred. Herzfeld admits that the Glendiot agnatic soi is not technically a corporate group since, for example, its members do not own common property; Herzfeld argues, however, that it is conceptually and ideologically corporate, with village neighborhoods being named after particular patrigroups and with their members engaging in group political activities.

[9] These are the quite standard affinal terms, i.e., gambros (ZH, DH), nyphe (BW, SW), kouniados (WB), kouniada (HZ), badzanakis (WZH), and synnuphada (HBW). It should perhaps be noted, however, that in Spartohori the term kouniada is also used for WBW, i.e., the wife of one's kouniados. This is not a particularly standard usage (one would expect simply the nonspecific sympethera, "female affine") and illustrates the Spartohoriot assimilation of the kinship terms for married couples.

of each sex (e.g., FBS, MBS, FZS, MZS) but *sixteen*, of which the extreme case would be an Ego's spouse's mother's sister's daughter's husband—a "first cousin" for all that.

Terminology is not, of course, the crux of the matter. The important factor is that for the Spartohoriots such affinal relatives—whether relatives of one's spouse or spouses of one's relatives, or both—are genuinely considered to be "family" and are treated in the same way as one's "own" bilateral kin. I noted that my old friend Michalis was drinking regularly with a young sailor, Labros. I commented on this, to which Michalis replied that he was drinking with his nephew. I protested that Labros was not his nephew. Amid a certain amount of laughter I was reminded that Labros had recently married the daughter of Michalis's brother (with whom Michalis was not on speaking terms)—ergo, Labros had become Michalis's nephew. The relationship was *phresko*, "fresh," but Michalis stressed that he was "very much an uncle" to Labros.

The consequence of this form of reckoning—which, so far as I know, is not uncommon in Greece—is to create a proliferation of uncles, aunts, nephews, nieces, and cousins: 16 genealogical specifications for uncles, 16 for aunts, 16 for nieces, 16 for nephews (and a further 64 for uncles and aunts, and 60 for nieces and nephews, who would be first cousins once removed in the cumbersome English terminology),[10] 32 for first cousins (male and female together), and 128 for second cousins (male and female together). But though such a form of reckoning may be reasonably common, its full effects are to be felt only in a relatively small community that, importantly, is largely and preferentially endogamous—in a community, say, such as Spartohori, where the total year-round population was only 551, and where in the case of 75 percent of married couples, both partners were from the village.[11]

The effect is an obvious one. One way or another, almost everyone is related to almost everyone else. Moreover, genealogical connections be-

[10] Greek kinship terminology standardly preserves generational differences by expressing the relationship between a cousin and the child of a cousin as one between uncle/aunt and nephew/niece (whereas, technically, in English they are reciprocally first cousins once removed—though in practice English "folk" usage frequently follows the Greek model). The Greek terminology thus makes the relationship between a cousin and the child of a cousin analogous with the relationship between a sibling and the child of a sibling—the logic of which, in structural terms, is perfect.

[11] This is, of course, an extremely crude index of endogamy, for among other things it excludes the marriages of all Spartohoriot women who have "married out" into other communities. On the other hand, it is reasonable to assume that the number of brides who left Spartohori would be roughly equivalent to the number of brides who married into Spartohori. I speak of women marrying out and marrying in since the inheritance of land and houses in Spartohori is basically patrilineal. Men are thus less likely to change location on marriage.

tween people are frequently multistranded—a folding-in of the community's kinship links such that people are related to each other *ap'tis duo meries*, "from both sides," as a result, for example, of the marriages of a pair of first cousins to a pair of siblings (not permitted by strict Church law) or of two pairs of first cousins (permitted by Church law).[12]

One way of gaining an impression of the degree of the Spartohoriots' interrelatedness is to take a single individual and to see the extent of his/her recognized kindred in relation to the village's total population. My old friend Michalis was fond of boasting that he was related to half the village. In his case—which I do not believe to have been exceptional—the boast was roughly true. Since Michalis had four sisters and two brothers who survived into adulthood, the number of his nephews and nieces was high. On the other hand, only one of Michalis's father's siblings, a sister, had survived to adulthood, and his paternal grandfather appears to have had no surviving siblings. The number of his patrilateral relatives was thus low. Moreover, neither Michalis's wife nor Michalis's mother appears to have come from particularly prolific families. The number of his matrilateral relatives and of relatives acquired by marriage was thus not out of the ordinary. Nevertheless, given the form of reckoning used, within the bounds of second cousin the number of Michalis's collateral relatives actually resident in the village was still 122.[13] But to these must be added a further seventeen *sympetheroi* (affines) resident in the village whose relationship with Michalis derived from the marriages of his son and daughter (themselves both resident in Australia). Including Michalis's own wife and his remaining bachelor son, the total number of Michalis's "family" within Spartohori was thus 141. But these were still less than the grand total of resident Spartohoriots whom Michalis could count as kin, for I have omitted, partly because of the inherent vagueness of the category, Michalis's many other sympetheroi who were relatives of his siblings' spouses or relatives of his affinal nephews and nieces (e.g., the relatives of his brother's daughter's husband). Minimally, then, Michalis's kin accounted for 25 percent of the village's permanent population, and if all sympetheroi were taken into account, it would probably not be unreasonable to say that he was related to half the village.

[12] My understanding of Church law derives from the *Pidalion* (8th ed., 1976, based on the 3d ed. of 1864), a comprehensive guide to Orthodox Greek canon law designed for the use of the clergy. The prohibition on marriage between a pair of siblings and a pair of first cousins is specifically mentioned on 748. It must be admitted, however, that actual practice in Greece often deviates from the regulations set out in the *Pidalion*.

[13] This is not exceptionally large for a bilateral kindred. Cf. Campbell (1964:38), who estimates that the average number of an individual Sarakatsanos's kind was 250. These were, however, dispersed among a population of some 4,000, which radically alters the situation (see below and cf. Loizos 1975:63 and 74).

Let me now turn to the definition of this word *family*, which I have been so freely using. *Oikoyeneia* is not a technical term. Its meaning is quite as sloppy, or at least as context-sensitive, as the English word *family* by which I have rendered it. Sometimes—and perhaps most commonly—*family* refers, implicitly at least, to the members of a household, the spiti. In practice this will nowadays mean a husband, wife, and children—i.e., a nuclear family.[14] Alternatively, it will mean the nuclear family with the addition of a grandparent or grandparental couple (usually the husband's parents) and possibly one or more unmarried siblings of the husband's, i.e., a stem family.[15]

I have said, however, "implicitly"; for in fact if the question were put to a Spartohoriot whether, for example, parents who happened to live in another household, or married brothers and sisters who had their own households, were or were not "family," then the answer would emphatically be that they were. "My family" may refer for most practical purposes to the domestic unit, but as soon as the definition of family becomes subject to any conscious reflection, it becomes more extensive. After all, except *statistically*, the spiti represents no particular configuration of kin, and Spartohoriots would never consider their mothers or brothers or sisters to be outside their "family" just because they happened not to be coresident with them. Important though the spiti may be as a social, economic, and moral unit, it cannot be made to yield the definition of *family*, which will always overflow its bounds. The spiti is essentially a de facto consolidation of kin whose unity, though underwritten by kinship, results from coresidence itself.

Given, then, that *family* always escapes the boundaries of the household, a more extensive definition might perhaps be supplied in terms of all those reasonably close relatives who are regularly addressed and referred to by means of a kinship term. In practice this *tends* to mean all a person's bilateral and affinal kin down to and including second cousins, and, indeed, such a grouping has some practical significance. When, for example, a family celebration is held—an engagement, wedding, or baptismal party—it is convention automatically to invite this group. Moreover, such a definition is also in at least rough accord with the incest

---

[14] There were 187 households in Spartohori that were occupied year-round by at least one person. Of that 187, however, 103 were occupied by either widows or widowers, or by elderly married couples whose children were normally resident in Athens or overseas. Of the remaining 84 households that might be considered to have something approaching their full complement of members, 46 consisted of nuclear families.

[15] Again, of the above 84 households, 16 consisted of stem families. It might be noted that a further 22 households contained two (or more) generations of married couples—though this domestic arrangement is clearly in decline and most newly married couples insist on neolocal residence.

prohibition, which does constitute an important boundary for the definition of *family*, since it is only when "the blood has changed" that a relative may be taken in marriage. Nevertheless, even the incest prohibition
will not provide the definition of *family* in Spartohori with the degree of
neatness with which it circumscribes the bilateral kindred in the case of
Campbell's Sarakatsani,[16] for the Spartohoriots' interpretation of the marriage prohibitions is such that they forbid marriage even between third
cousins. On the other hand, they will argue that third cousins are "not
really family." In short, the relationship of third cousin is clearly recognized in that it constitutes an impediment to marriage, but in most other
respects it is on the margins of what for day-to-day purposes is recognized
as "family." The incest prohibition and the working definition of *family*
are not entirely congruent.[17]

Some form of accommodation between an incest prohibition inclusive
of third cousins and the general feeling that the practical limits of kinship
are reached at second cousins could perhaps be arrived at by arguing that
although third cousins may not themselves marry, nevertheless their
households may unite and they may become sympetheroi through the
marriages of their children. However, any real attempt to equate the
marriage prohibition with the definition of *family* is thwarted in the other
direction by the Spartohoriots' practice of "double affinal" matches,[18] notably marriages of a pair of siblings to a pair of first cousins. Though in
breach of canon law, such marriages are not uncommon, and the children
of such matches will be related to each other on both their paternal and
maternal sides—*ap'tis duo meries*, as the villagers say. But if someone is
simultaneously Ego's patrilateral first cousin and Ego's matrilateral second cousin—or, to put the matter in a more telling way, if, given the
standard assimilation of kinship terms, Ego can marry his/her brother's
first (affinal) cousin—it becomes rather difficult to argue that the incest

---

[16] See Campbell (1963:80 and 86–87; cf. 1964:40 and 50–51).

[17] See also du Boulay (1974:145) for the ambiguous status of third cousins. It should be
noted, however, that the overall situation in "Ambeli" was somewhat different, since third
cousins were permitted to marry (as, with some reservations, were second cousins), while
in Spartohori the closest match allowed was between a third cousin and the child of a third
cousin.

The relationship between third cousins in Spartohori closely resembles the relationship
between second cousins among the Sarakatsani, where second cousins "are on the margins
of kinship, people who are nearly 'strangers' " (Campbell 1964:107). It should also be noted
that among the Sarakatsani the children of these second cousins may marry. The Sarakatsan
situation thus parallels at one generation's remove that found in Spartohori, where it is the
children of third cousins who may marry and third cousins who are "nearly strangers."

[18] This clumsy term is the best I can arrive at to designate the practice. Such marriages
are referred to in the *Pidalion* (744) as "*ex anchisteias digenon*"—"from double-familial affinity."

prohibition affords any definition of "family" by constituting it as an ex-
ogamous unit. Indeed, the very fact that people talk about being related
to someone "from both sides" shows clearly enough that in their appre-
hension of the matter someone who was "family" has married someone
else who was also "family."

I would prefer to argue that the incest prohibition, like the household
or spiti, does not define "family," but rather defines a particular grouping
of relatives in connection with a specific regulation—those who may
marry as opposed to those who may not marry. Such an interpretation
derives some support from the fact that although for day-to-day purposes
second cousins provide the rough limits of recognized kinship, in certain
circumstances the Spartohoriots are happy to acknowledge the possibility
that the lines of kinship could be traced more or less ad infinitum—to
third, fourth, and fifth cousins, and so on, into a realm where any precise
knowledge of relationships must be wanting but where the possibility of
relatedness can still be entertained. Indeed, in an admittedly rhetorical
manner it was frequently explained to me that the whole village was "all
one family." Clearly this remark was to an extent metaphorical, for it
formed part of an idealized account of the village (reserved for outsiders
such as myself) in which it was claimed that everyone cared for each
other, that everyone was bound to each other, that one person's sorrows
were the village's sorrows, one person's joys their collective joys. In
short, the village was *like* a family, which provided the most ready metaphor for its alleged solidarity. But such a metaphor also bleeds imper-
ceptibly into fact. When I was trying to sort out the village's tangled genealogies, my confusions would be met with laughter and the observation
that in the end I would find out that everyone *was* related to everyone
else: that (sentiment aside) they were "all one family."[19]

KINSHIP AND CAUSATION

In the preceding section I have tried to indicate two things: the extensiveness of Spartohoriot kinship and the indeterminacy of the concept of
"family." On the one hand, kinship virtually exhausts the space of the
Spartohoriot community; on the other hand, it fails to divide people into
discrete and definable familial groups. How does this affect the role of
kinship in structuring social action?

Let me start with a simple example. As I mentioned, it is conventional
for all relatives up to and including second cousins to be invited to any
major celebration, e.g., a wedding party. This parallels the Sarakatsan

---

[19] I suspect such a claim is not an uncommon part of Greek village rhetoric. Herzfeld
(1981:562) reports that the villagers of "Pefko" in Rhodes (a similarly preferentially endog-
amic community) refer to themselves as "one kin" (*mia singenia*).

case to the extent that one might feel confident in stating that major celebrations involve the participation of all members of the bilateral kindred
(due allowance being made for the fact that, given the Spartohoriot definition of the term, the "bilateral kindred" is not to be equated with the
soi). In Spartohori, however, the bride's family and the groom's family
hold a quite separate series of celebrations, each inviting their own kin.
Not infrequently it occurs that a particular individual will be quite closely
related to both bride and groom—uncle or aunt to one, cousin to the
other. Of course no real problem is created. The particular person attends the celebrations of the party to which he/she is most closely related, or attends some of the celebrations of both, or—a point of some
significance—attends the celebrations of whichever of the families he/she
is most friendly with. But although no social impasse is created (the Spartohoriots are a sensible people) such a situation at least demonstrates that
even when kinship is the explicit criterion of selection and inclusion, it
cannot be counted on to settle matters. Further considerations have to
be taken into account.

Let me now pass to a more complex matter, to one of those aspects of
village life that I suggested could not be understood without a knowledge
of kinship: namely, politics.

It would be insulting to suggest that the Spartohoriots do not have
strong political views and that for them politics is not a matter of party
ideologies and political philosophies. Nevertheless, they also admit that
politics can be a "family matter"—i.e., that votes can be and are mobi-
lized along kinship lines. In 1980, elections were held in the village for
the position of *proedros* or village president. Two *syndiasmoi* or "teams"
competed for this position and for places on the village council. In theory
the elections are supposed to be "nonpolitical," but the Left, and especially the students studying in Athens and the new Athenian-dwelling
class of businessmen and professionals (most of whom were PASOK sup-
porters), rallied round a certain Petros M, an old communist from civil
war days. The rival team, which centered on a shopkeeper, Gerasimos Z,
was also quite left-wing but strongly anticommunist. It also perhaps represented the more traditionalist villagers rather than the emergent bourgeoisie. Petros M and the Left won handsomely—an accurate enough
index of the political climate—but parallel to politics ran kinship concerns
that I was able to observe at close quarters, since they involved my host,
Nikos, and his family.

Nikos's wife's brother, Stathis, a man whom Nikos immensely ad-
mired, was a member of Gerasimos Z's losing team. The trouble was that
Stathis's younger brother, Babis, was also the son-in-law of the winning
candidate, Petros M. If politics had been simply politics, perhaps all of
these people could have voted according to their ideals and with a clear

conscience; but since kinship could not be discounted, Nikos and his family were quite literally placed in a genealogical double bind. The person in the most invidious position was of course Babis, who had to choose between his brother and his wife's father. I do not know on what grounds he based his choice, though I suspect they were ones of political conviction. At all events, he opted for his father-in-law and quite decisively. But if Babis's dilemma was resolved according to political convictions, this certainly did not prevent him from trying to further his cause through family connections. Indeed, he went the rounds of all his and Stathis's relatives and advised them not to vote for his brother. In this he must have been quite successful, for, as Nikos later explained to me, though Stathis made a respectable showing, the votes he secured were all *philika psiphismata* (friendly votes) and not *oikoyeneiaka psiphismata* (family votes). In fact the family had "brought him down."

Needless to say, my host, Nikos, was himself caught up in these unfortunate events and, with the rest of the family, voted against his relative Stathis, and for his (more distant) relative, Petros M. The exception was Nikos's wife, who voted for her brother Stathis. As Nikos explained, she could scarcely have done anything else—though, as he admitted, it did result in the embarrassing oddity of a husband and wife voting differently. As for Nikos's old mother, Stavroula, she simply voted for whom she was told—Petros M.

Stathis himself was outraged by this family betrayal and went so far as to boycott Nikos's kaphenio for several months. Nikos thus paid a price for his part in the family/antifamily pact—and it should be noted that the price itself was measurable in terms of the values of kinship: the loss of the patronage of his beloved kouniados. But the real interest of this episode lies in the fact that although it was clearly recognized that votes could be cast along family lines—hence Babis's visiting of all his relatives; hence Nikos's contrast between "friendly votes" and "family votes"—in the final analysis kinship was incapable of controlling the vote, and not because an appeal to kinship lacked persuasion or because individuals had their own political ideas, but because *kinship itself* actually split the vote. Instead of providing the basis for corporate action, the very complexity and multiplicity of kinship connections meant that, politics aside, people's loyalties were divided. Kinship could be appealed to; its weight could be thrown on the scales; but nothing resulted from it automatically. It might be expected that one would vote for a relative; but in the end one could only vote for the relative by whom one was most persuaded.

At this stage it is convenient to revert to the wine makers. It is perfectly true that their cooperation in the village was based on kinship, just as was their business enterprise in Piraeus. But again the constitution of this kin-based group was scarcely automatic. Between them the bilateral and affinal kindred of the three brothers would have accounted for well over half the village—but half the village was not in partnership with them. Those of their wives' brothers and sisters' husbands who were involved in the wine making were also those who, as high-ranking ship's officers, were involved in their shipping company—and they were all wealthy men. By contrast, their first cousin who transported the grapes across from Lefkada was not wealthy. He was a fisherman and storekeeper. Nor was he a member of the wine-making group. He was employed by it. That in itself might be construed as an example of the preferential extension of "favors" toward kin, and in fairness I should stress that while in the village the wine makers made every effort to comply with its egalitarian ethos. But what gave the wine makers their identity, what made them a recognizable group, what bound them together even in such village activities as wine making (and excluded their cousin), was the fact that they shared a common life-style and a common financial (and cultural) ascendancy. They were known as "the rich," "the Athenians." Not all even of their quite close relatives fell into that group. And just as with the village elections kinship could not determine who would vote for whom (since it fails to create discrete kinship groups), so with the wine makers kinship was so extensive that some other basis has to be sought to explain their solidarity—call it "class," or perhaps a common life-style and shared expectations, or, to use that least "structural" of concepts, just friendship. And here it is perhaps worth recalling Christos and Pavlos, the two brothers-in-law who together bought their new caïque. So far as they were concerned, they cooperated because they were "family"; but it should not be forgotten that the reason they became "family" was because there had been a prior history of friendship—because Pavlos and his sisters had been cared for and protected by Christos's father.

It may be objected, however, that in querying the determinant role of kinship I am neglecting an obvious point, for the examples of cooperation I have adduced are between close relatives—brothers, sisters, brothers-in-law, etc.—whereas my argument about the ineffectuality of kinship as a determinant of social relations has been illustrated by reference to the more distant ties of cousinhood and the like. To a degree this objection is valid. People are more likely to maintain that there *ought* to be cooperation between close kin than they are for more distant relatives, and obviously the further one moves from Ego, the greater the proliferation of kin and the greater, therefore, the necessity of choice.[20] As we have seen in the case of the village elections, however, the choice for Babis was between a brother and a father-in-law, both close relatives (even if

---

[20] Cf. Campbell (1964:107–109) and du Boulay (1974:150–152).

the latter was an affine).[21] But even among the closest of kin, genealogical proximity is no guarantee of good relations. If anything, the opposite is true. In Spartohori (as elsewhere in Greece) brothers are idealized as the very paradigm of disinterested affection, amity, and loyalty, and while they are young and members of the same household, this perhaps is true. But if one considers the serious rifts within the village—those people who are not on speaking terms, who have been "cold" toward each other for twenty years—then, for the classic reasons of property, inheritance, and its division, they are more likely to be brothers than anyone else.[22] This too is recognized by the villagers. A screaming match erupted one midday between two old men (amply supported by their wives)—brothers whose houses, exact divisions of a paternal spiti, adjoined. The immediate cause of the confrontation was a newly installed drain pipe that trespassed an inch or so over one property into the other. A crowd gathered. Some shouted "Shame!"; others took sides. One old woman, hands on hips, regarded the scene and commented contemptuously, "Hah, brothers again." The chances of brothers' being best of friends or worst of enemies are about equal—and it is the existence of those "chances" which I wish to stress. If, as an observer, one did not know who were brothers and who were not, one would never guess.

THE IDIOM OF KINSHIP (WITH APOLOGIES TO MARGARET KENNA)[23]

So what is left of kinship? Could one take it all away and leave everything just as it was before? In objective terms the answer might almost be yes. In ideological terms the answer is most certainly no. It all depends on whether one is concerned with reasoning or result, with motive or effect. "Family" are those to whom loyalty is owed. "Family" are those who owe one loyalty. Ideologically this is not open to doubt. Nor is it subject to empirical falsification. Betrayal by a brother is so much the worse because a brother betrays. Assistance from an uncle is so much the more welcome because an uncle assists. The statistical probabilities of either do not affect the response; nor do they affect the morality on which that response is based. The fisherman, waiting at dawn for the arrival of his cousin to make up our crew, is met instead by his cousin's little boy with the message that dad will not be coming because he is feeling unwell (and wants to stay in bed). Furious, the fisherman appeals to me, "You see! That's the sort of wanker he is. He does this to me, his *cousin!*" Conversely, I am done a favor by someone in the village and remark on it to

[21] In fact, the relationship between fathers-in-law and sons-in-law in Spartohori was particularly close. See Just (1980).

[22] Cf. Davis (1977:176–197).

[23] I borrow the title for this section from Kenna (1976b).

a friend—"Ah yes, of course. He's a wonderful boy. He's my nephew, you know. A good family!"

In short, the morality of kinship and the set of expectations that derive from it are not subject to empirical falsification (or confirmation) because kinship is a value in itself.[24] I should reveal that when my host, Nikos, voted against his kouniados, Stathis, he did have an ax to grind, for, as I have mentioned, Stathis's team was headed by a shopkeeper, Gerasimos Z, and Nikos and Gerasimos Z were fervent enemies. Since I was on good terms with both, both were somewhat circumspect in their criticism of each other, but Nikos would not even set foot in Gerasimos's shop (which had the tobacco concession) and so had to buy his cigarettes by proxy (usually me). But they were first cousins; or rather, Nikos's wife and Gerasimos were first cousins (which also means that her brother, Stathis, and Gerasimos were first cousins). Quite truthfully, then, Nikos explained to me that his personal reason for not having voted for his brother-in-law Stathis was that a vote for Stathis would have been tantamount to a vote for Gerasimos. However, he then went on to say that his unwillingness to vote for Gerasimos was based on the fact that Gerasimos had been proedros once before and had not proved particularly "energetic." Somewhat weary of this obfuscation, I suggested that the reason he had not wanted to give a vote to any team headed by Gerasimos was that he and Gerasimos detested each other. "No, no!" cried Nikos immediately, "Gerasimos is a very good man. Gerasimos and I are cousins, we're family."

But finally, and perhaps most importantly, in a village such as Spartohori where the links of kinship are so numerous, the morality of kinship is not falsifiable because kinship can always be strategically traced. Its value can be added when and where it is necessary. My old friend Michalis used continually to remark on what a fine family the Zs were. Integral to his explanation of their virtues was his own double affinity with them, for one of his daughters had married the son of a certain Nikos Z, while one of his sons had married the daughter of Nikos Z's sister. In short, Michalis's son and daughter had married a pair of first cousins. It also happened, however, that Michalis was a great personal friend of Nikos Z's brother, Thomas. Thus in praising his friend Thomas, Michalis would praise the whole Z family, and in praising the whole Z family, Michalis

---

[24] Cf. Davis: "Kinship carries with it some extra value which makes association with kinsmen more desirable than with others" (1977:222). In fact my conclusions closely accord with Davis's views: "Obligations are often ignored. Trust may be betrayed, the relation itself denied, but it is nevertheless true that men who wish to attract the support and cooperation of others will do so in the name of prescriptive obligation—and will express an even greater sense of betrayal than if they are let down by an acquaintance or friend" (ibid.).

would point out his double connection with them. They were fine people, and he was very much related to them.

But who were the Zs? Here the whole ambiguity of family comes into play, for though Michalis's daughter had certainly married a Z, his son had not—or rather, he had not married anyone by that name. He had married the daughter of Nikos and Thomas Z's *sister*, and Nikos and Thomas Z's sister was married to a certain Spiros V. Spiros V, however, was not a particular friend of Michalis's, and Michalis's reasons for construing his affinal relationships exclusively with the Zs rather than with the Vs *and* the Zs hinged simply on his close friendship with Thomas Z. In this construction his affinal connection with the Vs was politely ignored. So far as Michalis was concerned, his connections were with the Zs and via two paths—the marriage of his daughter to Nikos Z's son, and the marriage of his son to the daughter of the sister of Nikos and Thomas Z. Indeed, when this sister was referred to, she was referred to as a Z— which from one point of view, but only one point of view (and not perhaps what one might have taken as culturally the most likely point of view) she was.

ACKNOWLEDGMENTS

Fieldwork was conducted between April 1977 and May 1980. I should like to acknowledge the generous financial assistance of the Philip Bagby Trust, Oxford, and the UK Social Science Research Council, which made this work possible.

PART II

Gender and Kinship outside Marriage

Chapter 6

SISTERS IN CHRIST: METAPHORS OF KINSHIP
AMONG GREEK NUNS

A. Marina Iossifides

In this paper I wish to examine some of the norms defining kinship and kinship roles in a Greek village and to compare this with the relationships observed in nearby convents that use similar kinship terms. To say simply that the convents have modeled their social relations on kinship roles found in the secular community is, I believe, to miss the point of the relationships. Though the terms may be the same (as in *sisters* or *Mother Superior*), there is a shift in emphasis from the material world and life as an ever continuing "natural cycle," a view strongly held in the village, to an emphasis on the spiritual world toward which each soul strives or should strive in order to achieve grace and unity with God upon death, a view stressed in the convents. It is the distinction drawn between the *kosmikos anthropos*—the person of the world, that is the secular person—and the *pneumatikos anthropos*—the person of the spirit or of God: the monastic. This shift fundamentally alters how the terms are understood and used.

Essentially both the nuns and the villagers recognize the existence of a "natural" world and of humans' relationship to that world. For the villagers, nature and the natural aspect of human beings must be controlled. For example, sexuality, the most vividly discussed "natural" drive of humans, must be mediated through the spiritual and social rite of marriage to become a fruitful aspect of social and personal regeneration, of social continuity in spite of death.

For the nuns, however, it seems that "nature" and "natural needs" as the legacy of Adam and Eve, must be conquered, not simply controlled. The nuns' objective is to incarnate the union of person with God while living this life. They seek to live like the apostles in divine grace both of spirit and in body. They seek to overcome the passions that afflict the body, thereby transcending this material world and achieving eternal life in the next.

To explain the shift in meaning, I will be taking up the concepts of "substance" and "codes of conduct" as first introduced by Schneider (1980). The villagers' belief in blood as the defining substance of kinship, regardless of one's conduct toward one's kin, though adhered to by the nuns at one level is at another level subsumed by the belief that through conduct one can transform one's "natural" substance. In the convent it is held that with the guidance of Christ and one's father confessor and through careful vigilance over one's conduct, one may upon death assume one's place as an angel in the tenth *tagma* (battalion) of God. The human substance of this world is transformed into something divine. Conduct determines substance (see Nicol 1963:42).

What I am interested in examining, then, are some of the cultural constructs of kinship, to note how the kinship terms and their underlying meanings alter within the same society when used in two different contexts.

Fieldwork was conducted in a village located in southern Epirus, in northwestern mainland Greece, between January 1986 and May 1987. The village is near a town that serves as the commercial center of the region. Some village inhabitants are exclusively agriculturalists; the rest cultivate oranges and olives and, simultaneously, work as either craftsmen or as white- or blue-collar workers in the town. The villagers have no particular social or economic ties with the two convents discussed, T. and P., though some villagers do rent land from a third, smaller convent nearby. Of the two convents discussed here, T. is the larger, boasting eighteen nuns, and is located on the outskirts of the town. The convent of P. is high in the mountains to the west of the village some forty-five minutes' drive from the town and has fourteen nuns. It should be said that not all the nuns had completed high school and some had not completed grammar school. Others were educated and had been teachers or civil servants before entering the convent. Despite these differences, the nuns generally presented common opinions and views. Moreover, I was often referred to the abbot or abbess, who were considered better able to clarify points or answer specific questions.[1]

In the past, the villagers traded with both these institutions, as well as with other monasteries in the region, though not on a large scale. They also attended the various religious festivals held yearly at these religious institutions. Now, only a few people from the village visit either convent, though during the summer months people from villages all over the re-

---

[1] I should like to add that I am not attempting to write a theologically "correct" account of life in a Greek Orthodox convent but simply to present and analyze some of the beliefs and outlooks of the nuns whom I was privileged to meet. To a theologian, the "stories" and views expressed here might seem simplistic. This simplicity, however, must be understood both within the context of the nuns' and the abbot/abbess's attempts to explain their views and the nature of God to one who was completely ignorant, and within the context of these particular monastics' lives and background.

gion and from various parts of Greece come to the convents as tourists or as pilgrims.

Because of such visitors and because many of their needs are supplied by the town and the surrounding villages, the nuns have contact with and knowledge of the world beyond their convent walls. Moreover, many of the nuns come from Epirus or from nearby regions, though there are no nuns from the village where I did my fieldwork. Interaction among the villages, the town, and the monastic institutions in the region has taken place over many decades. I would argue then that general outlooks and values are similar, thereby justifying a comparison between the village's and the convents' notions of kinship.

This paper is divided into three parts. The first section will briefly outline kinship in the village. The second section will define kinship terms in the convent and the dichotomy expressed by those terms between the spirit and the body, or substance. The third section will attempt to show how the body and the spirit are reconciled by the nuns through their understanding of sin and their relationship with the Divine.

VILLAGE IKOYENIA

Kinship in the village is often expressed by the term *ikoyenia*. In this section I wish to give a brief summary of only some of the ways in which the word *ikoyenia* may be used in different contexts. *Ikoyenia* derives from *ikos*, meaning "house," and *genia*, meaning "birth" or "generation," and "race." It is a term resembling the English word *family*. The first question asked of an unknown villager is, "Piounou ise?" (Whose are you?), a question that asks you to identify yourself with a particular ikoyenia in the village. Personhood and identity seem to be closely linked with the notions of kinship and the ikoyenia. At the very crux of the iko-yenia is the ceremony of marriage, for it serves to unite a man and a woman under the watching eyes of the community and in the sight of God.[2] Within this socially sanctioned relationship, sexual intercourse is insisted upon, for it is only here that socially legitimate children are born and a new ikoyenia established.

Bearing children is the main aim and reason given for marriage. The core of the ikoyenia, the husband, the wife, and the children, must continually be re-created through marriage and birth. Aging and death destroy the ikoyenia. Birth and children assure renewal, continuation, and

---

[2] It was not until 1983 that civil weddings were recognized by the State. Until then only church weddings were binding. Among the villagers, church weddings are still the preferred form of marriage. The first civil wedding in the village was held in the summer of 1987.

life. Thus, marriage and the creation of an ikoyenia are said to be the goal and destiny of humans on earth.

Sexual needs and desires are seen to be natural and should be fulfilled in order that mental and physical well-being may be maintained. This does not mean that adultery is condoned. On the contrary, it is condemned as jeopardizing the ikoyenia with the serious risk of an illegitimate child. Couples who have sex without intending to marry are considered to be "like animals," unable to judge or control their passions. However, sexual relationships between young people are usually tolerated as long as the couple plan eventually to marry. For most villagers, then, the sexual act is not seen as harmful or sinful when associated in some manner with marriage. Underlying this is the importance placed on the stability of the ikoyenia and the fulfillment of the "natural" needs of its members.

IKOYENIA AS SYNGENIA

Syngenia[3] (*syn* + *genia*), similar to the English notion of "relatedness," means "of common stock, generation, or lineage." It is used to define relations through blood and marriage ties, though its primary definition implies blood relations (*eks ematos*), as they are considered closer than relatives by marriage (*eks anchisteias*). Relatives by marriage as well as by blood are referred to as one's ikoyenia in certain contexts, and people do trace their connection to a particular ikoyenia through marriage, blood, or both.

Blood is said to be transmitted equally to the child through both genitor and genitrix. Since the child and parent share blood, the emotional ties between the child and its parents are said to be the "strongest."[4] Siblings are also said to have "strong" ties between them because they have the *same* blood. They are said to understand one another, to feel deeply and strongly for one another. This tie should continue throughout their lives.

Blood relations in the village, taking Ego as a point of departure, ascend generations up to and usually including great-grandparents and outward to include collateral relations. Du Boulay (1984) points out that relatives often reckon their collateral relationship by looking up the lines of

---

[3] The term *syngenia* refers to "being related," or the state of "relatedness." *Syngenis* refers to those who are related, that is to say relatives.

[4] There are several instances of adoption in the village, though I know of no recent cases. An adopted child is known as a "soul child" (*psychopedhi*). It calls its adopted parents mother and father. It was the preferred practice to adopt the child from a sibling of either the wife or the husband such that a blood tie preexisted. This emphasizes the importance of children for the creation of an ikoyenia and the value placed on "blood."

descent to the original sibling group.[5] In this case syngenia is traced through to those with the "same" blood and thus to common origin or progenitors.

Among second and sometimes third cousins,[6] there is a strict prohibition on sexual intercourse and marriage. The syngenia is close, as these cousins are said to share to the some given degree[7] (*vathmo*) the substance of blood. Beyond this degree marriage is permitted. Though the blood relationship, syngenia, can be and is traced beyond third cousins, it is said that the relations are not close. It may be understood that the "original" blood has intermingled with so much new blood through marriage that it has been diluted. The relationship therefore is not very "strong." There is only a "bit of relatedness" (*mikri* or *liyi* syngenia).

Blood relationships arise from the combining of blood through sexual intercourse, a "natural" act, and the bearing of children, a "natural" outcome of intercourse. Blood relations are thus seen as "natural" and "immutable"; one cannot change the fact of one's genitor or genitrix, nor can one change one's blood or one's relations.

Relatives by marriage are those people married to one's blood relatives. This group may be expanded to include one's spouse's syngenis, for it is said that when one marries, one "enters" the ikoyenia of one's spouse. However, Ego's ikoyenia does not acquire syngenia with Ego's spouse's ikoyenia, though sometimes syngenia was loosely traced in this way. These groups are said instead to have *sympetheria* (affinity). To make clear the syngenia established between husband and wife by marriage, some informants quoted the marriage ceremony: "And the two shall become one flesh." The husband and wife become one body. Yet it was evident from the stories told that the couple were not fully united until the birth of the first child. Through that child they truly became one flesh, the substance of the parents combined in the flesh and blood of their offspring.

CODES OF CONDUCT

The phrase "codes of conduct" (Schneider 1980) refers to ways a person in a particular relationship is expected to behave. In times of trouble and

[5] This was also the case in the village I worked in, where I was often told such things as: "Oh, we are related. My mother and her mother were first cousins. That is, my grandfather and her grandmother were siblings."

[6] The ambiguity concerning second- and third-cousin marriages is discussed by du Boulay (1984:536–537).

[7] Degree may also be expressed in terms of "distance" that is, how "near" (*kontini*) or "far" (*makrini*) relatives are to Ego, and marks the extent to which people share common substance (Schneider 1980:65).

celebration, a person is expected to stand by his/her ikoyenia (the term here is used in its broadest sense), to lend assistance financially or emotionally in matters both public and private—for example, in voting for a relative or in helping in marriage or funeral ceremonies.

Codes of conduct may also pattern ways in which people are defined as syngenis. For example, I was told by one woman: "We don't have much contact with them and so the syngenia has left, has grown less. You can't really count them as syngenis even though they are second cousins." Thus, whether a particular person is characterized as a "true" syngenis or not depends in part on how that person acts.

However, when people are asked to name their syngenis, they respond with the normative definition of syngenis as defined by blood and marriage, and they admit that, no matter how a particular person behaves, a relative is always a relative. One can at most ignore the relationship, thereby putting social distance between oneself and that relative. The substance of syngenia does not alter.

HOUSEHOLD, MALE IDENTITY, AND IKOYENIA

Ideally, the husband, wife, and children should live together under one roof, sharing meals cooked by the women, and the food and money brought in by the working members of the household. Quite often the new couple may live patrilocally, with the husband's parents and his unmarried siblings. Only rarely will they live uxorilocally. Though it is recognized that both parents give equal amounts of blood to the child, and that both the mother's and father's kin are the child's kin, the child, especially in the past, was thought to belong to the father's house and to his ikoyenia. The emphasis was and is on the patrilineal line, and the desired child was and is a boy, though male offspring are not considered as essential as they were in the past. It is through the boy that the ikoyenia, here embodied in the "house" and the father's name (recall *ikos* = house, and *genia* = lineage), is continued. Girls give up the name "of the house" upon marriage, acquiring in its stead their husband's name, the name of his ikoyenia. In bearing children, they create a new ikoyenia foreign in name and house to that of their natal ikoyenia. It is only with the birth of children, especially males, that the new wife begins to be recognized as a member of the house, for she is now attached to her husband's ikoyenia through the children she has borne.

The village, then, as a structural and social entity, is made up of houses owned by the men and transmitted through the male line. And though houses may be sold, exchanged, or lost to a generation and may thus find their way into another ikoyenia,[8] it is the notion of the house and the patronym as expressions of the ikoyenia that is of paramount importance.

WOMEN, HOUSEHOLDS, AND LAND

At the center of the household is the kitchen, in the past identified with the hearth, or fireplace. It is there where the most important domestic or "inside" functions of the household take place. There the women cook; there the members of the household gather, eat, and occasionally sleep. It is there that the children of the household were born.[9] In all these functions the hearth comes to symbolize the centrality, sustenance, and continuation of the household. And it is women who fulfill these necessary tasks (see, for example, Dubisch 1986; Hirschon 1978:66–88, 1981:72–88; Rushton 1983). They transform raw food products into nourishing, often cooked, food sustenance. They also mediate between the material and spiritual worlds, praying for their families, going to church, keeping the fasts and name days, and caring for the household graves. Even the children they bear are the good and socially acceptable products of "natural" sexual desires.

The land around the village is continually changing hands through the women and their dowries.[10] All the villagers agree that, particularly in the past, women got the best and the greater share of the landholdings of their natal house, along with household goods and money which made up the dowries. Their brothers inherited whatever remained. It was and is the women who provide the land they work along with their husbands, which sustains the household economy.

To summarize: though the house and the name of the ikoyenia define male identity, it is the women who, like the land they bring with them upon marriage, vitalize the ikoyenia and provide the means through which it may continue.

LOVE AND PARENTS

Though love[11] should arise between the married couple, it is recognized, particularly among those in their mid-forties and older, that it is not

---

[8] As the generations spiral out and the blood is diluted, the link between a particular house and a particular progenitor becomes less important, more tenuous, and it will eventually pass out of living memory.

[9] Now almost all children are born in clinics in the nearby town.

[10] Such practices have changed somewhat over the last ten to fifteen years. Parents now tend to divide land and money equally among their children. However, a son will always be given a house in the village if possible, preferably his father's house.

[11] The word "love" here is used for the Greek word *agape*, which signifies a deep, abid-

essential. Rather, common goals and aims in life are what constitute a marriage. It is recognized that lack of love for your spouse should not deter you from fulfilling your roles as a parent and spouse, from fulfilling your aims in life.

The greatest expression of love in the village emerges from the conception of shared substance and nature: the mother's body. It is agreed among all the villagers that there is no love like that of a mother for her child. It is a love born from the fact that she carries the child within her for nine months. She suffers in giving birth; she holds the infant to her breast to feed and nourish it. The child is very much a "natural" part of her body.

A father is also said to love his children, but his love is generally not considered to be as "deep" (*vathia*) or "great" (*megali*) as the mother's. He is said to be more objective and logical in his love for his children. He is the final arbitrator, naughty children being threatened that their father will be told if they do not stop misbehaving.

It may be said that the parental relationship is a hierarchical one: the mother is the all-giving, comforting, and understanding figure; the father is the loving but sometimes strict disciplinarian.[12] Only when parents are very old is this relationship somewhat reversed, the children becoming responsible for the welfare of their parents.

DEATH AND TIME

Substance, blood, is thought to become diluted over time or through successive "degrees." This view necessitates a conception of time as a continuous process, a flow of events that can never be repeated. Substance cannot remain in its first "pure" form as it was given by the first progenitors. Yet substance, as a definition of kinship and ikoyenia for Ego within his/her lifetime, is considered immutable. How, then, is kinship defined?

In taking genealogical charts, I was often referred to older women who "could remember further back." Any further back than three generations led to a single anonymous couple who were considered the beginning of the ikoyenia. Beyond that was beyond memory: "Who remembers that far back? I didn't remember them" (*Pios thimate? Ego dhen tous thimithika*). What this statement implied was: "I did not know them."

It is the living people's memory of the relationships they had with those who have died that keeps the dead "alive." Death serves to sever

---

ing, and caring love. *Agape* may be contrasted with *eros* which is often, though not always, used to signify uncontrollable passion and sexual love.

[12] This is, of course, an oversimplification, for fathers, and men in general, are also seen as "softer" and more sentimental than mothers and women, though they may not express their emotions as easily as women do.

kinship links because it severs relationships (du Boulay 1984:533–556). This provides an understanding of the confusion expressed by parents reciting genealogies concerning whether or not to mention young people who have died. Infants are said to exist in a liminal state between this world and the "other world" from which they came. As such they cannot fully participate in a relationship with others. Young people who die before they have children, though they have been in relationships with parents and siblings, "leave no one behind to remember them" (i.e., leave no children). Moreover, the "cycle of life" (*kiklos tis zois*), in which adults give birth to new life, grow old, and die, is reversed with the death of a young, unmarried person. In this instance only the parents and siblings may include the young person in the genealogical charts, particularly if the death has been recent, for the deceased was an active member of the ikoyenia.

The importance of remembered relationships is also supported by the practice of second burial, which used to occur three to seven years after the first burial in the ikoyenia's plot. After this first period of interment, the corpse would be disinterred and incorporated into a common ossuary. The individuality of the dead person and the link with the ikoyenia would eventually be erased from living memory. The dead would become part of the linear time of history, distinct from the regenerating time of the ikoyenia. Beginning in the late fifties, the practice of a specific ritual of disinterment began to die out. This was accompanied by an increasing emphasis on the elaboration of the burial plots. Marble slabs and gravestones began to replace the simple whitewashed stones that had defined a plot's boundaries. Today the bones of the dead are removed only when a newly deceased ikoyenia member is to be buried. They are cleaned and placed at the foot of the new coffin and buried along with it in the plot of the ikoyenia. The bones are jumbled together: no attempt is made to keep bones belonging to different individuals separate and distinct. It would seem that the stress is now primarily on the ikoyenia and its continuity after death. In both practices, however, the dead is incorporated into a larger unit and his/her individuality erased as he/she passes out of living memory.

The concept of the ikoyenia as a particular entity within the community is maintained by the redefinition of who the "original progenitors" were. In other words, by repressing the memory of ascendant generations, people focus their attention on the children to come. It is through those children that kinship is defined. As the Geertzes (1975:162) put it for the rather different context of Bali, the catalog of identifiable ancestors is short-circuited in "a continuous celebration of regenesis."

Thus it may be said that it is not memory and death that create kinship in the village; it is blood. Blood is the vitalizing, life-giving force in the society, as du Boulay (1984) has shown and as is supported in church doctrines.[13] Passed on from parents to children, from generation to generation, it assures continuity. In this sense, to live beyond one's time is to live beyond the meaning of kinship. This was poignantly expressed by an old woman, said to be 105 years old, whose constant and bitter complaint was: "Is it right for a mother to bury all her children? Why didn't he [*Charos*, the personification of death] take me as well?" The old woman's children had died, and—as was pointed out to me—should her grandchildren become grandparents, these great-great-grandchildren, who would constitute her ikoyenia, could easily intermarry. Not only had she reversed the natural course of events in burying her children, but she was in danger of living beyond the time of kinship relations.

Having highlighted certain aspects of kinship in the village needed for the argument, I turn now to the kinship terms as they are used and understood in the convent.

CONVENT

When a woman leaves her secular (*kosmiki*) ikoyenia to enter the convent,[14] she may be said to adopt a new ikoyenia,[15] one created by the Church and the convent that will serve to define her as a person. In the secular community, as shown above, personal identity is realized within kinship. "Blood," considered immutable and "natural" in this life, is said to be the strongest substance binding people together. In the convent these blood ties, though recognized, are subsumed by spiritual bonds that serve to unite not only the members of a particular monastic community or all Orthodox monastics, but all human beings with the Divine, with God. However, and in this lies the paradox, the nuns use the notion of shared substance to support their claim that as humans we are all the descendants of Adam and Eve and also of Christ, Son of Man. In this sense, the "shared substance" is not diluted or weakened over time but equally strong now as it was in the past. On the other hand, it is believed that through one's conduct in life, one's material substance is transformed and one is able to achieve eternal life in the divine community. It is, then, the paradox of "material substance" that, on the one hand, it can

---

[13] Similarly "spiritual kinship" (*koubaria*), though created by the church ceremonies of marriage and baptism in which no physiological links are created, is informed by canon laws and by practices and beliefs in the village that serve to encompass the spiritual bond within the concepts of physical, "natural" bonds. The godparents are linked by a physical as well as a spiritual bond with the child. See du Boulay (1984).

[14] In Eastern Orthodox Christianity, there are no monastic orders, and both convents and monasteries are called monasteries. Here I use the word *convent* to avoid confusion.

[15] Might we say that the convent, because it seeks to transcend "substance," adopts children in the manner of psychopedhia?

be transformed in this life and, on the other, it serves as the link between humans and the Divine.

In Eastern Orthodoxy, though each convent and monastery has its own constitution outlining the practices and precepts of that institution, it is recognized that there is only one monastic tradition binding all monastics together in the eyes of God. And though rivalry between the two convents I studied was evident on occasions, ideally it should not have existed. In this way, the convent seems quite similar to the household in the village: both are separate entities yet part of a wider community.

Entering the convent, the young woman is entering what will be her "home" for the remainder of her life. Nuns may not leave the convent in which they took their vows. Only with great difficulty may they transfer to a new convent; nor may they renounce their vows. Renunciation may lead to excommunication and the eternal damnation of the former monastic's soul—for the nuns, a true eternal death. The scene is set. Let us examine more closely the convent community.

KINSHIP: SPIRIT OR SUBSTANCE?

In the convents of P. and T., the nuns address each other by name or as "sister" despite obvious age differences or differences of social positions occupied in their former lives.[16] And though a hierarchy seems to exist among the nuns within the convent, it is downplayed and particularly difficult for outsiders to detect. Ideally the nuns among themselves should be equal. As in the village, where a child should not be singled out from among its siblings by its parents since "all have the same blood and come from the same womb," so too in the convent should all the nuns be "one in Christ."

The term *sister* creates a metaphor that likens the relationship between nuns to that between "real" or secular sisters. Like all good metaphors, this one marks the differences as well as the similarities between the two entities (see Sapir 1977:6). Both the nuns and the secular people recognize that the nuns are not "real sisters." Yet by using the formal term of address *sister*, a term rarely used among secular sisters, the nuns mark their relationship. They emphasize their common, spiritual unity in God, an indissoluble unity that secular sisters share by blood, while simultaneously emphasizing an aspect of the codes of conduct expected of secular sisters but demanded of the nuns.[17]

---

[16] It should be noted that kinship is only one of the metaphors borrowed from the secular world. The nuns also use metaphors of polity and the army to describe their lives and their community. In this paper, I will limit myself to examining kinship.

[17] This kinship term applies not only to the nuns within any given convent but to all nuns

It is not only in the notion of sisterhood, however, that monastic relationships parallel secular kinship. The *Hegoumenos* and *Hegoumeni* (abbot and abbess, respectively) are said to fulfill roles similar to those of parents.[18] In the convent, the hierarchy is strictly maintained. Obedience and the subjection of one's will to others are virtues that the nuns struggle to cultivate. The Hegoumenos and Hegoumeni are said to speak with the enlightenment of the Holy Spirit. Their blessing is required for each action taken. Permission to work at a certain task, to be relieved of work due to illness, or to ask a favor from an outsider or another nun must be given by the Hegoumenos/i and is couched in the words, *Ean evloyite* (If it is blessed).

The commands and the occasional punishments of the Hegoumenos/i, however, are not meant to break or disillusion the nuns but to help them achieve the salvation they seek. And, powerful as their authority is, so too is their ability to forgive and to guide those who come to them. The Hegoumeni is *Mitera* (mother), and like a mother she cares for both the material and the spiritual well-being of her "children," the nuns. She must maintain order, but she must also help those nuns with spiritual anxieties and needs. She is responsible for the financial management of the convent. And if a nun should fall sick, she must attend to her needs by arranging doctors, medicines, and hospitalization, and also by offering prayer. In resigning their will to the Hegoumenos/i, the nuns also resign responsibility over their personal well-being to God and more immediately to their superior.

The Hegoumenos is the *Patera* (father), and in P. his role as confessor, as well as priest,[19] monk, and Hegoumenos, allows him to bestow absolution and grace in the name of Christ. Thus he ranks higher in the Church institution than the Hegoumeni, for it is through him that the soul is cleansed and receives the "second baptism" of the confession and the gift of communion.

---

and monks. All are sisters and brothers in Christ, and all who serve Christ as Hegoumenos/i retain this appellation beyond the monastic walls they call home.

[18] The Hegoumenos and Hegoumeni are addressed by many terms: for example, *Geronta* (fem. *Gerontissa*), meaning "Elder" and signifying not their age in years but their spiritual age, their acquired spiritual wisdom and maturity. In this sense, a young man or woman may be a Geronta/tissa if considered spiritually developed. The Hegoumenos may also be addressed as *Papouli* (little priest or grandfather) as well as by the formal term *Patera* (Father). The Hegoumeni may be addressed formally as *Mitera* (Mother) or informally as *Mana*. I do not have the space to examine the different meanings of the terms. Here I only wish to call attention to the emphasis placed on the metaphors of father and mother by the nuns. The more familiar terms express, I believe, a sense of ease and informality within the community that runs parallel to the deep respect the nuns have for their superiors. This duality also characterizes their relationships with the Divine, an issue that will have to be deferred to another paper.

[19] Monks are not priests unless they are so ordained.

This distinction stresses particular aspects of the secular roles of father and mother, while pointing equally to the differences between the secular and monastic worlds. In that the Hegoumenos is addressed by the formal term of *Father*, rarely used in the village, his role is marked as different from that of a blood-related father. The Hegoumenos is not simply like a father, nor does he take the place of the father as an adopted father would. Rather, he is better than a father, in a sense more a father than a secular father could ever be.

This is well expressed by the definition of *love*. In the convent, the greatest human love is that between one's spiritual Father, one's confessor (*pneumatikos*), who is always a man, and the person who confesses, addressed as "my child" by the spiritual Father. The nuns explained: "The husband loves the wife more than her parents can, for the husband has chosen[20] to marry her and to live and have children with her. The spiritual Father loves his spiritual child more than a husband can, for he cares for her soul. He prays for her and with the confession takes on the burden of her sins as well. His love is the greatest of all loves."

In other words, the parent loves the child because the child is a product of the parents' flesh and blood. The husband should love his wife in the spiritual sense as well as in the carnal sense. The spiritual Father, however, loves only the spirit and soul of the person. His task is to help his spiritual child find Christ who is within. Thus his love is said to be greatest. The nuns' views in this instance reverse those in the village. Emphasis in the village is placed on the maternal, "material" bond made through shared substance; in the convent emphasis is placed on the fatherly, spiritual bond. In the convent what is stressed is the voluntary act of love rather than the obligation, or compulsion, to love because of the material bond linking parent with child, or the carnal bond uniting spouses.[21]

The roles of the spiritual father and mother also point to a seeming contradiction in convent ideology. Since all are one in Christ, equal in the sight of God, how is it that there is a spiritual father or mother who must be obeyed? This contradiction was explained to me by the Hegoumenos of P. in terms of the light and shadows that played in the courtyard of P.: "God loves all people equally. But some are stronger than others, better able to receive Him. In death all will stand in the courtyard of

---

[20] Though in the village the majority of the marriages were formerly arranged by the parents, the children did have some say concerning their future partner. Today most young people choose their marriage partners. Ideally, in Orthodox Christianity, a marriage is contracted by two consenting Christians. They must choose freely to marry, for they are bound together in the sight of God and made one (Meyendoroff 1984:48).

[21] Of course this is never explicitly stated, as it contradicts the concept of motherly love as "natural" and "instinctive" and one of the lauded virtues of the *Panayia* (Virgin Mary).

Heaven but some will stand in the warmth and light and others in the shadows. Yet all will be equally in His presence." Some people, in other words, are capable of receiving more of God's grace than others. It follows that in this world the stronger must assist those who "stand in the shadows" if they are called upon to do so.

In the convent, this is seen in the case of the newly tonsured nun, who is less trained, less capable of following God. It might be said that like a child who must be initiated and socialized into the secular community, so too must the nun be weaned from the secular expectations and ties that bind her, that she may more fully participate in the spiritual community of God which the convent ideally represents. A brotherhood is not enough. There must be an ikoyenia with "mothers" and "fathers" able to "raise their children in God" (see Pennington 1979:42).

In the convent the use of formal kinship terms and their related roles—which arise from notions of blood and syngenia found in the village—coupled with the fact that there are no "natural" links binding the monastics serve to highlight the idiosyncrasies of the monastic relationships. The metaphor forcefully calls attention to spiritual unity as the binding element of relatedness, placing it by necessity above shared substance as a truer or higher form of "kinship."

Yet the significance of kinship terms in the convent is more complex than this. The story of Original Sin and the subsequent sacrifice of Christ was vividly related to me by the Hegoumenos of P. This is as close a rendering of his narration as is possible:

> There were once ten battalions [tagmata] of angels in Heaven who served God. But the leader of the tenth battalion chose to defy God and sought to equal Him, so he was cast down along with his followers. This was how the Devil came to be and the Devil is God's greatest enemy.
>
> God then created Man to take the place of the lost tenth battalion. He created him in His own image and He loved him very much. But man, through Eve, rejected God and God's love. For God in His great wisdom had forbidden Adam and Eve only one thing: they were not to eat from the Tree of Knowledge. Everything else was theirs. Eve, like a deceitful child, preferred to listen to God's worst enemy, the Devil, rather than to heed the words of her most loving Father.
>
> For defying God, Adam and Eve were punished and cast out of Paradise. They were forced to live and suffer on earth in exile where they must toil and where women must bear children in pain. This was the retribution demanded by Divine Justice.
>
> Yet God in His infinite love for humans, despite their rejection of Him through their disobedience, sent to earth His only Son and allowed that Son

to suffer and be killed. It was the sacrifice of Christ, the God-man,[22] a sacrifice that no human could ever match, that gave humans a second chance.

Thus, it is our duty not to deny God and His love a second time but to try to abide as closely as we can by His laws and in this manner become worthy to finally take our rightful place as angels in the tenth battalion.

In the convent, this story, besides showing God's love for humans, was also evidence that all humans are the sons and daughters of Adam and Eve, the original progenitors who, created by God, bear within them something of the Divine.[23] Similarly, Pennington (1979:75) notes that the monks of Mount Athos feel themselves to be in unity, as one body, with all Orthodox through time. The belief in a common kinship, though accepted by many of the villagers if they are asked to comment on it, is never volunteered by them in discussions on kinship or on religion. In the convent, however, it formed the basis of much of the nuns' thinking and of their discussions. Thus, whereas in the secular community "substance" serves to create separate, distinct ikoyenies, in the convent it serves to unite all humans through their original progenitors. As the nuns often stated, "We are all descendants from the same seed." Thus, the living nuns trace their human ancestry to the first humans and through them to Christ and to God the Creator.

This leads to ambiguity. On the one hand, it is as if humans are the children of God and related to Christ, Son of Man, since they are "all of one seed." Yet at other times their relationship with the Divine seems to stress the spiritual. For example, the Panayia (Virgin Mary; the word *Panayia* means all-holy or most holy of saints) is the Mother of all humans, for in giving birth to Christ she gave birth to humankind's salvation, to a spiritually reborn humanity. In one discourse, then, humans are all of one seed—the creations and children of God—and in another discourse they are spiritually united to the Panayia and the Holy Trinity.

This becomes somewhat more complicated when one examines a statement by the Hegoumenos of P. in which he described the Panayia as "people's gift to God so that He could become man." Could the Panayia be regarded as the new element added to the divine "line" allowing for

[22] Established in the Fourth Ecumenical Council of Chalcedon (A.D. 451) was the doctrine that Christ was consubstantial with the Father and consubstantial with humanity; that Christ had two perfect, indivisible but separate natures (Ostrogorsky 1956:55).

[23] Depending on the context, the nuns either seem to mean that all of humanity is related or that all people who are Orthodox are related. In the convent I sometimes got the sense that Catholics and Protestants were damned because, as Christians, they should see the truth of Orthodoxy and convert; Jews were damned for having killed Christ; Jehovah's Witnesses were the Antichrist; and members of all other religious groups were "savages," people who were ignorant of the Truth and thus not responsible for the sins they committed.

Christ's embodiment on earth and the redemption of humankind? It is through the Panayia that people could once again achieve grace and the possibility of eternal life. She is said to be the bridge between Heaven and earth. She links through childbirth the ikoyenia of humans with the ikoyenia of the Divine. Through the Panayia humans are, so to speak, in an affinal relationship with the Divine. As in the village, where the woman is the "outside," "foreign" element that is respected and adored as mother but who never completely enters into the ikoyenia, so too the Panayia is placed exceedingly high, but as a human, never part of the Trinity. She can only intercede, plead, and give assistance. But she is the most glorious of humans, having achieved the highest sanctity, having become a member of the divine male ikoyenia through the birth of Christ. Humans may be said to be both in an affinal relationship with the Divine (that is, different from the divine personages but still co-members with them) and in a consubstantial relationship (that is, having some of the Divine within them, being after all sons and daughters of Adam and Eve).

Moreover, metaphors of relationship—which describe God as Father and Judge of the Second Coming; the Panayia as mother, the caring and forgiving figure in the Holy Family; and Christ as Son of God, part of the Trinity, and Judge and Punisher of sinful men—make use of kinship terms to explicate how God, the Panayia, and Christ act in their roles as Father, Mother, and Son of God. Or, rather, the terms mark the relationships as being more potent than their human counterparts, while also serving in the nuns' eyes as examples, ideals toward which humans should strive in their own relationships. The metaphor is thus reflected back onto the secular community. The secular ikoyenia should be *like* the eternal, divine ikoyenia.

To summarize, the kinship terms used among the monastics imply one ikoyenia, with "fathers," "mothers," and "siblings." The convent members thereby mark themselves as a distinct group, spiritually bound, seeking eternal life. And since within this ikoyenia individuals are at different stages in achieving salvation, the use of the hierarchical model is apt. Also relevant is the use of the term ikoyenia for the Divine Family, the Father, Christ, and the Panayia, in a spiritual relation to humans. Through His Son, Christ, who was born to a human woman, God the Father is related to humans. The relationship is both one of affinity, through the Panayia, and one of syngenia, through Christ and also through Adam and Eve, the original progenitors.

What I hope to have shown thus far is that there is an ambiguity in the nuns' descriptions of their relationship with the Divine. On the one hand, it is a material relationship, founded on substance that has not been diluted over time, and, on the other, it is a spiritual relationship which encompasses this material unity.

BLOOD, FLESH, AND THE HOLY COMMUNION

From this ambiguity there arises a problem. Humans may trace their descent to God, yet it is understood that this syngenia may be lost through sin. Humans may be cast from the sight of God into eternal damnation as Adam and Eve were, but this time there will be no redemption. All people therefore must strive to maintain the bond they have regained with God through Christ in order to achieve a true and lasting syngenia, a syngenia that will be based first on spiritual unity and second on material unity.

In the following pages I hope to show how the material and the spiritual are linked by the nuns through the notion of the codes of conduct. We may start by noting that the material substance maintains its sanctity over time once it has been transformed spiritually. A simple example is given by a flask of holy water or oil. As a part of the oil or water is used for blessings or cures, it can be replaced by tap water or cooking oil without dilution of the substance's sanctity. Only a drop of holy water or oil is needed to make the profane substance pure and blessed.

In such a case as this, a distinction can be drawn between sanctified substance and earthly substance. For humans, however, this distinction is blurred, since humans are both earthly and divine in spirit and substance. Moreover, humans are differentiated from the rest of creation because they are said to have a will and intelligence enabling them to make choices—something oil cannot do.

Implicit in this notion of the human condition, as it is understood by the nuns, is the notion of syngenia with the Divine and the mutability of this tie during one's life. Christ, Son of Man, is believed to have shed His blood for the salvation of humankind, and this sacrifice is repeated daily or weekly in the liturgy. The act of communion is the partaking of the body and the blood of Christ. It is commingling, the incorporation of the body of Christ within the body of the communer. With communion you have become literally one with Christ. Your substance is transformed (see Bettenson 1967:75). But this oneness with Christ is said to last only for a short while, a day at most, for as humans we cannot avoid sin. Inevitably, we make wrong choices, thereby becoming once again less close to God, seeking to follow our own will rather than God's.

For the nuns, communion spiritualizes the mundane, lifting the society and people toward God. Prone as we are to sever ourselves from Christ as we once severed ourselves from Paradise and God, we must continually strive to renew our spiritual and material purity, a task requiring constant and untiring vigilance. It is only upon death and only if one is judged and accepted by God that one can enter into the Kingdom of Heaven, becoming truly and forever "one in Christ." In this instance, substance, blood and flesh, is permanently transformed through obedient adherence to the codes of conduct. It loses its earthly, inherited sinfulness and acquires everlasting grace.

This is quite unlike the villagers' idea that one's blood and flesh link one irrevocably with one's kin. In the village the fact of the material substance cannot be changed by the codes of conduct, while in the convent it is just this fact that the nuns seek to overcome.

BETROTHAL AND MARRIAGE

This endeavor informs the nuns' relationships with the secular world.[24] The nuns see themselves as occupying a liminal position somewhere between heaven and earth. By forsaking their secular ikoyenia, the nuns seek liberation from the secular bonds into which they were born. The tonsuring ceremony seems to resemble the secular rites of baptism, marriage, and funerals. This ceremony is too complex to be detailed here. Suffice it to say, however, that the nun thereby receives a new name, as in baptism, while for her relations "it is as if she has died." Nuns may not attend the baptisms, weddings, or funerals of even the closest members of their secular ikoyenia. Nor will they be buried in the plot of their secular ikoyenia, but in the convent graveyard. The social "death" marked by the tonsure may be likened to a nun's first burial: "Like an old woman burnt by Charos [a personification of death]," as the villagers say, the nun wraps herself in black vestments. Even the name for nun, *kalogria* (good old woman) signifies the separation. The nun is old, dead; her kinship with the outside world should therefore die. Like a young woman who dies without children, the nun should be forgotten in this world.

For the nun, however, central to the tonsuring ceremony is the imagery of marriage. With the tonsure she is said to betroth Christ, the "Eternal Bridegroom," and her eventual death is regarded as a summons from Christ to his pure and humble bride to enter into the promised and long-awaited union with Him, the Beloved. In becoming the "brides of Christ," the nuns enter more fully into the community of God. In sacrificing their youth (which the Hegoumenos says is the greatest sacrifice humans can offer to God) and submitting their will to God, they take the first and greatest step in denying the "natural" drives of the body, the

---

[24] It should be noted that in practice the nuns are close to their secular *syngenis* and that often their *ikoyenia* will supply the convent with foodstuffs and keep the nuns informed of marriages, births, and deaths which occur outside the convent walls.

secular aspect of their being. They, like the Panayia, in giving themselves to God, seek to act like a bridge between this world and the next. But Eternal Unity can only be achieved with their own rebirth as angels in Heaven.

As Maltz (1978) has pointed out, the image of the bride effectively portrays the nun's liminal position between this world and the next. A bride is in a transitional state: no longer the young girl innocent of any relationship, nor yet the fully mature woman and wife. The nuns, too, are in a state of transition. Through their betrothal, they signal their desire to become "one in Christ," yet because they are still prone to sin, still "of this world," they must struggle to achieve this complete unity. They must be in a constant state of preparation, ever diligent and ready to respond to the call of their groom.

It is interesting to note, however, that nuns comparing their position with that of secular women often say that they are married to Christ. By describing their state in terms of marriage instead of betrothal, they appropriate the social identity accorded to married women. They have simply chosen to bind themselves in this world to the Church and the life it dictates. Yet, significantly, though they speak of being married to Christ, they never refer to Him as their husband (*ton antra mou*) but always as their bridegroom. In this life, their relationship to Him is always that of a bride—that is, perpetually in the process of achieving unity. Betrothal frames the transformation from the earthly, potentially sinful state to a state of eternal unity in Christ, both in spirit and in body.

THE BODY

As we have seen, the dichotomy between the body and the soul, the material and the spiritual, is not clear-cut. And though both are involved in the process of redemption or damnation, the body often best serves to express these states of transformation. For example, the body's failure to putrefy after death may signal either salvation or damnation. It is recognized both by the nuns and by the villagers that a *vrikolakas* (loosely translated as "vampire") is someone who in life was very sinful and whose punishment now is to roam the earth, having a body but no soul; a being of pure substance without spirit.[25] In this instance, the body is a terrifying sight and has an unpleasant smell, evidencing spiritual damnation and arousing fear. Yet there are many instances as well in which humans were proven to be saints when their exhumed bodies were found intact and "a sweet aroma permeated the air for miles around," a clear sign of spiritual

[25] In the village no one has seen a vrikolakas, and no one admits knowing anyone who became such a creature. In general villagers were not terribly interested in the subject, though it was familiar to them.

grace. In both instances, the body is a sign of the dead person's spiritual state: substance has been transformed into something otherworldly.

The nun who renounces her vows and returns to the secular world may be said to acquire "more substance," losing the spirituality she had obtained through her vows. She steps down into the earthly world of material concerns from the "social death" and spiritual life she had acquired. Now, excommunicated, her body—her substance—is alive, but her soul is dead. Like the vrikolakas, the excommunicated nun becomes one of the living dead.

CONCLUSION

In this paper I have sought to bring out three points. Used metaphorically in the convent, kinship terms highlight the similarity between the ways people who are "mothers," "fathers," and "sisters" should act in the village and are expected to act in the convent. The Panayia and the Hegoumeni, like mothers, are expected to be loving, affectionate, caring, nurturing, and protective. God and the Hegoumenos, like fathers, are expected to maintain a loving discipline and order over their children. Nuns, like sisters, should be treated equally and should care equally for one another.

The differences highlighted by the metaphorical use of these terms in the convent center on the creation of "true kinship." In the village this kinship is created by blood, whereas in the convent it is held to be spiritual unity. Spiritual fathers, it will be recalled, are better, more truly fathers, than secular fathers could ever be. Thus, the convent's use of the term *father*—a metaphorical use from a secular viewpoint—comes to be, from the nuns' point of view, the primary referent of *father*, the example of how secular fathers should act.

A paradox arises from the use of these kinship terms, because spiritual unity is made intelligible by the use of the ideas of "common substance" and shared blood, as expressed in Holy Communion, or the notion of descent from a "common seed." In the convent, "relatedness" no longer circumscribed by death extends to encompass all humans, both living and dead. This, in turn, unites the ikoyenia of God with the ikoyenia of man through the Panayia, Christ, and ultimately the first progenitors, Adam and Eve. The fact of being human links us through kinship—the sharing of common substance, of "one seed"—with the Divine. Yet, in contrast to the village notions of kinship, this link may be severed by sinful actions in life. Humans can lose their kinship with God to suffer eternal damnation. In the convent, "substance" no longer bound by death or the "natural" world is regarded as transformable, capable of achieving divinity in an eternal and material, as well as spiritual, "kinship" with Christ.

ACKNOWLEDGMENTS

I would like to thank M. Bloch, M. Sallnow, J. Carsten, A. Papataxiar-chis, M. Phylactou, and the members of the Thesis Writing Seminar of the London School of Economics, 1987–1988, for their comments and advice. I am especially indebted to P. Loizos for both his comments and his encouragement. I am grateful to the Fulbright Foundation for funding me while I was in the field and to the Onassis Foundation for financial assistance during the writing of my thesis. I am especially indebted to the nuns of P. and T. and to the many people in the village who took the time and had the patience to answer my questions.

Chapter 7

FRIENDS OF THE HEART: MALE COMMENSAL SOLIDARITY, GENDER, AND KINSHIP IN AEGEAN GREECE

Evthymios Papataxiarchis

RECENT ADVANCES in feminist anthropology and the anthropology of gender have sensitized us to the study of phenomena with an explicitly gendered character and have further influenced every corner of anthropological thinking (Moore 1988). These developments have contributed to the emergence of a new anthropology of masculinity (Whitehead 1981; Brandes 1981; Herdt 1981, 1982; Herzfeld 1985a) that focuses on how men view themselves as male persons. This essay argues that the widespread phenomenon of friendship among men cannot be ethnographically analyzed simply in terms of politics or economics.[1] The case that I will consider here suggests that, far from being an appendix of male-centered structure, friendship is an aspect of the antistructure, allied with leisure, with commensality via alcohol or gambling, and characterized by the absence of significant economic functions. The fluid, "light" character of emotional friendship can be accounted for if the gendered nature of the relationship gets analytic emphasis. These emotional alliances make sense in the Aegean only in terms of their foundation in the ongoing construction of masculinity as this occurs in the subculture of male-dominated coffee shops and in practices of commensality. The making of masculine identity, then, and its gradual explication in structured patterns of commensality are dominant themes in the study of friendship between men.

---

[1] The ethnographic literature on male friendship in the societies of the northern Mediterranean and southern Europe focuses on the work of Pitt-Rivers (1973, 1977). Pitt-Rivers attempted to bridge the gap between a traditional emphasis on the institutional aspects of interpersonal relations (e.g., Foster 1953, 1960; Wolf 1966) and mainstream kinship analysis. The work of Brandes (1973, 1981), Gilmore (1975), and Murphy (1983), who studied exclusively male relations in Andalusia, profited from this reorientation. For the Greek case, see the brief but sensitive analyses by Currier (1974) and Loizos (1975:89–92) and the very interesting insights into friendship in Crete by Herzfeld (1985a). Campbell (1964) and Loizos (1977) reported the wide relevance of asymmetrical, contractual ties that often link the isolates of the family or the local community to the surrounding institutional complexes.

Mouria and Skala are two small, neighboring communities in northern Lesbos with a combined population of around five hundred people.[2] The two villages form a single administrative unit (*kinotita*), and their inhabitants engage in olive growing and fishing. The most remarkable aspect of social life is the extensive segregation of the sexes: women and men spend most of their time in same-sex contexts and identify strongly with their own sex. The nucleated village seems to be divided into sex-specific territories. The square in the center with the coffee shops and the marketplace is dominated by men. The houses that surround the square and constitute neighborhoods are small havens for women and children.

In these communities, it is assumed that women are inclined by their nature to exhibit the archetypical kinship feeling of "maternal love" in nurturing and bringing up children. Domestic kinship is thus of central significance in the attainment of female personhood. *Sigenia*, to be translated as "kinship," sets women together in matrifocal alliances made possible by a neolocality norm that favors women and by female dowries. Ideas about sexuality, pollution, and moral worth, the social configurations of conjugality, and the roles of women as dowry administrators and wage earners suggest the considerable domestic power of women, especially among the poorer strata.[3]

In the antagonistic engagements of the matrifocal groups that compete for prestige, there is little room for friendship. Married women often assume that a woman's sustained loyalties to her consanguines do not leave much scope for relating outside the house, a realm thought of as full of antagonism and gossip. Ethnographic evidence further shows that friendship among women grows in the gaps of matrifocal kinship, usually during courtship and, more rarely, in the first years of marriage. Female friendships involve women with minimal domestic obligations, such as students who travel together to the high school in a neighboring head-village, or young mothers who are outsiders and lack membership in a matrifocal network. Married women friends are conceived as of "the (same) house" (*tou spitiou*) and assist each other in tasks that otherwise are assigned to female relatives. Friendship among women, then, is a substitute for kinship, it is expressed in the terms of domestic kinship, it is susceptible to the fluctuations of domestic life, and it usually fades in time.[4] Intersexual friendships between married persons are rare and sus-

---

[2] I conducted anthropological fieldwork in northern Lesbos from September 1979 to May 1981.

[3] For an ethnographic account of social life in the two communities, see Papataxiarchis (1988).

[4] Kennedy, who studied friendships among women who marry outside their village of origin in Crete, has argued that the lack of research in this area arises from the rather

pect: an exchange between a man and a woman cannot evade sexual connotations. A woman treated to a drink by an unrelated man or a man
visiting an unrelated woman's house is assumed to be evidence of sexual
liaison.[5]

As domestic kinship is of greater significance for women, so friendship
is culturally acknowledged and extensively practiced by men. Men spend
a lot of time in the coffee shop, where they drink, chat, conduct business,
play cards, sing, dance, or even nap. For many men, bachelors included,
who are often conceived of as visitors to houses dominated by women,
the coffee shop is a refuge. Life in the coffee shop reflects the subtleties
of the commensal code of *kerasma* (treating to a drink). Kerasma embod-
ies the values of the gift: its application firmly establishes reciprocity in
commensality. It further opens the path to the assertion of masculinity in
an egalitarian context.

In this paper I analyze friendship as it is perceived and practiced in
the world of the coffee shop. I start by considering the demarcation of
friendship from economic and political exchange and its independence
from kinship; then I move on to discuss its developmental cycle and its
focus on the making and sharing of masculine identity. Friendships
among men in Mouria rest on a rich infrastructure of gendered emotions,
i.e., emotions that are thought to be exclusively held by men. Men as
friends "use" these emotions to make their experiences into solid frameworks of resistance against the threatening values of household and kinship, state and the market. In the conclusion, I draw on some of the
implications of this analysis for the understanding of friendship, in particular, and same-sex relatedness, in general. Emotional friendship is remarkably different from kinship in many respects: as a haven of egalitarianism, as an autonomous basis of personhood, and, in effect, as a
sentimental alternative to maternal love and the amity of kinship. This
represents an insurmountable problem to the placing of friendship on a
continuum with kinship. In the context of the coffee shop, gendered friendship appears to be an alternative to the kinship basis of personhood.

"androcentric" research assumption, "that women's social and experiential lives are limited
to the domestic context" (Kennedy 1986:121). Kennedy is not explicit on the relation between female friendship and kinship. Hirschon, however, regards "access to the home" as
indicative of the intimacy of friendship and sustains that "close friendships, in which serious
personal and family matters were disclosed, were described significantly in terms of kinship" (Hirschon 1989:185). Du Boulay (1974:214) speaks of companionship between women
who were "effectively on their own."

[5] An interesting Mediterranean example of intersexual friendship occurs in the context of
courtship between unmarried youth in Andalusia (Uhl 1985). Also see Cowan's analysis (this
volume).

STRUCTURE AND FUNCTION IN FRIENDSHIP

As in other societies in the Mediterranean, relations of male friendship in Mouria are regarded as the crowning expression of an ideology that stresses normative equality among all men. The relationship cannot be based either on the assertion or the structural premise of an inequality that arises from age, family background, social class, wealth, professional occupation, or marital status. Status differences are thought to divide men, while friendship is considered as the bond that resists all division.

Friends are usually of the same generation (*yenia*). They are equally involved in or distanced from the domestic sphere, this being dependent on number of children, the personality and kinship network of the wife, or the property situation. Marriage and the making of a household creates a serious imbalance in the friendship tie and puts the relationship to the test. Friendship particularly thrives in the large group of male bachelors who are structurally without households. In Mouria, out of fifty-five men, aged between thirty-one and seventy, twenty are single. Most of these men are among the most regular participants in coffee shop life and systematic exponents of the values of male autonomy.

Despite the recent decline of class inequalities, the idea of symmetry in class background survives as a guiding principle of friendship but adopts a new focus on the "professional" background. Wage earners, tree pruners, or builders who are friends may often be members of the same harvest team or work for the same boss. Landless farm laborers, dependent laborers, and builders (i.e., men with no land-based status) have a greater tendency to form friendships than middle-ranking peasants who are attached to land and the household. Yet men with noncommensurable status, such as the owner of the local olive-processing factory or the secretary of the cooperative, are perceived, and rightly so, as having no emotional friends. Men who are aggressively masculine are likewise thought to be friendless.

Differences arising from political persuasion or origins play a lesser role, especially if they are not part of the formative experience of friendship. Men can be friends even though they vote for different political parties, or are not of similar origin (the parents of one being refugees), or even have different class origins, which fade in time. The friendship of Aris Papas with Stamatis Psaros is a good example. Both men are in their middle forties, married, with a son and a daughter respectively. Their households could be described as equally matrifocal. Aris's wife, despite the fact that she is the youngest of five very poor refugee sisters, is one of the most dynamic and respected women in the village. Stamatis's household, on the other hand, is even more typically matrifocal, since it is under the control of his energetic mother-in-law. Stamatis could be described, although never referred to, as *sogabros* (groom who resides with his wife's parents), since he is from a neighboring head-village. Aris has a refugee background. The two men work together as skilled wage laborers in pruning or building; they are *sintrofi* (comrades), in this case partners. Their "partnership" at work apparently relies on a commonality of character, on the enjoyment of being together, and on the reputation they have for being emotionally involved in what they do. This certainly overrides their different formative experiences and their current political standing, which could be a source of friction. Aris is very active in the Communist Left, while Stamatis is a follower of the Center Left.

Male friendships are thought of as examples of voluntarism and openness. Whereas a man is born with kin, he "makes" friends. A man "chooses" his friends, while he may have been introduced to his wife or even have married by arrangement. Choice is somehow endemic in the relationship of friends. In a playful manner, old friends often act like new ones, thus lending the connection the fresh air of spontaneity and individuality. The commitment that binds the friends, however, remains throughout a voluntary one. As there is no obligation to remain friends, there are equally no penalties for leaving the relationship. No stigma is attached to the friend who chooses not to meet his companion or who concludes the relationship.

The stress on the matching of backgrounds, the absence of strict rules and jurally binding obligations, the reliance on sentiment and mood, to be fully discussed below, leave the impression of an inchoate, structureless relationship.[6] Elsewhere in the Mediterranean, it has been argued that friendship is a relationship that survives on credit from jurally based or contractual reciprocity or through affiliation to kinship. In Mouria, however, it appears to be emptied of both structure and function, to be separate from kinship, and to lack the contractual properties that might privilege it in counteracting the atomism of households by linking local society to the market or the state. Let us examine these points one by one.

First, among the Sarakatsani, Campbell (1964) noted an aspect of friendliness permeating the relationship of matrilateral cousins who neither grazed their domestic animals together nor shared a compound. In other respects the nonagnatic realm was considered hostile terrain. Thus little scope remained for friendships with non-kin. In Mouria (as elsewhere in Greece) the social realms of kinship and friendship are kept

---

[6] The general structurelessness of friendship gave rise to characterizations like "supplementary" or "interstitial" (Wolf 1966:2) or "residual" relationship (Pitt-Rivers 1968:413). Others take a more intermediate position stressing its quasi-institutional nature (Paine 1969:514; Hammond and Jablow 1987:257).

strictly apart.[7] The widespread assumption is that men who are kin cannot easily become friends.[8] Tension and conflict thrive in the relationships between fathers and sons, as well as between brothers. This is intensified when the closed and obligatory, materially binding and hierarchical nature of male kinship is applied and reinforced in economic cooperation. Mouriani often use commensality and friendship as a small haven from the troubled waters of kinship where they may freely complain about the excessive demands and the despotic rule of fathers or older brothers.

Interestingly enough, female kinship may indirectly support male companionship. This is the case of friends who are linked through the shared matrifiliation of their wives. These men do not regard their affinal attachment as the basis of friendship. It just makes it easier. There are cases of emotional friends sponsoring each other at marriage. *Koumbaria* (spiritual kinship), then, merely reinforces an already-existing bond. Ties of friendship do not, however, seem to affect relations between the wives, the relatives, or the children of the male friends.

Second, the mixing of the instrumental and the emotional dimension in the analytic definition of friendship is an important aspect of the anthropological theory of kinship and one that will receive further attention. Many ethnographers agree with Pitt-Rivers's (1973:97) assumption that "all friendship must be both sentimental in inspiration and instrumental in effects."[9] Yet Mouriani hold a concept of male friendship that devalues the instrumental side when it exaggerates the emotional. Friendships are applied in activities that are emically distinguished from economic cooperation and cannot be glossed as *sinergasia* (cooperation), or *sinalama* (exchange of labor services). The applications of friendship

[7] Herzfeld also noticed in Xiromeri that friendship and kinship are mutually exclusive (1976:196–197). Equally, du Boulay argues that in Ambeli, a village in Euboea, short-run friendships of practical expedience contribute to a continuing system of extramarital alliances that are in a continuous state of flux (1974:214–220). Olson (1982) reports similar juxtapositions of friendship to kinship.

[8] Nor do I think that it is adequate to consider friendship as "an escape from the press of life" (Wolf 1966:11), thus attributing to it the functions that cannot be attained by kinship. In a Protestant Irish community, Leyton (1974) describes friendship as a luxury and an alternative to kinship that aims to resolve conflicting role demands. Paine (1974:10) argues that noninstitutionalized friendship is a "refuge from the glare of public life and its burden of institutional obligations" in civil society.

[9] Also see Brandes (1973:758), who argues that "a friend . . . cannot and will not remain economically disinterested in the bond." This is certainly almost a consensus view among ethnographers of the Mediterranean. Another good example is Galt (1973), who describes interpersonal relations in the southern Italian island of Pantelleria along the lines of Foster's dyadic contract model. "People become friends and maintain friendships through the exchange of services or goods such as small gifts or even small loans" (327). For a different approach, see Wolf's (1966) distinction between emotional and instrumental friendship.

are usually qualified by an element of expressiveness and masculinity or the joint dependence on a social superior.[10] For example, friends may dance together or offer their services to the same boss at the same time; yet they rarely cooperate in fishing, in the olive harvest, or in the execution of special tasks. Nor do commensal partners engage together in spheres governed by the logic of economic calculation and self-interest that allegedly underlies relations between households.

Interested and disinterested reciprocity are symbolically distinguished by their respective association with different types of commensality. Cooperation between households or wage-labor arrangements are often marked by coffee commensality. After the completion of a task, the men who helped in sheepshearing or building may be invited to have coffee or a meal to conclude a session of cooperation. Commensality is arranged in return for practical help or even the skillful accomplishment of a paid task. It symbolically compensates for the extra input of personal effort. The code of commensality is exploited to symbolically "translate" economic exchange into the sharing of substance and therefore disguise the inherent asymmetries. *Raki* (a strong spirit distilled from grape skins) is avoided in these fundamentally asymmetrical exchanges and reserved to symbolize truly emotional, disinterested partnership.[11] In these instances where the friends unilaterally assist each other, the idea of reciprocity is fully suppressed. These are unplanned, almost spontaneous, and purely voluntary offerings of help that ideally derive directly from the sentiments of friendship. In effect, no record of exchanged services is kept.

Third, attitudes toward patronage are indicative of the nature of friendship, insofar as they reveal the utilitarianism of the latter. Instances of patrons and clients "dressed" as friends are frequent throughout the Mediterranean.[12] Mouriani, however, are very critical of patronage arrangements, which they consider damaging to a man's reputation for independence. The use of *rousfeti* (favor) stands in contrast to the male values of self-reliance, autonomy, and freedom. Rousfeti is thought of as an external importation into the local society and suggests a form of political dependence that is regarded as fundamentally immoral. Today asymmetrical exchanges with political significance are restricted to a specific pattern: fish are exchanged for "favors." The recipients of the fish are usually officials of the Agricultural Bank who arrange loans for fishing and

----

[10] See Campbell (1964) and Loizos (1977).

[11] See Papataxiarchis (1984).

[12] In the past, wealthy landowners from Mouria hired men and women of refugee origin to work for them as domestic servants or agricultural laborers and sponsored their marriages or baptized their children. Present attitudes toward patronage may well be a reaction to these cases of economic paternalism. For a good collection of studies on patronage, see Gellner and Waterbury (1977).

"mortgages" for the making of new houses or provide technical advice. Fish are sold in the market and usually cooked by women at home. The currency of political exchange is not part of the sphere of male morality, and therefore these exchanges are regarded as morally neutral. The gift of fish merely eases the flow of financial support from the state.

Outside these rather restricted asymmetrical exchanges of "fish for favor," there is little to remind us of the extensive use of patronage in other parts of Greece or Cyprus.[13] However, let us dwell on the exception and consider the only "proper" case of patronage that took place during my two years of fieldwork: this was the baptism of the daughter of a Mourianos by a local M.P., an event that was extensively criticized within the local community.

Pavlos Papadopoulos belongs to one of the well-off landowning families of Mouria and is patrilaterally attached to the leading surnamed group of local merchants. His father's patrilateral cousin is one of the big men as well as president of the community council, of which Pavlos is also a member. He is in his early thirties, has married into one of the nouveau-riche families of Skala, and, although he owns more than sixty *modia* of olive groves,[14] also works as warehouse foreman in the local cooperative. Having grown up in Athens and completed some years of high school education there, he is more cosmopolitan than most Mouriani and rather critical of mainstream politics in Mouria, which he considers an obstacle to the economic development and prosperity of the local society. In recent years, tourism started being a serious source of income for Skaliotes. Pavlos was among the first to spot the opportunity and decided to extend his dowried house and rent rooms. To do so, however, he had to get a loan; this, under the circumstances, would have been very difficult without *meso* (leverage). The opportunity was found when a member of parliament from the governing conservative party (New Democracy) visited Skala and undertook the baptismal sponsorship of Pavlos's daughter. The politician saw in this arrangement the means to gain political following, although Pavlos allegedly did not exaggerate the political benefits that would accrue to his protector. Equally frankly, Pavlos from the start made clear to his prospective sponsor what he wanted. Pavlos's initial contact with his patron was premised on the offices he held as local councillor and employee of the cooperative. In this capacity he extended village-wide hospitality to the visiting politician. Yet he soon turned a relationship of commensal hospitality into an asymmetrical political contract that served his *simfero* (private interest). The mixing of codes, unusual for the local culture, was subjected to severe criticism by fellow villagers and forced Pavlos to take

[13] See Campbell (1964) and Loizos (1977).
[14] One modi equals 640 kilograms.

the unprecedented step of baptizing the child in the church of a head-village fifteen kilometers from Mouria and inviting only the close family circle, who came to know about it a few days before the event. To my surprised reaction that I was neither informed nor invited—despite the fact that, as a regular visitor to their home and a commensal friend of Pavlos's, I had on many occasions shown my interest in the forthcoming baptism—Pavlos responded that it was nothing really serious or worth bothering about. Pavlos explained his decision in strictly material terms, stressing the calculative aspect and diminishing the moral content of the relation. He said that the baptism of the child and koumbaria did not really have any moral significance. This is why he had delayed the baptism for so long. Pavlos didn't boast or advertise his relationship with the politician, nor did he refer to him publicly as koumbaro. To his consociates he emphasized his different political stand, insisting that "of course" he would not vote for New Democracy. The koumbaria apparently made very little impact on the relationship of the two men. Pavlos assumed that he had in fact taken advantage of the weak position of the politician, who desperately needed a safe "welcomer" in Mouria.

The story of Pavlos's koumbaria illustrates the restriction of patronage to an act of exchange, a koumbaria for a mortgage, rather than an exchange pattern or an exchange-based relationship. The outside sponsor gained only an acquaintance, a person with whom he could exchange drinks in the coffee shop. The development of the relationship into a broader base for political support was blocked by the purely transactionalist spirit of the insider, who, having got what he wanted, lost interest in the perpetuation of a more or less problematic exchange. The contract operationalized an economic tie with the help of a symbol that in Mouria carries female normative power and meaning. For patronage to be effective as a mode of political exchange and incorporation, it is necessary for structurally asymmetrical reciprocities to have a moral influence. This is not so in Mouria, and Pavlos knew it very well.

ASPECTS AND TYPES OF MALE FRIENDSHIP

So far, we have seen that friendship is kept apart from kinship and is firmly insulated from the morally suspect practices of economic or political exchange. Friendship, then, seems to lack any firm roots in what we usually perceive as social "structure," nor is it subject to what we conceive as economic or political "functions." Both "structure" and "function" are relegated to domestic kinship, which is a concern of married women and of men who aspire exclusively to the values of domestic kinship. What, then, is the content of friendship in Mouria?

The normal habitat of friendship among men is the coffee shop, and commensality is both its base and its practice.[15] The very gesture of friendliness is articulated as a treat to a drink. Kerasma is a minimal expression of recognition, especially if it does not originate with a person to whom the recipient is already related. If the treat is more or less systematically reciprocated, it turns into a gesture of *sevasmos* (respect), a mutual acknowledgment of the relative position of the two men, the starting point for an exploration of personal character with the prospect of closer relations.[16] At this stage, there is a central concern for symmetry and equality, and the relationship is qualified by the subtleties of the code of kerasma.

Friendship stands at the outer boundary of belonging, and it conceptually qualifies the category of *xenos* (outsider), who in certain cases is addressed as *filos* (friend). In principle, the outsider is subjected to *filoxenia* (hospitality), which etymologically refers to a feeling of amity and friendship towards the xenos.[17] *Filema* (the very gift of hospitality) can be reciprocated only at the same level, i.e., when the host visits the community of his guest. Once the outsider is granted the right to treat, he is conceived of as a friend. The postman who regularly visits the village or the anthropologist after a period of residence is referred to as filos. This entitles the outsider to ask for the moral protection of the local society. At this level, the term for friendship is used as the most broad term of inclusion.

Elementary friendships of this sort can accommodate the exchange of services and are often embedded in a network of material reciprocities. A friend may ask for a *chari* (disinterested favor, the gift of casual service). A sack of olives is conveyed to the factory, or spare parts for the engine are bought from Mytilene. The offering of the service may be followed by a treat to coffee, yet the favor belongs to a network of reciprocities distinct from, and not commensurable with, alcoholic commensality. The exchange of drinks makes the flow of favors easier when the relationship is too rudimentary to accommodate more heavy pressures for cooperation.

These first, exploratory steps toward commensality often lead to casual friendship.[18] Two men start keeping company (*kanoun parea*); they ex-

---

[15] See Papataxiarchis (1984). Reciprocal drinking has often been associated with forms of friendship. For example, Aceves (1971:48) argues that "the offering and taking of beverages is part and parcel of the whole ritual of friendly social relations." See also the etiquette of drinking among *amigos* in Andalusian bars (Driessen 1983:128).

[16] These notions correspond to what Pina-Cabral (1986:155–161) glosses as "relative" and "absolute" respect in friendship.

[17] This level of friendship corresponds to what in Rhodes is called *yarenis* (ties of reciprocal hospitality) (Herzfeld 1989:78–79).

[18] I borrow the term from Gilmore (1975) who refers to this kind of friendship as "disin-

change drinks systematically and even suspend the use of the kerasma code itself: they split expenses (*refenes*) and do not distinguish the giver from the receiver. First names or nicknames are used as terms of address, implying familiarity, and the term *filos* may be used in reference. A man may have a number of casual friends with whom to associate in the same or different contexts, yet most of these ties derive from the same sphere of drinking companionship (*parea*) and are qualified by the sentiments of diffuse solidarity.

Among young unmarried men, who have completed their military service, the parea (drinking party) constitutes the section of the peer group from which casual friendships can develop into something more deep, affectionate, and important. Casual friendship serves as a testing ground to establish "who matches [*teriazi*] whom" in new avenues of masculine activity, such as excursions to the nearby town for a *glendi* (festivity) or flirting with women or dancing together the *zeybekiko*.[19]

A good example are the card-playing sessions that usually take place after work. It is mainly young men who assemble to play *xeri*: each man gets six cards face down and is obliged to turn up a card when his turn comes. If a player holds the same number or figure as the card played before him, he can collect all the cards that have been played since the last player did the same. Each card carries a certain value. At the end of each game, which involves two rounds of dealing from a single pack of cards, the score of each player is recorded. The games are repeated till the first player has reached an agreed number of points.

The card game of *poka* (poker) and the throwing of dice are popular avenues for competition among men. Xeri, however, is markedly different in many respects. First, it is the only card game that remains part of the realm of commensality, since no money stakes are used. What is at stake in xeri is the right to kerasma, awarded to those who lose. Xeri, then, focuses on the honorific side of kerasma. The defeated side honors the winners by offering them a brandy or a soft drink. The treating becomes a penalty for losing that does not require future reciprocation.[20] Second, the defeated party has the right to invite the winners to play a new round and the winning party is obliged to accept the challenge.

---

terested companionship" governed by "subtle etiquette" and "enmeshed in an on-going system of continual reciprocations" (315).

[19] The Zeybeks lived on the outskirts of Smyrna and supplied the local notables with hired soldiers during the eighteenth and nineteenth centuries. Their traditions won fame among the local populations because of their involvement in struggles against the Ottoman state. Among other dances, such as the *chasapikos* or the *nisiotikos*, zeybekiko is the most prestigious from the standpoint of masculine identity.

[20] Davis (1964) reports a more competitive type of card playing that is reminiscent of what Mouriani call *bilot*. In *passatela* the winner has the right to select his partners. See also Herzfeld (1985a:157).

Rounds of xeri are repeated regularly among the same men for long periods. Thus xeri leads to the formation of rather closed, although not formally exclusive, circles, which often coincide with a parea. The third and most important aspect of xeri is that the unit of participation is not the individual player but a team of two players. Ideally, it is a contest between two pairs of men who are, in effect, given the scope to test their ability to be coordinated, and to cope with the strains of competing together.

Through such steps, pairs of emotional friends are gradually delineated. If friendship in general relies on commensality, emotional friendship is described as stemming directly from the heart. This is certainly implied in the reference to the close friend as *kardiakos filos* (the friend of the heart). As a local saying puts it, a man's friend is *tis kardias tou o yiouldas* (the close associate of his heart). Sometimes, emotional friends use *akranis*, originating from the Turkish for "peer" or "equal," as a term of reference. They also use a term widely applied in Macedonia, *kardasi*, from the Turkish for "brother." Brothers may refer to each other as *adelfos* (brother), but they never employ the term to address each other. Friends, on the other hand, may use this term for purposes of address, but not to refer to each other.[21] Most often emotional friends call each other either by their first name or, in a more private context, by a nickname or even jokingly by surname, thus stressing the distinct individual identity of their partner.

In coffee shop discourse, ties of emotional friendship are regarded as enclaves of relaxation and intimacy and are often brought up as examples of trust, amity, and reliance, as well as cordiality and fraternity. Between emotional friends, "there are no secrets": the friend of the heart is the best confidant, loyal and supportive.[22] These properties seem to be linked to the strictly bilateral and exclusive character of emotional friendship. For it is thought to be part of man's nature to have an intimate "friend of the heart." Those without emotional friends are in danger of being likened to a man with no real emotional involvement, an *adiaforitos*. Those with long-standing friendships are pointed out and are associated with good luck.

The rhetoric of emotional friendship rests on the assumption that the "friends of the heart" have priority in demanding each other's attention and that they are closely attached when neither material interest nor bonding obligation demand it. This is well depicted in the image of being

---

[21] There is evidence to suggest that the term *adelfos* was used in the context of religious brotherhoods in a nearby head-village.

[22] Emotional bond friendship resembles the Andalusian *confianza*, "a dyadic tie leading to emotional fulfilment" (Gilmore 1975:317), which Gilmore juxtaposes to *compromiso*, "an instrumental bond between households" (315).

koliti (lit., "stuck together").[23] The separation of friends is described by the same term that applies to spouses: *chorismos* (parting). The usage *dikos tou*[24] (his man) employed to refer to a man's friend equally suggests the possessive quality of the relationship. Indeed, friendship seems to be characterized by an isolationist tendency, and there is concern that the friends do not gossip about each other and the relationship stays gossip-proof.

Friends do not extend their mutual loyalty to third parties; they equally avoid the interposition of third parties in their relationship. This is especially true in the case of women, who are often thought to have a negative influence on male relations. At a late-night post-raki discussion about sexual adventures during bachelorhood and current cases of adultery in the village, two friends came out with the categorical assertion that "you cannot go with the wife or the sister of a man with whom you drink every night." This is, in fact, the most sacred barrier to real as well as imaginary adultery within the village.

Therefore, the primary sanction in friendship is the individual sense of moral worth (*filotimo*). For plebeian men who value the sentimental bonds of friendship more than the hierarchical, encompassing, obligatory bonds of *ipochreosi* (obligation), the record of behavior in friendship is the sine qua non of moral worth and reputation. A good friend is a proper *anthropos* (man), a moral human being who deserves everybody's respect and trust. A man who betrays the trust and amity shown him by a friend is thought to be lacking filotimo, a *zöo* (animal).

Friendship initially appears as unstable and endemically fragile, full of anxiety and often jealousy. However, the very sentiment that creates the problem is the basis for facing it. Anxiety surfaces easily, complaints are stated, explanations are offered, and emotional settlement is usually reached. At other levels, there is considerable toleration of asymmetry. Occasionally, men buy their *mezes* (snack) from the grocery shop and bring it to the coffee shop. There were occasions on which the provider of the core mezes was the same person in successive drinking sessions. No notice was taken of this. Friends may share kerasma and act as collective hosts, providing mezes for the parea.

Thinking of men in Mouria or Skala, I find it easy and natural to rec-

---

[23] The element of time spent together and the significance of mutual attention for the validation of the bond of friendship is stressed by Currier (1974:148) and Brandes (1980:128).

[24] What is worth noting here is that this very interesting usage of this term of inclusion denotes a level of membership which is of a lower order than that of the family: this is the dyadic tie of friendship. Yet at this level "membership" equals "possession," and in this sense the reference to X's friend as dikos tou resembles reference to X's female erotic partner as *diki tou*.

ollect simultaneously their intimate drinking companions. These figures appear with an intensity and clarity that matches, and often supersedes, that of other characters, such as a mother or a wife. Indeed, male friendship has an implicit structure, symbolized by a particular drinking table. The metaphor of cohabitation conveys this image well. Emotional friends occupy their table with the consistency and regularity, not to say zeal, with which a conjugal couple occupy a house or even a bed. No particular rights attach them to "their" drinking spot, and no offense is taken if somebody occupies it in ignorance. However, every insider knows very well which table is attached to whom. Another equally consistent, yet more solitary, pattern is in evidence during the mornings: each solitary man claims a table that is customarily "his."[25] These uniform spatial arrangements provide the elementary social structure of the coffee shop.

The joint attachment to a drinking table is, then, a "structural" marker of emotional friendship in Mouria. This is, indeed, a very narrow basis for a relationship, but a significant one, since the table links and integrates the fragments of male experience. The perpetuation of the empathic, almost circumstantial, solidarity of commensality increasingly cements the bond, thus transforming occasional occupancy into the habitual. The principle at play is simple: the more and the longer one stays in the relationship, the stronger and deeper it progressively becomes.[26] The more it is occupied, the more the drinking table becomes the focal center of friendship, a kind of observation point from which all achievement as well as failure is accommodated, all experience is molded, and the distinct identities are blended into a unity.

As long as the table is occupied and the friends still enjoy being together, the feeling is that the bond cannot decline or break. And a special quality marks those friendships in which the friends have stayed together continuously. These relationships are brought up as examples of the resilience of filia.

FRIENDS OF THE HEART: THE MATCHING OF MASCULINITIES

As commensality is the basis of friendship, so the egalitarian aspects of the former provide the key to approach the latter. Students of New Guinea societies have noticed that the ceremonial forms of egalitarian exchange suggest the submersion of individual actors into anonymous collectivities (Forge 1972; Rosaldo 1983). This is the case in the multilat-

---

[25] A similar, even more fixed, pattern of sitting is evidenced in the church: each stall is repeatedly occupied by the same individual.

[26] Gilmore (1975) came near to these conclusions in conceiving of friendship as "the moral and modal basis" of alliance, "being a changeful state of mind and a *cumulative* feeling as well as a set of rules and roles" (322, my emphasis).

eral commensality of the drinking party (parea). In the dyadic drinking companionships, however, the egalitarianism of kerasma is pushed to the extreme form of sharing identity. Indeed, in the development of emotional friendship, the idea of symmetry and reciprocity is superseded by the more prominent theme of matching identities, of individuality achieved and shared in a relationship. And as the expressive side overrides the transactional one and the periodic allocation of the two partners to the giving and receiving poles ceases, a sense of "sameness" permeates the relationship. The friends assume that they reflect one another in terms of subjectively experienced and objectively demonstrated sentiments and conceive their relationship as one in which expressive potential is matched.[27] Through time friends of the heart appear to be of the same heart. To employ a Durkheimian metaphor, the matching of friends in Mouria resembles a situation of mechanical solidarity and therefore contrasts with the organic complementarity that Paine (1969) considers as a distinguishing feature of emotional friendship.[28]

The key to the expressive dimension in friendship is the notion of *kefi*. Friendship relies on kefi as well as being the social means of reaching kefi. Kefi, a multisemic gloss, originates from the Arabic *keyif* or *keyf* (pleasure and delight, humor, a healthy state, as well as a state of slight intoxication). In the eyes of Richard Burton, the nineteenth-century traveler, kefi is the core symbol of Eastern eroticism (Kabbani 1986:54).[29] Mouriani employ it to suggest an ideal mood of joy and relaxation, achieved when the worries and concerns of this world "are banished." It further suggests desire, as well as a symbolic physiology according to which the center of the male body is the heart. Lightness is associated with kefi and depicted in drinking as well as singing and dancing. The spirited body of the man who dances solo, a body animated by an all-embracing desire and elevated beyond earthly, material concerns into communitas proper, captures the aesthetics of kefi.

Kefi is the core notion of a wider constellation of meanings that, besides suggesting emotionality, constitute the moral sides of the self antithetically to the environment. Mouriani conceive kefi as the antonym of ipochreosi, the jural obligation that permeates the conjugal bond, and

---

[27] Kerasma is expression as well as exchange. In local exegesis kerasma is often paralleled to a gift-giving gesture of good morning, it derives from filotimo (love of honor) and male generosity, and it is part of inner and emotional (*endiaferon*) rather than external and material interest (*simferon*). See Papataxiarchis (1984).

[28] Kennedy (1986:130) notes that sharing is the distinguishing feature of women's best-friendships in Crete.

[29] I want to thank Michael Herzfeld for bringing Kabbani's work to my attention. For the cultural configurations of male sentiment and their contribution to the making of a symbolic basis for prestige, see Papataxiarchis (1985, 1988). Also see the work of Caraveli (1985).

Male commensality: Reaching kefi in the coffee shop

Friends of the heart

juxtapose it to simfero, material self-interest. Whatever gives rise to an
"obligation" cannot support kefi. Kefi represents a point of view and a
rationality that is different from, not to say antithetical to, the rationality
of status and role; it is part of an antistructure, especially appealing to
lower-class men, who experience as impositions the hierarchical structures of state, work, and domesticity.

Most important, kefi symbolizes masculinity. This infrastructure of
emotions distinguishes men from women and further grades men by
pointing to the agonistic aspects of manhood. Therefore it is men who
adopt kefi as a program for action against work, domestic obligations, or
dealings with the state that weigh down and pollute the heart. The very
pursuit of kefi provides the subject matter of friendship.

The sharing of emotional states and moods that suggest masculinity
underlies male friendship. Friends of the heart share what lies in their
heart. Men of a roughly identical background are expected to face similar
problems and reach commensurable moods. If they have moods that cannot match because they arise from fundamentally different worries and
experiences, then they can hardly reach together the expected level of
jollity. Men friends become light (xelafronoun) in each other's company
by giving away the emotional waste they accumulate; thus they circulate
emotional strain, suffering (vasana), and complaints (parapona) without
fear of rebuke or humiliation, in the atmosphere of simpathia, the liking
that arises amid those who have identical worries as well as mutual trust.

Verbal communication between friends is qualified by the sharing of
moods. The competition of alternative discourses in the coffee shop is
thought to be a source of friction; it suggests an antagonism incompatible
with friendship. Therefore, male friends avoid debating issues, yet they
participate in kouvenda (conversation). Kouvenda is an ongoing commentary on events or people, premised on an already-shared point of view.
The expression kouvenda na yinete suggests a purposeless discussion that
leads nowhere: the words exchanged in kouvenda carry no binding force.
What is most characteristic of kouvenda, however, is that words capture
moods. This is why kouvenda can be qualified by the prevailing mood
into "light" and "heavy." By exchanging words, then, friends just share
their verbalized moods.

More than anything else, however, moods inform the very experience
that is the basis of friendship. Friends sometimes are of the same sira
(lit., "rank"). Sira refers to the actual quarter of the year one is con-
scripted, as well as to the group of men who serve together. The term
sira is used in different contexts, to refer to the order of marriage priority
among sisters, the turn of treating to a drink, or even as an indicator of
class status. In all cases, therefore, a kind of rank order is implied, and
the individuals are differentially placed in accordance with it. In friend-

ship, however, reference to rank connotes similarity instead of difference. Friends who have been in the army together may refer to each
other with "He is my sira" or may call each other sira. Apparently, sires
are age-mates, and the application of the term points to a camaraderie
that has emerged during army service and is subsequently projected into
the social life of the village.[30]

However, there is something more important than the acknowledgment of comradeship in the use of the term. In the last analysis, men of
the same sira were previously classmates at school for many years. Why
don't they use symbols from that era to mutually identify each other?
What distinguishes sira is that it is usually associated with the first call
out of the local society. The year before beginning military service, candidate conscripts are called to Mytilene for a physical as well as written
examination by the Periodevon, as the unit of examiners is called. In the
1960s, this was the first visit to the provincial capital for some of these
young men and thus a highly significant moment in their lives. It was,
further, the first authoritative and even traumatic test of the young men's
masculinity. What survives in the memory of the candidate soldier is the
physical comparison with the rest of the men who sit naked in a row, and
the examination of the anus to diagnose signs of homosexuality.[31] Despite
its traumatic nature, this visit to the Periodevon marks both a confirmation of physical masculinity and probably the first, most important, formally approved transcendence of the local boundary and a prolonged separation from "home."

A similar basis of mutuality is observed in the cordial friendships that
arise after army service. Men friends who worked together as *gastarbei-
ter* in Germany in the early sixties, or earned their living as builders and
construction workers in the Athens of the late sixties or in Macedonia in
the mid-thirties, or even "went up into [*vgikan*] the mountain" as guerilla
fighters of the resistance and later of the Democratic Army, regard these
experiences as formative of strong, emotional ties. What distinguishes
these relations is the sharing of movement. The actual transcendence of
the local, geographical boundary is regarded as symptomatic of freedom-
loving male nature.

In this respect, forms of male mobility are thought of as special rituals
of masculinity. Today adolescents are initiated into this "mobile" version
of masculinity during military service. This may be followed by a number
of years of work in the merchant navy. Working away from home ideally

---

[30] There is a close similarity to the Spanish *quintos* (strictly translated as "conscript" but
extended to mean "age-mate"). See Brandes (1973:752 and 1979:6); Murphy (1983).

[31] The inspection of the anus as diagnostic of homosexuality emerged at the end of the
eighteenth century when homosexuality was perceived as physical illness and thus as susceptible to clinical examination. See Aries and Bejin (1985).

precedes marriage and thus characterizes the years of bachelorhood as years of mobility. However, a number of men assert these essentially male practices after their marriage in the face of open disapproval from their wives and relatives. Despite the fact that some of them exploit the idiom of obligation to the household to mask these exoduses, in more private discussions within the coffee shop it became clear that these were moves to reassert their masculine "freedom."

At the conclusion of their lives, men in general, and especially those who have traveled a lot and seen a lot, are "full of *istories* [stories]," which usually focus on a single theme: the making of the male self as that process was jointly experienced by friends.[32] Emotional friendship is the social medium of a folk notion of history (*istoria*). Men tell istories that focus on male achievement. These are narrative representations of a fundamentally open and biographical order of reality. Friendship in Mouria appears as a relationship full of "history" because it is the filter through which personal history is both made and collectively experienced. Its existential status corresponds to what men in Mouria think is "their" history. This native concept of history is the privileged terrain for recollection. It focuses on events, things, and people that are conceived as different or even exceptional, timeful parentheses in a timeless order, bearing always the indelible mark of the individual protagonist. Despite its female gender as a word, istoria originates in men's actions and is extrapolated in equally male memories. At its heart lies the idea that the most interesting and attractive source of history is what is associated with either becoming or being a man. In other words, what men love to narrate are events that are of emotional significance. This particularly male emotional overtone links these stories to a genealogy of experience that is worth remembering.

During the formative years, friendship corresponds to an open and dynamic definition of male identity. However, in later years it appears that friendships are more fixed, as unchanging senses of the male self are brought together. Men have stopped growing in masculinity. This is reflected in the closure of the boundaries of friendship. Friends of the heart exclusively relate to each other, avoiding the company of other men. The closure of ranks is accounted for in the statement made by two septuagenarian friends. "You know, we usually have three rakia. And we want to drink them *me tin isichia mas* [at our own pace]. This is why we avoid mixing with others." In other words, the habit of being together is reflected in what they drink and in what quantity, when and at what pace. Men say that they have neither the emotional interest nor the courage to

---

[32] On the sharing of experience through talking see Herzfeld (1985a). Also see Zinovieff (this volume).

step outside this orbit of drinking habit and explore in new directions. Of course a good friendship extends the drinking career of men who would otherwise be forced to leave the *rakadiko* (raki drinking place) because of the lack of a partner. And it fades out when the elderly partners conclude their alcohol-drinking careers.

FRIENDSHIP IN THE CONTEXT OF GENDER AND KINSHIP

The analysis of friendship is often premised on two assumptions: first, that friendship is inextricably linked to reciprocity and, therefore, can be approached from an exchange point of view; and, second, that the sentiment of friendship is culturally commensurable, if not reducible, to that of kinship, both relationships being part of the same moral system. The latter assumption originates in Fortes's (1969) widely criticized universalist thesis that the prescriptive altruism of the biological kinship tie between mother and child is the archetype of all amity and, in this capacity, that it is the moral gloss attached to other relationships, such as friendship.[33] The former assumption is exemplified in Pitt-Rivers's (1973) argument on consubstantiality. Relatedness equals an extension of the self through a similarity achieved in the sharing of substance. All morality, therefore, including that of friendship, is somehow trapped in reciprocity, since giving and receiving are the only means of testing sentiments and relating in a morally significant way.[34]

   In this essay I have analyzed the developmental cycle of "heart-friendship" and focused on how it is subjectively experienced by men. What emerges so far is that the subjective meaning of friendship is disproportionately stressed vis-à-vis its structural significance and that, as a distinct cultural form, it is more widely acknowledged among men than among women.[35] Here I will attempt to account for what is distinctive of friend-

[33] The criticism of the Fortesian model for conflating notions of gender with the idea of kinship domain in general and, in particular, the gendered character of the domestic/politico-jural opposition has been pursued at a conference on feminism and kinship theory. See the excellent paper by Yanagisako (1987). For a wider critical discussion of the Fortesian thesis and its relation to the Euro-American ideology of kinship, see Rapp (1987). It is worth mentioning that a prominent critic of Fortes, Schneider (1969), also assumes that kinship is the paradigm of morality.

[34] In this respect Pitt-Rivers replaces Fortes's naturalist perspective with one that focuses on exchange. Pitt-Rivers's continuum of "moral reciprocity" and the anchorage of friendship between kinship and patronage is, as Paine (1974:4) points out, essentially Aristotelian. In a moral, utilitarian framework, Aristotle examines friendship as the link between ethics and politics. Similarly Wolf's (1966) distinction between affective and instrumental friendship echoes Aristotle's distinction between the moral motive of "good" friends and the utilitarian motive of "useful" friends.

[35] This strategy of analysis is influenced by the way Whitehead (1981) handles the issue

ship in Mouria by placing its relational and experiential aspects in the
wider context of ideas about kinship and gender sentiment. The crux of
my concluding argument is that the sentiment of friendship does not belong in the same constellation of cultural meaning as the sentiment of
kinship. "Friendship" and "kinship," rather than being different points
on a single continuum, are clearly demarcated as aspects of different gender ideologies and juxtaposed as essential components of different pro-
grams for prestige-oriented action.

To summarize some of the main points of the argument: first, the world
of the coffee shop is predicated on the absolute opposition between the
hierarchical forms of contract such as wages, loans, or patronage, on the
one hand, and, on the other, the properties of equality and sameness that
are inherent in masculine practices. Second, these attitudes are expressed in friendship, which is based on sameness, marked off from contract, and increasingly freed from reciprocity. The meaning of sharing
alcohol is transformed as the code of kerasma ceases to apply to close
friends, who do not "treat" each other. Third, sharing is linked to "matching." Friendship becomes increasingly independent of any material
proof; it relies on a past and present "matching" of identity that is vindi-
cated by its very perpetuation. All interaction between friends of the
heart—joint activity in the coffee shop, shared movements outside the
locality—are fused with male sentiment and thought of as experientially
constitutive of the male self. To share, then, means to look alike. And the
more you share, the more you become the same. Fourth, "sharing" has
an expressive, not an instrumental content.[36] As it is mediated by living
in a "structure" of commensality, sharing in friendship suggests the demonstration of masculine feelings.

The last point takes us to the theme of folk exegesis of sentiment and
becomes clearer if kinship is added to the picture. On one level the notions of "family" (ikoyenia) and "kinship" (sigenia) organize the sharing of
biological substance. In this respect these concepts give rise to relations
that are perceived as ascribed at birth and thus involuntary, nontermi-
nable, deeply hierarchical, and in the last analysis incompatible with the
values that govern the formation of male identity. In contrast with
women, men find it very difficult to sustain their relations with male
kin.[37] The notions of "heart-friendship" and "companionship" (parea), on

---

of why the berdâche gender-crossing status is more fully instituted for men than for women
in native North America.

[36] Many anthropologists, including Pitt-Rivers, seem to be in agreement with Sahlins
(1972:194) who defines "sharing" as an ethnographic formula that indicates the extreme case
(in the continuum of reciprocities) of a putatively altruistic "transaction."

[37] Murphy (1983) notices how peer friendship escalates the father-son conflict, as the
young man pursues his way to masculine autonomy. The incompatibility of agnatic kinship

another level, organize commensality via alcohol and relations that are thought as voluntary, open, freely terminable, deeply egalitarian, and the preserve of personal autonomy.[38] In relational and even behavioral terms, then, friendship is clearly demarcated from kinship and contrasted with the latter in terms of equality versus hierarchy. The contrast, however, becomes sharper if they are placed in the context of two distinct indigenous theories of sentiment that provide the core notion of femaleness and maleness.

Elsewhere I have shown that the sentiments of filiation and parenthood are phrased in the idiom of offering.[39] The sentiment of kinship is best captured in the idea of maternal sacrifice (*thisia*) and pain (*ponos*). The mother and, secondarily, the father are expected to sustain through life a unidirectional flow of service embodying parental love and care to the children. Maternal love appears as an unconditional offer that in principle does not demand reciprocation of the same kind. It will be principally reciprocated in the future when the receiving generation takes its turn in the position of generator/distributor of kinship sentiment. The altruism, which is predicated on the sharing of blood, flows down the generations.[40] This is especially true of daughters who pass to their offspring what they previously received from their mothers.

This systematic coincidence of sentiment with a practical manifestation that does not require reciprocation has a powerful effect. On the one hand, it masks the extreme form of asymmetry that exists in the relationship. Indeed, the institutionalization of the maternal gift can hardly be disputed or questioned. On the other, it has structural implications, since it binds the daughter and sometimes the son to the mother with lifelong ties of faith and loyalty, which, as the daughter raises her own household, develop into a joint division of labor. Therefore, the sentiment of kinship constitutes the domestic domain primarily around female, uterine ties while fragmenting the women's world across kinship lines and limiting

---

with commensal friendship is certainly less exaggerated in Lesbos than in Seville. However, conflict becomes endemic in relations between close kinsmen when they cooperate in joint ventures that rest on an intensive, rigid, hierarchical division of labor. The succession of the hierarchical father-son bond by egalitarian ties of emotional friendship is sensitively depicted for Turkey by Olson (1982:50–51). On the father-son avoidance in a different part of Greece, see Just (1980).

[38] For another, yet quite different, case of juxtaposition between the nonamity of "kinship" and the amity of "companionship" or sharing of activity among the Buid of Mindoro in the Philippines, see Gibson (1986). In the same direction of depicting discrepant discourses on emotion, see the work of Abu-Lughod (1986) and Brenneis (1987).

[39] See chap. 3 in Papataxiarchis (1988).

[40] Fortes's (1969) notion of "prescriptive altruism," Sahlins's (1972) notion of "generalized reciprocity," and Pitt-Rivers's (1973) notion of "undifferentiated reciprocity" capture the essentially hierarchical and one-sided nature of kinship sentiment in Lesbos.

for women the scope of relatedness outside kinship. Women's celebrated
emotionality is effectively invested in the making of domestic structure.
In this respect, as other ethnographers of Greece have noted, ties of domestic kinship are of special significance to women's identity.[41]

While "kinship," therefore, falls into Pitt-Rivers's category of "moral
reciprocity," "friendship" (*filia*) contradicts it altogether. For "friendship"
cannot be approached from an exchange point of view, since it totally
negates and transcends reciprocity. And, further, it draws on a folk exegesis of male sentiment that conceptually demarcates it from kinship. Indeed, men are distinguished for their emotionality, yet their emotions
are thought to differ from women's and to be primarily articulated outside kinship.

Heart-friendship stands for an unstructured and inchoate yet strong
feeling of camaraderie, commonality, and trust among men who see each
other as mirror images of themselves. Filia is pure sentiment, the standpoint of straight emotionality from which men view society and its various structural arrangements that relate to household, work, or politics.
In filia men express their feelings, not to one another, but *with* one another. The feeling is not just independent of material validation or practical consideration; it is also free of jural guardianship. The relationship
is its own sanction.

In friendship the feeling *is* the relationship. The vocabulary of friendship is fundamentally an emotional vocabulary illuminating the states of
the heart and forms of emotional experience, as well as the modalities of
an emotional structure that stands for masculinity and demands relatedness outside kinship. Only a heart that achieves its natural state of kefi
can support the extension of the self and the creation of the emotional
bond. Filia, then, is the social symptom of kefi. The joyful sentiment is
recycled in the bond of friendship: friends love to be together because by
being together they can love. In masculine life kefi is both motive and
reward. Men who do not live as men should live do not and cannot have
friends.[42]

In this paper I analyzed heart-friendships to suggest that a gender- and
person-specific perspective is more suitable than an exchange one to
bring out the underlying thought system, with its discursive emphasis on
the emotionality of men. Emotional friendship is a principal aspect of a
set of ideas that demarcate a folk psychology and a prestige structure for
men only. What is remarkable is that friendship is not just pure senti-

[41] See, for example, Dubisch (this volume).

[42] The sentiment of friendship is close to what Fortes (1969) calls "amity" (and probably
what Schneider [1969] terms "diffuse solidarity"). The local usage makes sense both in
terms of the etymological affinity of *filia* with the Greek term for amity (*agapi/agapo = filo*)
and the derivation of the English gloss "amity" from the French term for friendship.

ment but the social explication of a gender construct as well. It is both the framework of becoming, and being, a man and the very social outcome of the symbolic claims to masculinity.

ACKNOWLEDGMENTS

A draft of this paper was presented to the symposium entitled "The Horizons of Current Anthropological Research in Greece," organized by the Department of Social Anthropology, University of the Aegean, in September 1986. I wish to gratefully acknowledge financial support by the London School of Economics including the Suntory-Toyota Centre (ST-ICERD), the Central Research Fund of the University of London, and the Wenner Gren Foundation. I would like to thank Alexandra Bakalaki, Maurice Bloch, Janet Carsten, Mari Clark, Michael Herzfeld, and Peter Loizos for their helpful comments on earlier drafts.

Chapter 8

GOING OUT FOR COFFEE? CONTESTING THE GROUNDS OF GENDERED PLEASURES IN EVERYDAY SOCIABILITY

Jane K. Cowan

My efforts to understand the ways gender is socially and culturally constructed in Sohos,[1] a town in central Macedonia, led me to investigate the social organization of trivial pursuits. In this community, despite a long tradition of waged female employment outside the home,[2] leisure pursuits—like the everyday activity of coffee drinking—are both gender-segregated and encoded with notions about gender difference. In this essay, I explore how dominant ideas about female sexuality, moral virtue, and autonomy are embedded in the practices of everyday sociability; yet I argue, too, that it is precisely through mundane but recontextualized acts like drinking coffee that such ideas may be contested.

Although consideration of everyday sociability has not been absent from ethnographic accounts, the insights of social analysts like Bourdieu (1977), Foucault (1978, 1979), and Gramsci (1971; cf. also Williams 1977) enable us to examine in more sophisticated ways the power relations animating these apparently everyday forms. As Bourdieu argues, it is over

---

[1] I lived and conducted field research in Sohos between February 1983 and February 1985. Sohos, located on a mountainous plateau about forty miles from Thessaloniki, is an old Balkan market town of 3,500, which is today a commercial and administrative center for the surrounding district. Roughly half of its households are involved (full-time or part-time) in family-based agricultural production (mostly tobacco, cereals, and fruit orchards) or livestock raising (dairy cattle, sheep, and goats). However, most households have at least one member involved in wage labor (periodic or permanent) or in family-based entrepreneurial activity.

[2] Sohoian females have long participated in waged employment, primarily in tobacco production (within Sohos and, seasonally, on the larger estates in nearby villages and towns) and as "domestics" (mostly in Thessaloniki and Athens). However, since working girls ("girls," *koritsia*, being in local usage a term designating all unmarried females, regardless of age) traditionally tended to leave waged employment upon engagement or, at the latest, at marriage, female waged employment did not challenge the "ideal" of female domesticity so much as constitute a phase *preceding* it in the female life cycle. Since the 1950s, various wide-ranging social, economic, and ideological changes have complicated this picture; today, although many women continue to work after marriage, the majority work in low-paid, insecure jobs, e.g., in piecework at home or in small workshops.

trivial matters of form and formality that those in power "extort the essential while seeming to demand the insignificant" (1977:95). Indeed, the very "triviality" of many of the things people do, doing what "proper" and "good" people should, not only block them from consciousness, since they constitute acts of utter common sense, but also serve to trivialize any protest.

As an anthropologist and a feminist doing fieldwork in the early 1980s, I hoped to discover something of how the world looks and feels to those Sohoians who were born female, to grasp and give voice to a female experience that, as some had argued, remained "muted" in ethnographic writings (Ardener 1975). Although the gender ideology described in virtually all ethnographic accounts of modern Greece had portrayed women as fundamentally inferior and weak, spiritually and morally, in relation to men (cf. especially the "classic" texts: Campbell 1964, du Boulay 1974, Peristiany 1965b:9–18), the works of Ardener and others prompted me, as it did several other ethnographers reexamining gender issues in Greece (cf. especially Dubisch 1986a), to ask certain questions about the established literature and about my own research: First, was this gender ideology merely an "androcentric" version, counterbalanced by an alternative, but as yet undefined, "gynecocentric" version? Second, if it was not—if, in other words, females acknowledged and helped to perpetuate negative images of their own gender, as well as structures that restricted their own lives—why and how did this occur? I found unexpected clues in the routine of everyday sociability. Indeed, after sharing endless cups of coffee I too came to feel enmeshed in its meanings and reciprocities. And I witnessed my companions' myriad small gestures of deference to the gender ideas and relations embedded in these quotidian sociable encounters.

In part, this essay is about "reproduction," about how everyday sociability is organized in terms of, and then reproduces, dominant notions of male and female "persons" (cf. Mauss 1985, Carrithers et al. 1985). If the "triviality" and taken-for-granted quality of these ordinary activities contribute, paradoxically, to their persuasiveness, they are often pleasurable, as well. It is therefore important that we consider the role of pleasure in *this* sort of reproductive process, while recognizing that the way the pleasure of a particular group—in this case, female members of the community—is defined and articulated, by themselves and by others, is a political matter most fruitfully examined in the context of power, needs, and interests (Lukes 1974). This essay is concerned, also, with how gender ideas are challenged and changed. After discussing how everyday forms of sociability *reproduce* gender notions, I explore how the appearance of a new sort of leisure establishment, the *kafeteria* or coffee-bar, creates a new *discursive* space in which dominant definitions of female personhood are made explicit and sometimes contested.

FOOD, SPIRITS, AND ENACTMENTS OF PERSONHOOD

A centrally important context within contemporary Greek society for expressions of "personhood," both as ideally conceived and as practically negotiated, is that of commensality, the sociable sharing of food and drink. That such exchanges define and maintain social relationships is, after Lévi-Strauss (1965), an anthropological commonplace, yet each society has its own gastronomical language and its own rules for giving and receiving. In Sohos (as has been noted, also, elsewhere in Greece; e.g., Herzfeld 1987 and Kenna 1990), townspeople frequently assert the exemplary moral worth of their town qua town using the idiom of feeding. Comparing themselves collectively to other communities in the area, they would insist that Sohos was more honorable and worthy (*pio filotimo*). Since *filotimia* is a polysemous term of moral value, whose specific meaning varies according to situation and across communities (cf. Herzfeld 1980), I sometimes pressed them to explain what this meant. Many gave a reply similar to that of the man who answered, "If you were a stranger to the village and I saw you on the street, I would take you home to my wife, who'd give you something to eat." Indeed, townspeople frequently defined filotimia as synonymous (in this context) with *filoksenia* (love of the stranger), the word most often glossed as "hospitality." Offering such translations, Sohoians were stressing how being "proper human beings" requires generosity: those who are filotimi should "feed"—rather than "eat" (i.e., betray or steal from) others.

The conventional practices of eating and drinking in Sohos give this emphasis meaning. Uncooked foods (salads, raw vegetables, breads, sweets) and tidbits, which are not considered "food" (*fai*), are usually eaten outside the house. By contrast, "real" food, in the form of meals, is prepared by the mother or daughter-in-law to be eaten only by members of the family and any houseguests, who are temporarily reidentified as honorary family members. In this community, it is rare to invite a fellow townsperson casually for dinner. Dinner parties as purely social events are not a part of local practice. The fact that sharing food within the house is so strongly associated with everyday familial conviviality is an important aspect of the meaning of ritual occasions when this convention is broken.[3]

Everyday exchanges among individuals of separate households involve

---

[3] An analysis of the rich symbolic language of food and drink exchanges within ritual contexts is outside the scope of this paper.

not "food" but special, abbreviated forms of it (sweets and tidbits) and drink. The form of the exchanges typically reflects the pervasive reality of a sexually segregated spatial world: women and men imbibe separately. Moreover, gender difference is codified through the foods and drinks that appear in these everyday exchanges. The association of men with pungent and salty substances and women with sweet substances is pervasive.

This is clearly exemplified in the formal *kerasma*, the customary offering of hospitality. When I visited women in their homes for the first time, I received this kerasma in its most elaborate form. The first item offered by the woman of the house (or sometimes, a daughter) is a tiny glass of a syrupy, usually fruit-flavored liqueur called, revealingly enough, "the womanly drink" (*to yinekio*). It is always served in a richly adorned thin-stemmed glass, silver or crystal, from a tray held by the hostess. Many women produce their own liqueur from local fruits. The second item offered is a chocolate candy wrapped in metallic paper. Such was the conformity among households on the details of this procedure that nearly every hostess served the same brand of chocolate, a trapezoidal cube with a hazelnut center, wrapped in shiny green foil.[4] The third item, and the symbolic focus, is a piece of jellied fruit, usually homemade (often from produce raised on the household lands), and bathed in sugary syrup. This jellied fruit, called *ghliko* or "sweet," is in Sohos prepared from many kinds of fruits and nuts, including cherries, figs, quinces, eggplants, tomatoes, and walnuts. Preparing this sweet is a hot, time-consuming, and not inexpensive project; the gluey but perfectly preserved fruit is widely considered an emblem of the housewife's artistry and skill. Finally, I would be offered a glass of cold water, not to be drunk at leisure but instead, after a conventionalized toast to the hostess and her family, to be downed in a few gulps. After all of these sweet things had been eaten, I was offered coffee, with the perfunctory query, "You drink it sweet, don't you?"

This kerasma was virtually identical in every house I visited for the first time. It is customarily offered to any stranger, male or female, on his or her initial visit. Though it is not mandatory for subsequent visits, the woman of the house liked to serve this to me, and to other female visitors, during even impromptu, everyday visits. Since a typical afternoon's round of visiting could, for me, easily include two or three houses, I sometimes found the local housewives' famous generosity something of an ordeal. My attempts to refuse the afternoon's third ghliko (in a cultural context where refusing hospitality is always problematical, cf. Kenna

---

[4] Other brands of chocolate were available, but this was considered "the best."

1990) were likely to be greeted with surprise. After all, women "liked" sweets!

Sweet substances are the medium of everyday female exchanges. Ingesting them, Sohoian girls and women literally produce themselves as properly feminine persons. Consuming sweets, they do what they "should" (observe the etiquette of guest-host relations) as well as what they "want" (since they are thought "naturally" to desire sweets), a conflation of moral propriety and desire that obscures the coercive aspect of such consumption. The association of femininity with sweetness is encoded in substances and practices outside the context of everyday sociability, as well. The shopkeeper who sold me wine characterized the sharper, drier, and stronger red wine, the *brusko*, as "harsh and manly" (*skliro, andriko*) and the *imighliko*, a sweeter and milder variety—which he thought would most interest me—as softer (*pio malako*) and "more womanly" (*pio yinekio*). Similarly, women and girls eating at a celebration or in a tavern conventionally mark their avoidance of too much or too strong liquor by diluting and sweetening their wine with Coca-Cola.

The symbolic association of maleness with salty and pungent substances is evident in everyday exchanges between men. *Kafenia*, where men gather, do not serve sweets and pastries. Rather, exchanges typically center on coffee (prepared according to each man's taste but tending to be less sweet than women's) and ouzo, a clear, distilled, anisette-flavored brandy. Ouzo is of key importance to the understanding of male conviviality: it is the central object of reciprocal—and sometimes competitive—hospitality in the kafenia. Its potency is recognized as a force that suspends inhibitions between men, facilitating sociability, yet also, with excess, causing them to forget their manners and lose control. Ouzo is always consumed with "tidbits" (*mezelikia*) to counteract ouzo's corrosive effect on the stomach and to soften the high it produces. These customarily include bits of sausage and cheese, olives, smoked fish, raw vegetables (like tomato and cucumber), and bread. It is not merely the alcoholic potency that renders ouzo a "male" drink, however. Like wine, which is distinguished according to sweetness into "manly" and "womanly" varieties, ouzo is conceptually opposed to "the womanly drink" (to yinekio), the category of syrupy sweet fruit- and mint-flavored brandies.

COFFEE, LOVE, AND PASSING THE TIME

In the symbolic universe of commensality, coffee is an element used by both men and women. This simplest and most commonly shared beverage is the obligatory offering among women visiting each other's houses, and among men congregating in the kafenia. It is clearly a quintessential symbol of everyday sociability. Yet for female Sohoians, the act of drinking coffee is rich with morally ambiguous connotations.

Married women who live in close proximity frequently gather in each other's houses for coffee. Informal visiting may occur during the late morning (after the morning chores have been completed and the midday meal is on the stove), after lunch during the midday rest period (particularly if the men of the house are not home for lunch), and in the evening.[5] These breaks from the daily routine provide a chance to relax, to commiserate, and to exchange news. In the mornings, such breaks may be rather brief, as there is housework to complete, but midday breaks may last an hour or two, and evening visiting—when done among neighbors and relatives—even longer.

During these visits, women "pass the time" in each other's company. Passing the time, in this context, is not explicitly goal-directed; rather, being with others is valued for itself. The townspeople use a Turkish term for "conversation," which they identify as a distinctively local usage, to highlight the pleasurable and comfortable intimacy of this sort of talk. They say, "We are making *muhabet* [*kanume muhabet*]."

Yet in a community where competition among families for prestige and wealth is taken for granted, talk is often focused on the exploits and misfortunes of others. Significantly, many people identify malicious and mocking talk as a feminine activity. Thus, it is frequently said—by both men and women—that women get together in their neighborhood "to drink coffee and gossip." The coffee-drinking event, on the one hand an emblem of intimate sociability, is now redefined as an index of women's easy life and idle talk. Sohoians attribute women's proclivity to gossip both to their "envious" natures (*zilia*) and to their need to find release from the boredom of a routinized and restricted existence. Many women accept this definition of themselves as "gossipers" (*kotsoboles*) as at least partially valid. And while some women view men's propensity to spend long hours and often considerable amounts of cash in the kafenio as a vice equal to their own, others regard this as a man's privilege.

One of the ways coffee is used among girls and women, but almost never among men, is for divination. Strictly speaking, reading the coffee grounds is forbidden by the Greek Orthodox Church as a pagan form of magic oriented to unraveling a future that only God may know. Though pious individuals strongly disapprove, most townspeople—male and female—regard "saying the cup" (*lei to flitsani*) as recreational, if slightly shameful, though more for its connotations of superstition than of sin. It

---

[5] More formal visiting (as for name days), in which women predominate, often as representatives of the household, occurs during the early evening (*apoyevma*) from about 5:00 till 8:00 P.M. For this, the visitor dresses up and often presents a gift of sweets or flowers to the household she is visiting.

is regarded as a way in which silly women pass the time. The technique is simple: Greek coffee, a finely pulverized coffee boiled with sugar and water, is served in demitasse cups, and the grounds are allowed to settle, making a thick mud on the bottom. If one turns the cup over, rolling it as one allows the slightly moist grounds to run out into the saucer, the sediment that clings to the sides of the cup forms patterns of light and dark spaces and vaguely shaped objects. There is a restricted vocabulary of symbols that can be discerned, and, depending on their location in the cup, they can be "placed" in time and in social space (i.e., near or away from the "house"), and their significance can be construed.

For my purpose here, the significance of the coffee cup does not depend on the degree to which girls and women believe in or deny its power as a tool to divine the future. Rather, the coffee cup is significant as a focus of, and catalyst for, talk about emotions and relationships that preoccupy them in the present.[6] A good deal of my experience in observing coffee-cup readings was obtained in the company of one particular group of young women, aged twenty to thirty-two, most of whom were unmarried. Though our homes were spread far apart in the town, we managed to meet nearly every afternoon for coffee, and "saying the cup" was a crucial moment in this daily ritual. The diviner of the cup might be a mother or other older female relative, a neighbor, or one of the group of contemporaries, but the themes of the cup barely changed from one day to the next. Readers often saw rings or a table filled with people (both signifying engagements), male figures of various proportion and coloring, letters of the alphabet (both references to a prospective suitor), and crosses or coins, which indicated good news or good fortune. There were also signs for news or letters from afar (white or black birds) and for money (a pattern of bubbles at the top of the cup). "Roads," understood in the widest metaphorical sense, might be "open" or "blocked." More generally, the reader interpreted the emotional state of the cup's owner, both present and future, by the overall color of the grounds, "light" or "open" cups indicating joy and "dark" or "closed" cups indicating anxiety or sorrow.

The crowning moment occurred at the end, when the reader asked the owner of the cup to impress the sedimented bottom of the cup lightly with her finger while silently making a wish. The bottom inside of the

---

[6] I am indebted to conversations with Alexandra Bakalaki, who has also written about women's coffee-cup readings, for the insight that stories created from the cup refer not to the future but to women's and girls' *present* experience. In this respect, coffee-cup readings bear similarities to the Cretan scapulomancy discussed by Herzfeld (1985a:247–258). As an intimate context in which female emotions and relationships are explored, coffee-cup reading may be compared to the informal recitations of personal love poetry among Bedouin women analyzed in Abu-Lughod (1986).

cup is believed to be the "heart." The pattern left by the finger was then interpreted by the reader, who usually saw a letter or a face or figure, this customarily attributed to a romantic interest, whether nearby or remote. Since the reader tended quite often to know many personal details about the young woman whose cup she was reading, she would in her interpretations allude vaguely to these personal details. She frequently asked the young woman to concur or elaborate on her interpretations. If, on the other hand, the reader was not well acquainted with the owner of the cup, she often asked leading questions in an attempt to feel out the situation and garner information.

I always asked for my cup to be read, and I noticed that this was a forum in which various female acquaintances tried to find out information about my marriage, my feelings about my husband and our physical separation, and my general emotional response to being so far away from home. I often felt the same ambivalence about volunteering detailed personal information that I noticed among my female friends. This was an occasion of great intimacy but also of vulnerability and danger. To readers they did not fully know or trust, my friends gave vague, cryptic answers with as little detail as possible, even as they listened intently to every word of exegesis. With readers they trusted, interpretation was a dynamic, shared project.

Coffee drinking among female Sohoians, then, is a focus for "passing the time" and resonates with the moral ambiguity which that notion implies for them by virtue of their gender. It is associated with pleasurable sociability, but also with idle and malicious gossip. Finally, it is a context for—and the coffee cup a symbolic focus of—the exploration of emotions girls and women experience toward individuals loved or desired. That is, it elicits talk, sometimes clothed in highly metaphoric or elliptical language, of love, sexuality, and the directions of female destiny, talk that reiterates traditional notions of the contours and limits of female experience.

THE MORAL GEOGRAPHY OF PUBLIC LEISURE SPACE

One of the most powerful manifestations of gender thinking in Sohos occurs in the domain of space. Most ethnographic descriptions of contemporary Greek society, particularly those concerned with rural communities, typically portray women's concerns and activities as centered on the house and neighborhood and the church, while men spend their time in public areas. The categorical and situational semiotics of gender and space are currently a subject of vigorous debate within Greek studies, and the collective discussion has made it possible to revise, refine, and historicize these broadly defined dichotomies. My own discussion here is confined to a consideration of how gender thinking organizes *public* "leisure space" in this community.

The quintessential institution of male social life in Greece, as in most Balkan societies, is the coffeehouse, or kafenio. It is here that manhood is performed, reputations are negotiated, and social relationships are enlivened through endless card playing, political debate, competitive talk, and reciprocal hospitality (cf. Campbell 1964; Herzfeld 1985a). The ambience and social meanings of the kafenio space can vary, regionally and individually; in Sohos, unless it was being used for a special event, like a wedding or a carnival celebration, the kafenio was regarded as unambiguously male space. As the ethnographer (*laografos*, lit., "folklorist") and resident foreigner (*dhikia mas kseni*), I was given the courtesy of limited access to these sites. I even frequented one kafenio renowned for its singers and storytellers on a fairly regular basis, becoming a sort of adopted daughter to the predominantly elderly clientele. However, I never saw another girl or woman from the town enter as a casual patron. Most avoided entering its doors at all, preferring—on occasions when it was necessary to fetch a male relative—to stand outside an open door or a window while attempting to win his attention by gesturing or hissing in a stage whisper. Women and girls insisted that they could not imagine going into the kafenio, that even the souvlake grills—less definitively "male" spaces but still dominated by men—in which girls might order sandwiches "to go," made them acutely uncomfortable. "*Drepome*," they asserted ("I am embarrassed/ashamed.") They felt, they explained, intimidated by the stares of the men and uneasy about talk that would follow.[7] The boundaries of the kafenio as a male space, though largely implicit, were absolute and almost sensually perceptible. With rare exceptions, females expressed little desire to intrude.

Nonetheless, in this community and throughout Greece, women see the kafenio as a symbol of men's freedom of movement and of the legitimacy of their association in public space. It is true that as physical entities, kafenia tend to be simple and functional. Rickety wooden or metal tables and hard, wooden straight-backed chairs stand on a constantly gritty floor covered with street mud and cigarette butts. The walls are characteristically painted a nondescript chartreuse, and in winter, with heating expensive or inefficient, they can be uncomfortably chilly. Yet

---

[7] Foucault has explored the relation between vision and control in a highly provocative and convincing way (1979). Certainly, in a small Greek community like Sohos, "being seen" may be experienced alternately as a sensual, social pleasure and an annoying, even intimidating, intrusion. This is very much intensified for females, who speak constantly of the sense of being watched and who are frequently and unreservedly asked (usually by older women), when walking down the street, to explain where they are going and what they plan to do.

the dearth of creature comforts only serves to highlight the kafenio's human focus, announcing this bare and unpretentious space as a setting for the serious business of male sociability.

While the discussion in the preceding section explored women's coffee drinking as an ordinary activity that occurs daily within the house and neighborhood, it does happen, on an occasional basis, that women also "go out" to establishments in the community. Most married women rely upon their husbands to "take them out" now and then, and sensitive husbands feel this as an obligation (cf. Hirschon 1978). The site of such an outing, often a Sunday afternoon event, has typically been the "sweet shop" (*zaharoplastio*).

Though they coexist in public space, the zaharoplastio stands in conceptual opposition to the kafenio, according to the symbolic association of women (and, here, also children) with sweetness, and men with pungent and salty flavors. Gender difference is also apparent in patterns of use. Men not accompanying women rarely spend time in the zaharoplastio unless it is to keep company with the owner. Both men and women, however, may enter its doors as customers, to buy chocolates, rich and elaborate tortes, or bottles of liqueur as gifts to be given when visiting.

The contrasts between the one Sohoian establishment that explicitly identified itself as a zaharoplastio and local kafenia were remarkable, though this must, in part, be attributed to the unusual artistic sensibility of the zaharoplastio's proprietor. Located slightly up the hill from the central square, the zaharoplastio consisted of one large and airy room, whose windows overflowed with large, luxuriant plants. Sunny and spotless, it featured a massive color television set hung high on the wall.[8] I came here several times with my mostly unmarried female friends to share an indigestibly sweet local speciality (*tulumbes*), sausage-shaped and fluted pieces of fried batter soaked in sugar syrup, a delicacy whose marvelous shape evoked a good deal of mirth and bawdy punning. However, the shop was usually empty, used by families and groups of young women only occasionally. In the cities, this contrast is even more elaborated, but it is clear enough in Sohos. Always pleasant, sometimes elegant, the zaharoplastio is conceived as an airy, refined, respectable contrast to the smoky, noisy, and often volatile kafenio.

THE KAFETERIA

In the period between my second visit in summer 1978 and my return for extended fieldwork in early 1983, a new kind of establishment appeared in the town. In 1978 I had been the guest of Mihalis's family, and

---

[8] During the period of my fieldwork, none of the kafenia had television sets.

in 1983 I stayed with them again. On the day of my arrival in 1983, Mihalis, now thirty-five, and his first cousin took me on a walk through the town center to see "how things had changed." Chilled and tired, we walked down a steep side street and stopped in front of what I remembered as the German garment factory. Cheap velour curtains that hung unevenly across the windowpanes hid the interior space, but opening the door I found a huge wood-paneled room hung with scenic posters of forests and rivers. A few clusters of men sat on wide plush chairs around low metal tables, and in the center an enormous spotlit fountain sprayed tiny blue jets of water. Far in the back was a cocktail bar and, on the back wall, a television and VCR. We sat down, I—as the only female in sight—rather self-consciously, and ordered not Greek coffee (which was not on the menu), but the more "modern" and "European" Nescafé with milk. This, I learned, was the kafeteria, the largest and most popular of three now operating in the town.

The kafeteria, whose genesis was in urban Greece, is a hybrid combining aspects of a bar and a zaharoplastio. I noticed such establishments first in 1975 in student-dominated areas in central Athens, near the university. They catered to an identity and sensibility familiar among students by creating an ambience both "European" and "sophisticated." They tended to serve tea and coffee (but only Nescafé, occasionally espresso, rarely Greek coffee), "European" aperitifs like cognac, whisky, vermouth, and only sometimes the indigenous spirit, ouzo, canned juices (sweetened, yet noticeably different from the carbonated soft drinks of the zaharoplastia), and *tost*, a grilled sandwich of cheese or salami that was just emerging as competition to the traditional, and still popular, cheese and spinach "pies" (*tiropites, spanakopites*). They were often at basement level, or at least closed off from the street by curtains or paneling. In contrast to the bare, glaring light bulb characteristic of the kafenio, the kafeteria was very softly lit and often featured jazz playing quietly in the background. It was, in the Athenian context, a place for students, male and female, to spend long hours in conversation. Its Italian etymology notwithstanding, this seemed a Greek analogue of the Parisian café, with similar connotations of cultural sophistication, political activity, and sexual freedom.

In the years between 1976 and the beginning of my fieldwork in late 1982, kafeteries began to appear in the cities and the countryside. Most could be identified by their attempt to create an ambience of urban, European sophistication. In the cities, the kafeteria has become a new haven, along with the bar, for working-class youths, for whom kafenia hold little interest. In the countryside, the responses have been curious and mixed.

WHEN WOMEN DRINK COFFEE AT THE KAFETERIA

All of Sohos's three kafeteries are dominated by adolescent males and adult men. One of these is patronized almost exclusively by the high school crowd. While even this space is at times aggressively male space, groups of girls congregate here after school to socialize both among themselves and with their male classmates. In the other two, though, the dominant clientele comprises youths and men in their prime.[9] Scattered among this dominant group, on any given weekday afternoon, are a cluster or two of girls. They are almost without exception unmarried. They sit for a juice, a soft drink, or a Nescafé; they talk for a while, joking and laughing both among themselves and with acquaintances they see in the kafeteria, yet always conscious of the eyes of the men around them. They arrive and leave in groups of two or more, never alone.

As an establishment that does not slip neatly into the familiar classification of gender and space, the kafeteria is something of a talking point among Sohoians. Ostensibly a discourse on the moral tone of the place, its subtext concerns the nature of the categories "man" and especially "woman." "Is it a good thing or not for female Sohoians to pass their time in the kafeteria?" Sohoians disagree. I juxtapose five voices, each of which articulates a distinct position on the subject of woman and the kafeteria. Three uphold the dominant ideology, though each for different reasons. Two challenge it—one begrudgingly, the other with conviction. The polyphony of opinion can be heard as an argument about woman's nature, rights, and place generated in a historical moment when a new socialist government committed to "equality" (isotita) between the sexes was implementing major legal and economic reforms affecting women, men, and the family (cf. Stamiris 1986).

The first voice belongs to Katina, the wife of Mihalis, the man who first introduced me to the kafeteria in early 1983. Katina herself never goes. One day I was discussing with Katina and her mother-in-law the vicissitudes of life for girls in the town when the conversation turned to the perils of narcotics. "Things are very difficult for young girls," lamented the elderly mother-in-law. "They go into the kafeteries, and in the cigarettes they are offered, or even right into their sodas, men slip in drugs." In emphatic agreement, Katina told me the following story: A girl of a reportedly "good" family commuted daily from a neighboring village to attend the high school. One afternoon, she left her group of girlfriends to buy a pastry and was approached by a man in the kafeteria that she had briefly entered. Every morning thereafter, instead of going to school, she met him there. When one of the teachers noticed her extended

---

[9] Elderly men remain attached to the kafenio, though they visit the kafeteria occasionally.

absence and ascertained her whereabouts, he informed her grandfather (who was at that time acting as her guardian, as her parents were guest workers in Germany). Horrified at this news, the old man vowed to catch her in the act of leaving and drag her away by the hair. The teacher calmed the old man, and together they apprehended her. Katina ends the tale of woe this way:

> They got hold of her, and she confessed [pause] that in that place where they were going, in the kafeteria, they had found drugs. And in this way, they had corrupted the girls. And it wasn't only her, there were six other girls, too. . . . They put drugs [narkotika] right in the orange soda, or in the glasses they offer the girls. They can put in anything they want, are *you* going to realize what they're opening up and putting in?

The way Katina used the word "confess" surprised me. Given the way the story was unfolding, I expected the girl to "confess" to her illicit relationship with the man. But Katina portrays her as confessing to being victimized. While the couple's sexual involvement is taken for granted, the girl in Katina's story has defined her own role as passive. If she was involved in indecencies, they were "being done to her," presumably while she was in a drugged stupor.

Katina tells us of girls who are vulnerable, not treacherous. Such an attribution, under the circumstances, seems remarkable. But it seems to me that this perception of the female condition predates the story. Married women, particularly mothers of teenage girls, constantly fret over their daughters' vulnerability. "Girls are a worry" (ta kortsudhia ine fovo), mothers often lamented. One woman, who had remarked that "a girl is dangerous" (to koritsi ine epikindhino), clearly did not have in mind an image of Eve-like sexual destructiveness, for she paraphrased this statement by listing all the things that could be *done to* a girl. To the contrary, these women who stress girls' vulnerability perceive their entrance into the dangerous and unsupervised space of the kafeteria as threatening not to men nor to the "moral order" in the abstract but to the girls themselves. In this explanation, the implicit source of danger is the voracious and predatory sexuality of men!

Yet if this fear or worry acknowledges the very real dangers—to her reputation and to her person—a girl faces in a patriarchal society, it does little to challenge that society's dominant assumptions. Girls, echoing their mothers, laughingly confess to being afraid of "being watched," "wolves," "the dark," "everything!" This sentiment of fear expressed *by* girls can be interpreted as a claim of virtue (cf. Abu-Lughod 1986:158). Linking vulnerability with virtue, the sentiment of fear articulates a girl's dependence and calls forth a protective response. And while apparently sympathetic to girls' less powerful social position, this sentiment claimed

by—but, more often, on behalf of—girls nonetheless upholds their traditional banishment to domestic or female-dominated space.

The second voice is less ambiguous, certainly less ambivalent and un-
doubtedly much more familiar. It belongs to Stellios, a fifty-year-old man
who participated, along with five others, in a conversation *in* the kafeteria
about the kafeteria. The context of our conversation is significant, as it
occurred just after an afternoon speech held in March 1984, in honor of
International Women's Day. The speaker had intended to explain to the
townswomen why they ought to organize and what the present government was doing to further their interests. The speech was badly attended, and the few women who *did* attend felt that the absence of their
female fellows had much to do with its location in the kafeteria. I took
the opportunity, nevertheless, to talk with the women and girls who attended to find out what they felt about various feminist issues. I asked
two girls, Amalia, aged seventeen and Soula, aged twenty, to discuss
with me (as I tape-recorded them) what it was like to be girls growing up
in Sohos. Stellios, amused and skeptical, listened from a distance. Gradually, he became uneasy with the girls' assertive rhetoric, and he began
to protest with his own stories. In one, he told of a woman who, despite
her husband's constant and severe beatings, was uncontrollable. She left
the house altogether, ran around with other men, and eventually drove
her husband to his death from shame and defeat. Stellios's portrayal of
"woman" left to pursue her own whims and desires outside the controls
of society (especially as expressed in the husband's authority) was of a
being thoroughly incorrigible and treacherous. When we began to explore the specific issue of women drinking coffee in the kafeteria, he became adamant:

> Do you know where all this leads to, everybody? It leads to filling up the
> orphanages, the homes for abandoned babies, that's where it leads to, all
> this kind of thing. Because today we start coming here, tomorrow we come
> again, we start talking. . . . Either because I'm good at talking, or maybe I
> find that she speaks attractively, now, day after day, surely some kind of
> flirtation, some kind of love will start up, and since they [sic] fall in love,
> what happens? The kids are left out in the street. You mark my word!

Ironically, Stellios's explanation not only casts the woman as naturally
treacherous but also as the guardian of moral order. It is a peculiar contradiction of the dominant ideology that although women are held to be
guilty somehow for luring a man into sex (their "temptress" quality), they
are also responsible for keeping him *out* of trouble (their rational and
tempering influence).

Stellios believed that a woman would wish to go to the kafeteria for
one reason only: to pursue sex. This belief no doubt drew upon a ste-

reotypical scenario in popular culture—in jokes, stories, films—that portrays a man and woman drinking coffee together as an erotic encounter, be it an inconsequential game of flirtation, an initiation of courtship, or a prelude to seduction and adultery. Stellios believed that this compelling attraction between a man and a woman could not be resisted. In his view, women demonstrated that they were good by repudiating such a place, indeed, by not "wanting" to be there at all. Hence his report about his wife:

JANE: Tell me, did your wife come to the speech?
STELLIOS: No, she heard about it—I was sleeping—and she told me about it. So I say, "Why don't you go with the neighborhood women?" She laughs. "To do what?"
JANE: Why didn't she want to come?
STELLIOS: "To do what?" she says. I say to her, "Maybe you have some kind of complaint about the situation at home?"
AMALIA: Ah, bravo. Why do you think that just to come listen means she must have some complaint?

His wife, Stellios tells us, ridicules not only the kafeteria and the speech on women's issues but, indeed, any implication that she is dissatisfied with her personal situation at all.

This, I think, is the third voice. In some sense it is fitting that—though the speech of a woman, a wife—it is uttered by a man. For this feminine voice, the married woman's voice, is most invested in male discourse, and most tongue-tied and ambivalent (cf. Irigaray 1974). To her husband and perhaps to other women, a married woman might well deny any interest in going to a woman's meeting, or going out for coffee. She might even mock those who do, labeling such desire as a challenge to the implicit contract whereby the woman exchanges her good behavior for her husband's protection and respect.

Yet does this denial of interest (a *moral* act) necessarily indicate a lack of desire? Certainly, younger married women often enough complained to me of feeling bored and restricted, and of how they wished there were places a woman could go to get out of the house. They admitted that there was now much greater freedom to go out with their husbands to clubs or to attend the formal dances sponsored by local civic associations. Indeed, they knew that their expectations for entertainment were comparatively greater than were their mothers' and grandmothers'. Yet they felt that in terms of everyday socializing, people still did not acknowledge their right to enjoy the small pleasures. Such women often noted, disparagingly, the taboos against women's movement in public as indicative of this community's grinding conservatism. "In other places," they sometimes remarked, "married women can go out for a cup of coffee, but here? *Po po po!*" They thus indicated—but with some contempt—the disapproval that would greet *them* were they to act out this desire. In so doing, they marked the quality of the desire as unrealizable, fantastic, in relation to the world they inhabited.

A married woman's confession of interest to me, the ethnographer, and sometimes also to her peers, does not match, in this "third" voice, with her public proclamation of disinterest. Why should this be so? Partly, I would argue, this reflects her quite correct sense of the politics of interpretation. For one of the ways that those with conservative interests *use* a social definition of space (in this case, one organized by gender) as a system of control is by controlling meaning.

Thus a woman may have her own reasons for wanting to drink coffee in the kafeteria: she may want to visit with her friends, to assert that she is independent, to get out of the house, and to relax over a cup of coffee in a pleasant place "like a human being" (*san anthropos*). She may even wish to flirt with a man. Yet her own reasons are not recognized. Her act is given a *public* meaning, indeed, a *predetermined* meaning, the only meaning allowed plausibility. Moreover, the triviality of the desire makes its predetermined meaning even more difficult to challenge. It is not as if a married woman must go into the kafeteria to do anything serious, like earning a living or accomplishing important work for the family.

The use of the word *pareksigo* is especially telling. It is usually glossed as "I misunderstand." But, rendering it in a slightly clumsier but perhaps more precise way, we might read it as "I mis-explain." Consider Soula's explanation of how people view an older (thus, probably married) woman who goes out to a kafeteria with a female friend:

SOULA: In Kladia [another village] women go out regularly, that is, as men do. Yet here—I don't know why men have got it in their heads this way—they think the woman should be in the house. They've twisted things. I have a sister married in a village near Drama, and there women—thirty, forty, fifty years old—they'll go out to a kafeteria by themselves and drink coffee.

JANE: Alone? [I ask because the meaning of this word is ambiguous: it can mean "a woman by herself" or "women without a man."]

SOULA: In a group, only women. Here, for a woman over twenty-five—I'm not putting the age even lower, as I might—to go out with her friend, they'll "mis-explain" her [*tha tin pareksigisoun*].

By changing the translation slightly, I want to emphasize that *creating* a meaning out of her coffee drinking is an active process, an assertion. Mis-explaining is not merely befuddlement. If it were, the woman could presumably state her case and clear up the problem. In fact, mis-explaining her coffee drinking is an accusation, yet it is hardly ever *directly* made. It is perfectly effective even when it remains as innuendo; indeed, existing in that cloudy world of the implicit, it seems almost superfluous to name. Our conversation continued:

JANE: What would they say of such a woman?
SOULA: A thousand-two things. [Pause.] What can I tell you now? [embarrassed laughter]
AMALIA: I already told you [i.e., earlier she had told me they see this woman "as a whore"].
JANE: That she's, shall we say, "of the road"?
SOULA: Ah, bravo. [They say,] "How does her husband allow her to go out?"

Soula and Amalia are quite well aware of the moral framework in terms of which the married woman's action will be explained. They also recognize the possibility of the gap between what she "wants" when she goes to the kafeteria and what the community *says* that she wants. Married women are aware of it, as well.

The third voice, then, is one that states publicly that a "good" woman does not refrain from going to the kafeteria because she is prevented; rather, it asserts that she does not *wish* to go. It is a proclamation of virtue. The virtuous woman is—so goes the claim—in perfect harmony with her husband (who is always presumed to disapprove of her entry into the kafeteria) and has no desire to jeopardize her family's well-being for some trivial desire (cf. Campbell 1964:268).

Married women have very real and concrete interests in preserving the *image* of a harmonious family, for inasmuch as the woman is perceived as responsible for the house, family problems reflect negatively on her. As women often repeated to me, "People will say that 'the woman is to blame.'" This is not, however, merely a matter of performance, for women's status and sense of self-worth may be largely rooted in making this image a reality: in managing family relationships and concerns successfully, and in being a competent, successful, and respectable wife and mother.[10] Consequently, while some women may—genuinely—have no desire to go to the kafeteria, it is not a statement that should necessarily be taken at face value. For the formation of desire (or its absence) must be examined in the context of the married woman's powers, needs, and interests in the real world. The denial of interest articulated in the "third voice" is, furthermore, contradicted by many women's private confessions that they would *like* to go but do not out of fear of possible consequences: gossip, censure, mockery, angry scenes at home, verbal or

[10] Indeed, gender categories for females (and *not* males) reflect how it is marriage, rather than age, that precipitates the status change from "girl" (*kopella* or *koritsi*) to "woman" (*yineka*). For most women, marriage is a prerequisite to achieving the status and potential benefits of full adulthood.

physical retaliation from a husband or parent-in-law, problems for their family. This voice, coming *from* women as well as being attributed *to* them, upholds the dominant gender ideology, because—if I may phrase it somewhat oddly—for the married woman, it is against her interests (as a wife, mother, and a lady of the community, a *kyria*) to assert her interests (as a woman, an autonomous "person"). And the response to this contradiction is a form of what Connolly calls "anticipatory surrender" (1974:91).

The first three voices, even with their complexities and ambivalences, reaffirm the validity of the segregation of unrelated men and women in public leisure space. Although they articulate this in part by assigning a moral quality to the kafeteria as a space, at the crux of their arguments is a particular conception of the female and of the meaning of her action in the world. In this, the female person actively "taking her pleasure" in the kafeteria constitutes a metaphor for an aggressive pursuit of sex. Thus, Stellios (voice 2) speaks of her as the archetypal and insatiable temptress; Katina (voice 1) defines the girl as a sort of "victim of pleasure," and the third voice describes the married woman as one who "repudiates" (this sort of) pleasure.

The fourth and fifth voices describe the kafeteria as a slightly different sort of place and the female as a slightly different sort of being. It is, in fact, in the fifth and final voice that we first hear that she ought to be encountered not merely in terms of her sexuality but "as a person" (san anthropos). The fourth voice remains ambivalent about the motives of either sex toward the other in the kafeteria, but because he finds the place agreeable, contemporary, a sign of his own sophistication, he is unwilling to show himself as an old-fashioned patriarch.

Yorgos, a young single man in his early twenties, worked in the kafeteria but was also well acquainted with the others in our group. In the dynamics of the discussion, Yorgos was in a medial position, sometimes derisive of the girls' claims and opinions, sometimes agreeing with them against Stellios. His ambivalence, which really shows his assent to two mutually exclusive positions, is revealed in two statements.

The first was uttered at a point in the conversation when the girls were insisting that most married men of the town did not consider the needs of their wives for entertainment and release from the daily household routine. They felt that the men considered their obligations fulfilled when they took their wives out a few times a year, "on Christmas and Easter," Soula remarked. This irritated Yorgos, whose retort showed not only that he found their complaints exaggerated, but that he himself recognized a woman's need for getting out (something Stellios explicitly denied) and would be quite liberal about permitting her to fulfill them.

[Here you are, talking so much], how do *you* get to come to the kafeteria? My wife, the young woman I'll marry one of these days, I can't—I'm not going to drag her along with me like a handbag. Let her take the kid, get her girlfriends, and come to the kafeteria for a cup of coffee. What, do I have to drag my wife along with me? Let her come.

Later on, however, after Stellios has pronounced that the woman in the kafeteria is the wrecker of marriages and happy families, Yorgos argumentatively asserts, without a hint of embarrassment, what he (and all men, and probably all women) are *really* after in this sort of sociability.

Let me tell you something. Every man, no matter how old, his mind is stuck on women. If I go into a store, to shop, even, or to the kafeteria, it doesn't stop me from seeing any woman that walks in, married or single, if she isn't accompanied [i.e., by a man], I go for her. It's in my mind right away and I stalk her, like she's a chick, I don't regard her, in other words, as a woman. That's all natural, everyone more or less thinks this way. And don't forget that a person today [*i simerini anthropotita*] is mainly concerned with partying, with eating, and with figuring out how to make love with a woman and have a good time. I don't think he considers anything else. He doesn't see the woman, he sees her as an object, and thinks how to have a good time. Since he's had his good time, afterwards, he acts as if he doesn't even know her.

In this very aggressive monologue, Yorgos tells us how he thinks the world works. It is not a vision sympathetic to women. Indeed, in seeing women as objects of men's pleasure, it teeters toward the vision that Stellios articulated. The difference, perhaps, is that it discards the rhetoric of virtue, propriety, and complementarity and portrays the antagonistic struggles between men and women in all their rawness. It is also a significantly more individualistic vision, focused on desire and personal interest.

The fifth voice is that of the two girls, Soula and Amalia. Though they have commented throughout on other people's interpretations, they have a personal vision of what a female is, and this they articulate both in what they say and what they do. First, they *go* to the kafeteria. Amalia, an extremely articulate high school senior, and Soula, a bright girl from a somewhat more liberal than average family, are striking as individuals, but in coming to the kafeteria they are not unique. To be sure, girls constitute a small minority among the patrons, and their presence remains controversial. But townspeople identify the kafeteries as a meeting place of young people, and they recognize, though they may disapprove, that girls increasingly spend time there.

Significantly, the girls' use of the kafeteria was viewed with a relatively greater tolerance, grudging though it was, than was granted to married women. Parents admitted that their children's reality was not the one they knew as children. They also recognized that girls have a comprehensible, if dangerous, interest in seeing and being seen by young men. Being seen is, of course, an ambiguous process. Parents may quarrel with their daughters over what the latter "have been seen" to be doing there—like smoking or flirting—whether this be rumor or fact. But the consequences for an unmarried girl are less serious than for a married woman. As in the case of the girl corrupted through her drug-spiked orange soda, the affair was "mended" when the grandfather pressured the man to marry her (cf. du Boulay 1974:116).

It is also clear that despite its indisputably sinful connotations, the kafeteria carries prestige as a symbol of modern sophistication and civilized luxury. In a community that prides itself on being a bit of a bustling metropolis (a *komopoli*) compared to the small sleepy villages surrounding it, yet one which is always painfully aware of its "backwardness" compared to the modern city of Thessaloniki, the kafeteries are part of Sohoians' claim to being progressive. This explains, at least in part, why I (even as a woman) was taken there my first day by Mihalis, and why the mayor, an urban-bred and "progressive" man, arranged for the Women's Day speech to be held there. It is a lever that the girls use, as well, when they want to go there and to make their presence legitimate.

The image of the woman upon which Soula and Amalia wish to model themselves is informed both by a feminist discourse that emerges in the media and in the political agenda of the two major left-wing parties, and by the social position these girls occupy by virtue of their age and gender. Neither Soula nor Amalia is committed, in terms of interests or obligations, to a nuclear family in the same way that a married woman is. Soula is contemptuous of the way people censor their own actions because of their fear of public disapproval:

> In the village, the one thing that people think about, whether it's to marry, to get engaged, to separate, or for the girl to do whatever, is other people. What will people say if I smoke, what will people say if I get engaged after I turn twenty, what will people say if I get engaged and break up, what will people say if I marry and get divorced, what will people say? They never say, what shall I do to make myself happy?

This complaint will sound familiar to anyone who has spent time in a Greek community of almost any size. But the assertion by a young woman that her own individual needs and desires ought to take precedence is not typical.

Soula and Amalia claim that a woman should make decisions about how to act according to her own needs, desires, and interests. They see the concern with reputation as hypocritical and conformist, and they find it unacceptable that women organize their lives in terms of it. They do not believe that a woman betrays her husband when she expresses an interest in a women's meeting or in a cup of coffee with her friends. Their sense of what they want in a relationship with a man (which is not necessarily what they think they can expect) is strikingly egalitarian and mutual compared with the hierarchical, if complementary, marriages they see around them. Adopting a more individualistic rhetoric, they speak forcefully of the woman "as a person."

After Yorgos's bleak description of the antagonism between men and women, and the "natural" objectification of the woman, Soula responded. She argued that "equality"—a word they had been debating all afternoon—was not a matter of sameness, of identical physical capacities. Equality meant regarding the woman not as object but as subject.

> But Yorgos, *this* is what we want to do [i.e., as feminists]. To make it so that a man doesn't look at a woman as an object no matter what place she walks into. Why should he see her as an object? We want to get to the level where the man looks at the woman as a person.

Amalia—shyly, tentatively—added her own remarkable assertion. She argued that a female's desire and her right to "act upon it" should in some way be allowed and recognized as legitimate. After the men had smugly quipped to Soula that "the woman also sees [i.e., desires and objectifies] the man," Amalia countered:

> You know what happens? Everybody says, it's men who tease girls, and boys who tease girls, but if a girl likes someone, for her to approach him first, he'll think she's "easy." If she's known as easy, that's it, she's had it . . . and yet that guy, he might not ever make the first move.

Soula and Amalia reject the equation of female moral goodness with passivity, even as they feel it impinge upon them. In embracing an alternative view of the female person, they redefine her power, her interests, her desires, the meaning of her sexuality and of her actions in the world. They *enact* their own independence by coming to the kafeteria, and then (provoked by me, the anthropologist) they use it as a forum to articulate and explore what "woman as person" means. Their voice—weak, inchoate—draws out and makes audible the contradictions that are only indirectly expressed in the other voices.

AMBIGUITIES OF RESISTANCE

Embedded within the practices of everyday sociability are socially constructed meanings about gender and sexual difference. Because activities like coffee drinking are both pleasurable and seemingly trivial, Sohoians tend to portray participation in them as freely chosen, a consequence of individual preferences. They explain that women prefer sweets, which houses and the zaharoplastio provide, while men prefer the pungent and salty substances served in the kafenio. They insist, furthermore, that males and females feel more comfortable in their own spaces. Such explanations not only justify the status quo, they also veil the ways power, needs, and interests are at play when people define what males and females want or—more to the point—*should* want (Lukes 1974). Using gender as an adjective applied to material objects (for instance, calling certain drinks "manly" and "womanly") further blurs the natural with the moral. Even so, this language elaborates certain aspects of a culturally constructed femaleness at the expense of others. Sugary images evoke the domesticated woman: "delicious" (*nostimi*) to men; yet good, safe, and unthreatening. Ingesting and enjoying sweets, a woman shows herself properly socialized as well as sociable.

What happens when a new leisure space appears in the town? Sophisticated, European, and modern in its symbolic nuances, catering to a new kind of person as it engenders, in Raymond Williams's (1977) striking phrase, a new "structure of feeling," the kafeteria confounds neatly commonsensical gender boundaries. As it conceptually irritates seemingly rigid categories of gendered space, the frictions extend to the felt and experienced everyday world.

The voices of variably positioned and unequally powerful speakers talking in and about the kafeteria articulate the complexity of gender ideas, relations, and experiences entailed in the trivial act of drinking a cup of coffee. Some use the occasion to contest hegemonic notions of women's nature and women's place. Others reassert the validity of these notions, or accept them simply because contestation is too costly. The different voices make clear that we cannot assume consensus about the meanings of male and female in contemporary Greece. Nor can we portray this lack of consensus as a consequence of two distinct, unified yet opposed perspectives, the androcentric and the gynecocentric. Gender is a site of ideological struggle in which divisions among women and among men, and alliances across lines of gender, are evident.

The entrance by young women into previously male-controlled public leisure spaces is, undeniably, a potent symbolic act of protest against locally configured patriarchal restrictions. But should we see the kafeteria as heralding a new era of liberated pleasures for women? Such a conclusion would be both facile and insidious, resting as it does on the simplistic assumption that gender inequalities reside *uniquely* in societies with traditional forms of gender segregation. And it implies that through the adoption of Western—what scholars and Sohoians alike have often called "modern"—ways, the position of women is automatically improved.

The implications of such acts of resistance are, in fact, more ambiguous. Though a site where the traditional restrictions of a local gender ideology are being contested, the kafeteria is hardly a revolutionary institution. On the contrary, and with no small irony, the recent appearance of kafeteries in Sohos exemplifies the hegemonic penetration of one particular Macedonian community by urban Greek and European institutions, symbols, and forms of sociability that are effectively displacing their indigenous counterparts. The kafeteria offers a new model of human "being" stressing leisure and luxury and celebrates a capitalist culture that, although it encourages males and females alike to show who they are by spending and consuming, also entails other forms of gender inequality. Yet those who would contest traditional gender meanings must draw upon whatever alternative discourses are available to them. Their efforts to imagine and to put into practice new ways of being female will inevitably reflect, as they engage with, the contradictory dimensions of their everyday reality.

ACKNOWLEDGMENTS

The fieldwork upon which this paper is based was conducted in the central Macedonian town of Sohos between February 1983 and February 1985. I am grateful for the support of a Fulbright-Hays Fellowship for Doctoral Dissertation Research and an NSF Dissertation Improvement Grant (for video equipment and support). I wish to thank Diane Bennett, Charles Gore, Michael Herzfeld, Kris Hardin, Gregory Jusdanis, Margaret Kenna, Peter Loizos, Susan Rasmussen, Donatella Schmidt, Anthony Seeger, and Cathy Winkler for helpful comments and criticisms on an earlier version of this paper. This paper is itself an earlier version of what appears as chapter 3, "Everyday Sociability as Gendered Practice," in my book *Dance and the Body Politic in Northern Greece*. Copyright © 1990 by Princeton University Press.

Chapter 9

HUNTERS AND HUNTED: *KAMAKI* AND THE AMBIGUITIES OF SEXUAL PREDATION IN A GREEK TOWN

Sofka Zinovieff

A KAMAKI is a harpoon for spearing fish, but the word is also used metaphorically in Greece. It describes the act of a Greek man pursuing a foreign woman with the intention of having sex. There is an implied use of cunning, and of mastering a physical interaction, as there would be in this type of fishing. The expression "to make kamaki" (*kano kamaki* or *kamakono*) has entered the Greek language and is now used frequently and in a more general way. For example, it can be applied if a woman is flirting with a man, or when a shopkeeper or restaurateur calls in customers off the street. In Platanos (a pseudonym), and in other touristic areas of Greece, kamaki has developed over the last twenty-five years, since tourists began to arrive in significant numbers. While anybody can (and many males in Platanos do) *make kamaki*, there are certain men who are known to be *kamakia* (plural of *kamaki*). These "hunters" systematically attempt to have sexual relationships with tourist women, rather than with Greek women, and are well-known in the town as playing a specific game, and leading a particular sort of life. Most Plataniotes and kamakia explain the game as being "just for sex," but the way that kamaki is played reveals underlying issues of class division, and of male beliefs in gender and prestige.

This paper has three main themes. First, it shows that kamaki is a system of male competition, whereby men without material and social status establish other grounds for prestige. Second, the act of kamaki highlights the sense of antagonism that many Greeks have toward "Europe" or the West. Kamakia may see themselves as belonging to a poorer, inferior society, and by lying to, tricking, and sexually conquering foreign tourist women from the supposedly superior societies, they have some revenge.

The third theme is the desire of many kamakia to change their lives, to escape, or to take material wealth or prestige from the West. When these men marry foreigners, they are uniting two worlds that were previously separate (marriage/household/Greek, and sexual freedom/tour-

ism/foreign), and their attitudes towards different categories of women
are revealed.

PLATANOS AND THE HISTORY OF KAMAKI

Since the 1960s Platanos has been a stop on the "classical tour" of archae-
ological sites in Greece, and many tourists only stay for one or two days.
The dramatic increase in tourism in Greece, from 1.6 million in 1970, to
6.75 million in 1985 (EOT 1985), has affected some areas far more negatively, especially those which are beach resorts. With a population of
about 10,500, Platanos is an important regional center.

The elegant, neoclassical old town is the center for the thriving tourist
industry, and, famed as a noble and historical place, it is also the home
of a few remaining "good families" (*kales oikoyeneies*) or "aristocracy"
(*aristokratia*). Although a mixture of classes lives in the old town, a rivalry
and even slight hostility exists between "real" Plataniotes and those who
are from the suburbs (also given pseudonyms), where approximately half
of the town's population live. The close-knit, historically working-class
district of Old Suburb has existed since the 1830s (established for Cretan
refugees of the War of Independence). The Refugees' Neighborhood was
first inhabited by refugees from Asia Minor in the 1920s but has expanded with incomers from villages and other areas of Greece. The third
main suburb is the new part of Platanos, composed of blocks and flats,
and still spreading steadily outward over the former marshy area. The
old town is also divided into neighborhoods, with the Fishermen's District being a predominantly poor area.

Platanos is not a typical resort that provides the "four Ss" (sun, sand,
sea and sex) of tourist literature. Nevertheless it is known to be a kamaki
center, and, since the early 1960s, Plataniotes have indulged in the activity. Some men give a practical explanation for the early years of the phenomenon: young Greek women were extremely restricted, and their
parents did not allow them to go out with men. (For the numerous
references in Greek ethnographical literature to the emphasis placed on
the sexual purity of Greek women, and how the honor of their menfolk
rests on their sexual shame [*dropi*], see, e.g., Campbell 1964; du Boulay
1974; Hirschon 1978; and Dubisch 1986a.) Thus the apparently freer and
more sexually liberated tourist women provided an opportunity for female company, if not for sex. At this time, a number of young men established a kamaki club called "Octopus," allegedly with rules of membership and codes of behavior. These pioneers contrast themselves—they
feel that they were more romantic and humane in their intentions and
methods—with the young men today who are only interested in sex.
Drakontaeidis wrote a newspaper article glorifying (though somewhat

ironically) the romance and conceding the paucity of sexual conquests made by himself and other members of the Octopus Club in 1961–1963. The present-day kamaki is presented as playing an entirely different, cruder, and (at least metaphorically), a more violent game (Drakontaeidis 1986). It is also said (in many cases erroneously) that the twenty or so members of Octopus were generally from "better families" and were well-educated compared with the typically poor, uneducated modern kamakia.

Native men pick up foreign women in many countries with tourism, and methods vary according to the social system, morality, and availability of the female tourists (e.g., see Cohen 1977). This sexual pursuit is known to many tourists, and foreign women may compare the techniques of, say, Italians and Greeks. Therefore, to the outsider, kamaki has other unique implications. To be a kamaki means to carry out a particular and named process, distinct from other, apparently similar ones (for example, a gigolo has different intentions), and to be identified by others (especially the peer group) as being a participant in what has become a popular summer activity and a male subculture in Greece.

A mythology of sorts, fed by various sources, has grown up around kamaki. "Fishing stories," especially from the era of the Octopus Club, have become legends, and not only in Platanos, as this subject is covered by television, writers, and journalists. Misconceptions abound—for example, that a national society of kamakia exists—and magazines and newspapers regularly perpetuate inaccurate clichés. Even foreign women (Joseph and White 1974) have published humorous, if insulting, exaggerations about overenthusiastic Greek men and tourist women in Athens. A television documentary (considered to be scandalous, and abruptly removed from the air halfway through) was made a few years ago, and it publicized Platanos, among other places. It depicted kamakia as being like male prostitutes, who used foreign women only for their money. The writer Vassilikos wrote a book of stories about kamakia in Platanos and has also perpetrated the notion that these men are well-organized "professionals" who hunt their victims with calculated, unemotional skillfulness.

Most Plataniotes have an idea of the kamakia that is based more on a national stereotype than on knowledge of the reality around them. Although a kamaki has a bad reputation in society, in general, men hold fairly tolerant or positive opinions. Women of all ages and social backgrounds tend to view kamakia as being inferior or inadequate men, who are unable to find Greek women. Moreover, these women impose their own sexual standards and assume that tourist women (*touristries*) are tricked or lured into having sex with the crafty, untrustworthy kamakia. Among the most positive statements by Greek women on this topic was that "kamaki has taught the young men to wash and be clean, whereas previously they and many Greeks were dirty."

The Men

Superficially, the focus of kamaki appears to be on relationships between men and women, but, in reality, it is on male alliances that use women as pawns. In general a kamaki is part of a *parea* (company) of men with a common identity and set of motives, and it is more common to make kamaki with others than entirely alone. While the ambition is picking up foreign women, it is the male friendships, the planning, the discussions, and the competitive equality that form the base of the activity. One of Vassilikos's stories portrays an autumnal meeting of a kamaki society, where the members discuss their summer catch: "A total of 3,262 foreign women were '*kamakied*' " (*kamakothikan sinolika 3,262 xenes*). The need to study "female psychology" if one is to succeed as a kamaki also comes under their scrutiny (Vassilikos 1978:101–103). In many cases, a kamaki will learn his techniques and a little English with other older kamakia, and different generations of kamakia are clearly identified, with their own characteristics and heroes. In Platanos the kamaki do not form a team, and although they are united in their goal, they do not all compete together. Rather, there are various groups of men who are linked, through neighborhood, school days, or work, who meet together in leisure time for this summer activity and for its winter reminiscences.

Being a young foreign woman, I was playing an incongruous role by associating as a friend-anthropologist with kamakia. When I first arrived in Platanos, I was approached by kamakia as a prospective "catch," but after I became a more permanent figure in the community (i.e., not a tourist), and did not fulfill kamaki expectations, this behavior diminished dramatically. While I was unable to participate fully in the activity of kamaki from the side in which I was interested (that of the men), I was able to gain access to this world by other means. Some friends allowed me to be with them while they discussed and carried out their "hunting," and in a few cases I was even used as a decoy to encourage tourist women to join a parea of otherwise more threatening men. My fieldwork was carried out for about two years from late 1985.

A sample of 31 men who were known as kamakia revealed various common factors in background and occupations. The information was gathered from a variety of sources and in many cases was related by friends, wives, and fellow kamaki of the men involved, rather than by each individual man. The men were aged between 20 and 40, with a preponderance around 30, and the majority (21/31) worked in tourist-related occupations. Of these 21, 12 were waiters or employees in bars, hotels, or tourist shops, and 9 were owners of establishments such as bars and tourist shops. The rest were half employees in the tourism business and half in miscellaneous occupations. The majority of these kamakia were from outside the central old town, with 17 originating from Old Suburb, 3 from Refugees' Neighborhood, and 3 from villages. A minority of 8 men originated from the old town, and half of these were from the poorer Fishermen's District. Thus most of the kamakia are from poor, working-class backgrounds, and, correspondingly, only 11 out of the 31 finished secondary school (*gymnasio*), with many leaving school at the age of 13 or 14. These figures indicate that in Platanos, the reality upholds the stereotype; that kamakia are usually men who lack material wealth and social status, at least in their origins, and who are frequently uneducated. Some kamakia show an awareness of the class element in their behavior, but with varied interpretations. One man argued that "Greek women only want rich men, and so we have to go with foreign women." In spite of this opinion, the same person (along with many others) is positively keen to meet tourist women rather than females of his own nationality. Thus the statement is more a comment on the class system in general than a report on actuality.

In the light of the kamaki's background, his procedures can be seen to exist, in part, as an alternative system of prestige. Papataxiarchis (1985) has suggested that just as "material components of status" can be transformed into social recognition, so too can "symbolic capital" of various sorts. In this case, prestige is not based on belonging to a "good family," or having money or education, or on fulfilling society's expectations as head of a household (*nikokiris*) with a respectable family and life-style. Instead, the kamaki wins success by "scoring" women. Furthermore, measurements of success vary according to how an individual operates and how he relates to his peers; in other words, the demonstration of his "performative skill in public" (Herzfeld 1985a:139).

A kamaki wishes to conform to the criteria that are deemed significant, and this includes physical appearance. It is highly preferable to have a "good" body and well-developed muscles, and many kamakia engage in bodybuilding·and weight lifting, which are believed to increase their eligibility as prospective lovers. One kamaki (whose nickname refers to his strong body) tells stories of foreign women in discotheques who left their boyfriends and went with him because they saw his amazing biceps when he removed his jacket. It is also said that women are attracted to men with large penises, and appropriate measures are taken, especially with swimming costumes—padding is even used—to achieve the maximum effect. Naturally, the beach is a favored parade ground for those with the right credentials. Another element is cleanliness, and most kamakia wash frequently, and (at least when encountering women) have a well-presented appearance. Great importance is also attached to whether a tourist woman is "clean" (*kathari*), which is usually judged by appearance rather than by how often she washes.

In establishing ground rules for being a good kamaki, these men are using certain gender characteristics to gain kudos (see Strathern 1981b:178–179). The competition does not exist between kamakia, but implicitly between them and men of other classes. Lower-class men are better kamakia than upper-class men, who cannot really compete. In general, men who have high social status in Platanos would not make kamaki within the town, as they fear for their reputation; there are no known upper-class kamakia. Similarly, married men normally have a need for secrecy and discretion, and both these categories of men are more likely to make kamaki outside the town. In contrast, men who use the activity as a prestige system are usually members of some sort of team or partnership, and they are more obvious and keener to declare themselves. A substantial element in the game is sociability with other kamakia and the public declaration of one's occupation; thus, in this paper, I have felt justified in leaving out (and perhaps not knowing some of) the more marginal players. A man from a different social milieu would also have difficulty in joining a parea of players. One educated man (who had been to a university) joined some kamakia friends to meet tourist women and was criticized for his conversational technique with women: "You don't screw with books" (*dhen gamas me vivlia*). In other words, there are standard expectations of how a real kamaki should behave with a woman, and of how to trigger the desired response.

THE HUNT

Part of the delight of making kamaki is the sensation of hunting. As the word implies, the intention is to metaphorically spear the "victim" (*thima*), and therefore the foreign woman is seen as being lured or trapped, and not as a willing partner herself. As an insult to touristries, kamakia sometimes say that "they all come to Greece for sex," but the idea of the woman as hunter spoils the chase. A common belief is that the earlier in her holiday a woman is approached, the more innocent and the more likely a victim she is. Some men are even said to go to Athens airport with this in mind. In Platanos, kamakia often search for women in a pair or a small group, and tourist women who arrive without men frequently travel together in this way. However, part of a sophisticated collaboration is knowing when to retreat: if three men meet two women, one man has to agree to leave in order for the process to advance properly. While the preferences of the women must be taken into account, there is a tendency for women to be viewed almost as units of exchange between men. If a man (one works in the tourism business, say, and has easy access to foreign women) manages to organize dates between his friends and foreign women (xenes), he may say, "You owe me three." The friends are in debt and should try to find new women to repay the first man.

There are many ways to find and meet touristries, but great store is placed in tricking them into a relationship. The largely unsuccessful line "Do you want to have coffee?" is still commonly used, but a more imaginative opening attack is preferable. This is said to depend on the nationality of the woman, and some men claim to vary their behavior accordingly. Perhaps for this reason, another favored beginning is "Where are you from?" If the woman turns out to be Italian or, worse, Greek, the chances of success are said to be very slim, as these women know the tricks of their own men too well. Americans are said to be direct and straightforward and may play the kamaki themselves. Various opinions exist as to northern Europeans, but they are thought to be impressed by romantic, hot-blooded, Mediterranean spontaneity. One set procedure described by a kamaki goes as follows: "Where are you from?" is followed by a compliment or a joke, such as "Are all the girls in Germany as beautiful as you?" If the woman has not left, there ensues the almost unavoidable "Will you come for coffee with me?" Many kamakia also frequent areas such as the bus station, the post office, or the steps to the fortress in Platanos, and can then ask, "May I help you?"

Some kamakia are known to have their own style and methods, or as being especially successful at tricking xenes into conversation and later into bed. Stories have entered the folklore of the participants themselves and are even known by Plataniotes. For example, tales of traps and conquests of the Octopus Club still circulate, more than twelve years after the demise of this "virtuoso" group. In one procedure, the kamaki goes to the beach with a half-painted picture (some say of a shark, others, of the sea) and waits until the most attractive woman goes into the sea. He then places himself directly behind her belongings, and when she returns he remarks, "You weren't in the picture yesterday." An even better ploy is to encourage the woman to make contact, by making her curious about the painting or about some other activity. Once a conversation has begun, half the battle is won, and many kamakia aim to have sex with their prey in the same day or evening. In some cases this is vital, as so many tourists stay for only one or two days in Platanos, but it is also a sign of prowess and conquest for the man.

In the ideal case, where a pair of kamakia meet two foreign women, they will frequently make a date for the evening. This gives the men (and the women) a chance to present themselves at their best, and for the men (as Greeks and locals) to introduce the tourists to the Greek way of life, and to work together as a team. If the kamakia are conscious of their actions as performance, they will probably take the women to a taverna, and then perhaps to one of the "boites," to hear Greek music and perhaps to try some dancing. The kamaki must live up to at least some of the fantasy that the tourist woman might have about Greeks, and he may resort to clichés. In other cases, the new couple may visit one of the many new, European-style bars, or a disco. Some kamakia claim that they can understand what a woman wants, and when is the right moment to "attack." As one man said, "I would not touch a woman before I know that she is ready. I can see it in her eyes and her behavior." On the other hand, men can become annoyed when the so-called easy tourist women "play games" (*paizoun paichnidhia*) and appear reluctant to go home with the admirers. Younger kamakia tend to live with their parents, which obliges them, at least for their brief adventures, to go to the woman's hotel, or commonly to the woods surrounding the beach, if they want to have sex. If the woman rejects the kamaki sexually, it has been a complete waste of time, and he may say to his friends, "I ate dog poison" (*efaga fola*).

A kamaki will rarely establish a real relationship with a tourist woman, and in extreme cases he may reject her after the first night. "How can I have respect for a woman if I screw her?" (*pos boro na echo sevasmo yia mia yinaika an tin gamao*). Once conquered sexually, she has become equal to a prostitute, and therefore worthless and without challenge. If the man stays with the woman for a short time, he will continue the game as he began it: telling lies to the woman and using her in his relationship with his friends ("A conscious kamaki must not ever fall in love"—Vassilikos 1978:36). Kamakia back each other up in making up false stories about themselves for the women. For example, they may say that they are doctors, architects, policemen, and even the mayor of Platanos, and that they own smart cars, or attractive shops or cafés. The occupants of one beautiful old house by the port received many letters addressed to men who did not live there, as it was common at one time for kamakia to claim the house as their own.

The lies told by kamakia illustrate the occupations and life-styles that they see as prestigious, as well as the belief that tourist women are impressed by their social standing. Greek men may express surprise when they see a foreign woman "go with" (*paei mazi*) a man of low social and economic status. It might, though, be said that she may have come to Greece with notions of romantic simplicity, and that if her holiday lover is a fisherman or a waiter rather than a doctor or an architect, this fits her preconceptions better. The same might apply when a kamaki does not speak English (or another foreign language) very well, and the stereotyped kamaki does not. A magazine article on kamaki writes that "fifty words are enough," with all these condensed into three: "me, you, bed" (Georgeles 1986). However, in the survey of thirty-one kamakia in Platanos, the overwhelming majority spoke English moderately to very well, and in some cases French in addition.

Kamaki lies are only one aspect of a relationship based on deceit. The touristries are used to articulate the relationship between men and may be endowed with anonymity ("They are all the same": suntanned, scantily dressed, and searching for freedom and adventure on their holidays). A woman may be paraded as a trophy in prominent places such as the waterfront (*paralia*), which is also a popular hunting ground, as it is lined with cafeterias. The kamaki will speak Greek to his friends in front of his foreign "chick" (*gomena*), probably discussing or insulting her, and making vulgar jokes, while appearing innocent or affectionate. Different groups of kamakia support one another, and a network of information exists revealing whether likely women are in the town and, more important, whether they have already been appropriated: kamakia attempt to respect one another's rights. Vassilikos declares that "a kamaki does not 'take out the eye' of another kamaki. This is a general axiom. A kamaki would never 'eat the woman' of another kamaki, even if she provoked him with her eyes or a whisper" (Vassilikos 1978:67). This may be a slight exaggeration, but is true in principle. Male solidarity is also expressed in the parallel and sometimes allied occupation of "peeping Toms" (*banistirtzidhes*). Not only do men spy on couples in the woods, on topless sunbathers, or with binoculars into houses, but some make arrangements to "peep" (*pairnoun mati*) on one another. A kamaki may agree to let his friends hide and watch him having sexual intercourse with a tourist woman.

The woman's role as a form of symbolic currency allows a kamaki to be generous with his friends. Not only may he provide them with "dates" and entertain them with jokes and stories, but he can give them visual access to the sexual act (comparable perhaps to shared viewing of pornographic films and magazines). In some cases two men may "share" a woman sexually: sexual encounters may involve more than two people (*partouzes*), or the woman may be passed on from one man to another. However, this is a delicate transaction, and, with the victim existing as "property," such an exchange is likely to happen rarely, and only between good friends. It is said that a kamaki may feel cuckolded (*keratas*) if his "chick" goes off with another man, but this depends on the circumstances.

The process of kamaki indicates certain beliefs about status and prestige. Kamakia are challenging and antagonistic not only toward higher-class men in their own society, but toward the women who come to Greece on holiday from other countries. They are also indirectly insulting the foreign men, who are implicitly indicted as sexually inadequate, unable to look after their women or to prevent them from going off in search of supposedly superior Greek lovers. The general reasoning for preferring xenes to Greek women is that they are "easy" (*efkoles*) and "free" (*eleftheres*) sexually, that they will not demand a serious relationship ("They always leave"), and, some say, that they are more beautiful. Depending on the speaker and the situation, foreign women may be characterized as more intelligent than their Greek counterparts or as more stupid.

Underlying these ideas is the rationale that xenes are superior because they come from superior societies, and that Greece (along with its people) is economically, politically, socially, morally, and culturally "behind" (*piso*). Therefore an unconscious sense of frustration and even inferiority exists on the part of the kamakia, who take a number of steps. They raise themselves to the supposed social and economic level of the women through lies, and they take revenge on the women (and thus on their countries) by insulting and tricking them, and by conquering them sexually and metaphorically.

KAMAKI DISCOURSE

A vital part of being a kamaki is talking about it, regaling the male parea with stories. "Both the event and the narration of event are social constructions, each reinforcing the other" (Herzfeld 1985a:207). Stories are expected to have plenty of "sauce" (*saltsa*), rather than adhering strictly to the facts. For a large number of these men (those who work in tourism), the winter months are a dormant period, without work or the prospect of making kamaki. After a long and often tiring period of working and making kamaki, men gather in cafeterias and bars and discuss their summer encounters.

The language used by kamakia is often aggressive and crude in relation to women, and violent metaphorical terms are used for picking up and having sex with a woman: for example, "to slaughter" (*sfazo*), to "throw or pull down" (*richno*), "to roast" (*psino*), or "to hit" or "beat" (*chtipao*). The xenes may be referred to as "whores" (*poutanes*), "chickens" (*kotes*), "dirty women" (*vromiares*), "women of the street" (*allaniares*), or more generally as *gomenes* (a widely used expression describing girlfriends or sexually attractive "chicks"). Vassilikos makes extensive use of kamaki vocabulary in his stories and shows how it reveals some of the irony and even hatred that exists in this activity. In addition, it is common for English to enter into the language of men who tend to associate only with foreign women (and usually in English). One kamaki told his friend that he was unable to say "I love you" in Greek any more, as it sounded stupid and had no meaning for him.

Stories concerning kamaki achievements are told after the event in predominantly male company; they tend to take a particular form and to focus on certain parts of the procedure. The men are identified (probably with nicknames), and the scene is set. For example, "We were sitting on the paralia at such-and-such a cafeteria." Then the women are spotted, and a description is given of their appearance (especially their bodies, which might be given marks out of ten, and their clothing, which determines whether they are "clean" or "dirty"). The next part of the story concerns how the introduction took place, which tends to raise laughter. For example, "Yiorgos, 'O Psilos' ["Tall One"], went up to the girls and told them that we were journalists interviewing tourists about their views on Greece." This preamble presupposes that the women accepted the invitation, and the tale progresses. The main theme of kamaki stories revolves around male cunning, how the women are wooed, where they are taken, how "easy" or "difficult" they were; and it is sometimes noted if the women had some special attribute, such as wealth. The supposed climax of the whole enterprise, the sexual act, may be covered in a throwaway line ("and we went to play chess"), after exhaustive attention to previous details. In some cases, however, this may have been influenced by my potentially inhibiting female presence.

There is much room for exaggeration in accounts of conquests with xenes, and, through this narrative style, a kamaki can present himself in a particular light. The measure of a "good kamaki" is not only in qualitative behavior (for example, he is preferably to be tough and nonchalant with the women), but in quantitative achievement. "Those young kids [*paidhia*] are no good; they only go with one or two girls all summer." Similarly, in order to be a "good lover" (*kalos erastis*), a man should have intercourse a number of times consecutively: "I threw (or knocked) her four" (*tis erixa tessera*). There is little mention of the woman's experience, but rather a focus on male preoccupations such as the size of the penis and the number of ejaculations.

Storytelling serves to unite "companies" (parees) of kamakia, and to give them a solidarity through shared experience, language, mentality, and ambitions. In addition to a unity of purpose in pursuing foreign women, the men also join forces in expressing their boredom or even disgust with the whole affair. "I have got tired" and "I have got bored" (*echo kourastei* and *echo varethei*) are frequently asserted, as is "Kamaki is wearing" (*to kamaki einai fthora*). At these moments, the foreign females are insulted, being described not only as "easy" and "whores," but as "dirty" (*vromikes*), and potentially dangerous and polluting. Tourist women can be seen as crossing many symbolic boundaries: they are women who enter a male world, they are supposedly superior and richer, but they are also "dirty whores." Thus in keeping with Mary Douglas's theories on pollution and taboo, they are symbolically dangerous and threatening (Douglas 1966).

These attitudes concerning sexual danger are reflected in writing on the subject and especially in connection with the increasing awareness of AIDS. A recent magazine contained an article on the fear of AIDS on the island Mykonos, which is renowned for its homosexual and generally sexually uninhibited tourists. The writer linked the attraction of *"beautiful male and female tourists"* with the *"danger* of the terrible disease" (Stavropoulos 1987). It is certain that the fear of AIDS will influence the way in which sexually available touristries are perceived, but it is still too early to tell how the kamakia will react. The number of cases of this illness in Greece is still relatively low, and there has not been a great deal of state campaigning against it. In Platanos, it is still more common for kamakia to make humorous statements of bravado than to voice genuine fear. In a similar vein, Vassilikos expresses Greek sentiments of fear and disgust through the words of a fictional mother whose kamaki son has venereal disease. "All that shines is not gold"; "They [the tourist women] all come here and pollute our country, turn the heads of our lads, and give us their cholera" (Vassilikos 1978:167).

EXPECTATIONS AND ESCAPES

If the first specific explanation given by kamakia for their occupation is sex, the second is the potential usefulness of a foreigner, the attraction of having a contact abroad. The woman ceases to be an anonymous foreign "chicken," picked from a flock of potential prey, and becomes a chance to gain something, or to escape. Cohen writes of a comparable situation concerning Arab boys and tourist girls in Israel, where the girls act as "a window to the wide world" (Cohen 1977:224). A large number of kamakia have dreams of leaving Platanos and of going to America (or northern Europe), where they will make money and lead a luxurious, superior life. An even larger number are eager to travel and to take winter holidays in these countries, and the touristries are a means to this end. Few kamakia are gigolos (i.e., are paid for their services by usually older women), but in some cases the hope of receiving presents, a ticket to travel, or hospitality abroad is a powerful motive. (A few older men reverse this pattern, and are known to spend money in order to impress foreign women.) The consciously ambitious kamaki offers favors and hospitality to the xenes, in the hope that they will later do the same for him in their countries (see Herzfeld 1987). Therefore it can be doubly in the interest of the kamaki to put himself at an advantage with the woman by playing up "traditional

Greek hospitality": he expects both sexual rewards in Greece and some reciprocal generosity later.

There is another side to the stories of touristries paying for their holiday lovers to stay with them in the "colder countries." It is said that some women are entirely different when they are back in "reality" at home, at work, and "in the cold." They are no longer interested in someone with whom they had a brief affair while escaping from normal life, on holiday, and in the sun. Presumably both the kamaki and the tourist woman desired a brief sexual relationship, but it may well be the man who has dreams or expectations for the future. Furthermore, it is the woman who leaves the man and returns to her regular life, whereas the kamaki must wait for the next woman to appear, or for the last one to invite him to stay. It is the women who control the fundamental conditions (arriving, leaving, accepting or refusing the advances of the kamaki), and thus the kamaki ideology of control and male domination can only really be sexual, and it is frequently based more on fantasy than reality. In these circumstances, the Greek lover has become the victim: used, and then rejected, and unable to make his own escape to the richer, more advanced countries of his fantasies.

KAMAKIA AND MARRIAGE

Given the strong basis of antagonism and violence that is present in kamaki attitudes toward their "victims," it seems extraordinary that many kamakia actually marry foreign women. Nevertheless, this is quite common, and long-term relationships do develop out of the unpromising beginnings. A kamaki may marry a foreign woman for a variety of reasons. In some circumstances a man may declare that he became tired and bored with his superficial and promiscuous way of life, and that he wanted to settle down. With marriage as a possibility, he may approach tourist women with attitudes and ambitions different from those of a typical kamaki, and there may be less of a contradiction. The desire to settle down is commonly given as a legitimation for marriage in general, but it does not address the issue of why a foreigner is chosen. In other cases, the couple fall in love and then decide to stay together. More rarely, a kamaki marries a foreign woman to enable him to leave Greece and pursue his dream life abroad.

In a sample of 46 past and present kamakia aged 20 to 60, 21 had married foreigners, with the trend beginning 15–20 years ago and continuing up to the present. Only 3 of the men married Greeks, and a further 4 had permanent foreign girlfriends. The relationship based on kamaki (a performative act) can therefore be transformed and formalized, with the focus changing from man-man (with women as units of prestige) to man-woman. The bond also loses what is the essence of kamaki—its temporary nature—and the goal can no longer be conquest through sex. An ex-kamaki married to a foreign woman declared that, if he were young today, he would not be interested in foreign women, because Greek women are now able to have relationships with men before marriage, and there is no *need* for kamaki. Despite the variety of pressures to prohibit unmarried Greek women from being "sexually free," it is true that the necessity for men to choose between foreign female company and none at all is not nearly as absolute as it was 10–15 years ago. In this light, the choice by large numbers of men, not only to have sex with, but to marry foreign women, indicates a deliberate preference.

The foreign woman is seen as very different from the Greek woman, both by the kamakia and by Plataniotes in general. As already indicated, the xenes are assumed "better" in some ways (more sophisticated, freer, cleaner, and from richer, more advanced societies). In contrast, the Greek woman is said to be "difficult," "cunning" (*poniri*), and restricted within the house where she must guard her sexuality. Herzfeld has noted an analogy between the "Greeks' model of female identity—cunning illiteracy (*agrammatosini*), deprivation, and lack of self-control"—and the Greeks' view of their own cultural and political subordination to "Europe" (Herzfeld 1986a:221). When a kamaki approaches a woman who turns out to be Greek, he may return to his friends, and say disparagingly, "She smells of sheep" (*mirizei provatila*), an insulting reference to Greece as an agricultural society, and to its backward womenfolk.

Alternatively, the symbolic, moral, and physical inferiority of Greek women to men is transformed when they become spiritual and physical guardians of husband, home, and family (a transformation of their role as "Eves" to one better identified with "Mother of God"—the *Panayia* [du Boulay 1986:139–144]). Moreover, as women "of the house" (*tou spitiou*), they are also protectors of cleanliness, a preoccupation of many Greek housewives. The foreign woman may be seen as superior (sophisticated and clean), or inferior (promiscuous and dirty), as it suits the Greek. Nevertheless, she does not fit the image of the "sacred ideal of womanhood," which has the Panayia as its symbol (Dubisch 1983:195). She is not Orthodox and is not associated with the kamaki's notions of the family (perhaps particularly as she does not have one in Greece), the all-important household, or marriage. In the circumstances in which a Greek man meets a tourist woman, she is "of the road" (*tou dhromou*). This is a place without order or cleanliness and is associated with prostitutes: another category of women who are part of the male world of sexual freedom and lack of domesticity, outside the home. When a woman loses her reputation, according to Hirschon, she is associated with the road, "an area of dangerous forces and temptations" (Hirschon 1978:81).

The "nature-culture" debate in anthropology has indicated the danger of assuming a universal symbolic association of male with culture and female with nature, along with the culturally rooted history of these terms (see Bloch 1987). Alternatively, as open symbolic categories, between which a mediation can exist, the nature-culture polarity is conceptually useful. (For different angles on the debate, see Ortner and Whitehead 1981; MacCormack and Strathern 1980; Strathern 1981b; and Dubisch 1983, among many others.) In the case under discussion, an oscillation can be observed: the Greek woman is unsophisticated, and "behind" (of nature), compared to the superior foreign woman (of culture). Yet the Greek woman is able to transform into the creator and protector of the household and family (culture), whereas the foreigner remains outside in the undomesticated, "natural" world of the street and unrestricted sexuality. Similarly, the stress placed on the virginity of the Greek bride is another aspect of the purity developed by "cultural" morals and values. Therefore, when a Greek man marries a foreign woman, it is problematical for her to change from "Eve" to "Mother of God," and to become "of the house" (tou spitiou) in the Greek sense. It is surprising that the kamaki is able to suppress his earlier opinions concerning the inferior nature of foreign women and, presumably, to focus on her superiority. His behavior in marrying a woman who might previously have been labeled as a "whore" is a blatant contradiction, but one that is not normally perceived. It is a good example of the gap that may exist in society between what is expressed verbally and actual behavior.

The proverb "[Take] shoes from your own place, even if they are patched" (papoutsia apo ton topo sou, ki as einai balomena) is sometimes quoted by Plataniotes. It refers to the advantage of marrying someone "from your own place," because even if a local woman is not so good or attractive, you at least know what you are taking on. The foreign wives in Platanos (about thirty-five to forty in total, although no one is sure) are usually referred to as a marginal group, who rarely enter the town life fully, and who are dissatisfied with Greece and their marriages. In a number of marriages, it is recognized that the wife was well-educated or from "a good family," and certainly the majority appear to be middle-class and have not come from problematic or marginal backgrounds. Some Plataniotes question in astonishment what they see as these women's unbelievable choice in marrying "uneducated, stupid, and poor kamakia." Although some of the marriages are successful, a number of the wives themselves suggest that, in the unsuccessful cases, there had been a large degree of fantasy and illusion in the beginning. For these women, it had been a question of falling in love under romantic circumstances in a foreign country, perhaps with men who could not speak their language.

It was only later, often after the birth of children, that the problems and the reality became apparent.

There appears to be a contradiction in many marriages between Greek men and foreign women in Platanos. At one level, the man chooses a marriage that is "different" and marks himself out as being special. The foreign wife may be desirable because she brings a degree of prestige for the kamaki (at least in his eyes), as a foreign car might. It is also implied that he is not a common Greek, because he managed to "spear" and keep a (supposedly better) foreign woman. The kamaki declares by his marriage that he has opted out of the mainstream values of marriage in Greece, and he remains as marginal as when he was unmarried. He has achieved or maintained a form of escape, and his stranger-bride enables him to move further from roots that he may see as undesirable. A few kamakia emigrate and live in the countries of their wives, and others do this for a while and then return to Greece. However, the majority of married or ex-kamakia stay in Platanos and often retain their former social circle of friends, and they may well have family and relations nearby. Thus (unlike the foreign wife), the kamaki has a support network and does not become more marginalized by marrying a foreign woman.

A further contradiction exists because although the foreign woman is "better" because she is "different," in marriage she is expected to be in many ways "the same." To marry the "free" foreigner who "always leaves" is to capture her, and to close her in a house, where symbolically she does not belong. Thus, whereas a Greek woman is characterized as being cunning and as trying to find herself a husband, the foreign woman is the reverse, and the kamaki who marries his "victim" is continuing his conquest along a new line. The majority of kamakia-turned-husbands expect their wives to conform to the rules of Greek marriage, which include staying at home and being the domestic and children's caretaker, while the men go out. On the other hand, the foreign wife is unable to become a wife and domestic figure in the neighborhood or town with the ease and understanding of a Greek wife, and thus she cannot experience the advantages. She lacks not only the background and knowledge (and, in the most unfortunate cases, at least in the beginning, the language), but also the support network of the female relations and friends. She will always be "So-and-so's wife," and to the Greeks around her she will remain a stranger or foreigner (xeni) for the rest of her life in Greece.

Foreign wives may stop being the threatening, polluting, and profane "Eves" they were before marriage, but it is difficult for them to become "sacred" "Mothers of God." The women themselves face the unanticipated problems of the notorious mother-in-law, of small town mentality and gossip, of husbands' restrictions on their movements, and often a lack of the romance that attracted them in the first place to stay in Greece. Furthermore, the element of revenge that plays a part in the act of kamaki can develop within the marriage. Some men continue being kamakia after marriage, and this behavior is socially easier and morally less threatening to other Greeks (and perhaps to the kamaki himself) if their wives are from abroad. In these marriages, the kamaki has resorted to the old game, which is sometimes described (by kamakia and others) as resembling a habit that is difficult to give up. The wife is excluded from her husband's male companies (*parees*), just as she always was as a tourist, but she is trapped in a way that she was not when she was "of the road." The only threat she can wield is that she will return to her own country, and while this does occur occasionally in "mixed" marriages, divorce is not common. Time will tell for those who have married more recently. It should be added that some kamakia give up their pursuit of touristries and establish close-knit marriages based on a northern European pattern, with the married couple having a social life as well as a domestic one.

CONCLUSION

As with many subcultures and minorities, kamakia establish a morality and code of conduct of their own, at variance with that of the dominant society. A man may identify himself with this subculture and make kamaki, or he may enter it more fully and become a kamaki. Men in the latter category are often labeled for life, but in most cases the degree of activity declines with age. Tourist women provide an opportunity for uncommitted sex, they act as units of exchange to articulate male friends, and they are used to achieve a particular sort of reputation. Moreover, the women, who are only equivalent to prostitutes or pawns in a game, can offer a route to various forms of escape through their gifts of money or hospitality, or even through marriage.

Tourists use Greece as a sunny playground for escape and fantasy, and they have become one of the most dramatic forces of change in the modern Greek environment, economy, and society. Kamakia have created a game that, in turn, uses tourism as its playing field. Within the context of pursuing and having sex with tourist women, kamakia are able to demonstrate their feelings of male friendship, reciprocity, and competition. In addition, they are expressing antagonism, and taking symbolic revenge, as members of an underprivileged social and economic class and a disadvantaged European nation.

ACKNOWLEDGMENTS

The research for this paper was carried out in Greece between 1985 and 1987, with a grant from the E.S.R.C. Among the many people who helped me with the writing, I would especially like to thank Akis Papataxiarchis, Alan MacFarlane, Michael Jackson, and Dimitris Karonis. I am of course eternally grateful to the people of "Platanos."

Chapter 10

GENDER, SEXUALITY, AND THE PERSON
IN GREEK CULTURE

Peter Loizos and Evthymios Papataxiarchis

At the beginning of this book we questioned the ethnographer's fascination with the household-centered model of gender, and then we went on to analyze domestic ideology and place it within a wider framework of variations and transformations. In fact we opted to distinguish between dominant and alternative discourses of gender and to discuss gender practices in a range of contexts. We saw that the dominant conjugal model is premised on the necessity of men and women coming together in a formal, sanctified union which is the very basis of their respective personhoods. Alternative ideologies of gender seem to occur in contexts where the sexes are kept apart, and these inform notions of personhood between people of the same sex. In new and changing contexts, alternative forms of sexual behavior between men and women are also observed.

Caplan (1987a:16–17) invited us to consider the relation between sexuality and gender, assuming that these are treated as independent variables. Recent and very important historical research in Western societies has demonstrated that there is impressive variation in sexual ideology and practice (Cott 1978; Flandrin 1979; Stone 1979; Shorter 1982; Aries and Bejin 1985). "Having sex," i.e., coitus, cannot be assumed to be simply "innate" and "natural," nor is there a "correct" fit between physiological sex and sexuality. Sexuality is culturally constructed (Caplan 1987a): a set of ideas that depend on context and inform behavior which bears on gender identity. Here, however, lies one of the difficulties. Sexuality and gender often coalesce in people's minds, while the ethnographer has to treat them as separate sets of meaning. This is not a matter of determining which comes first but of establishing connections that are analytically meaningful.

Here we want to enlarge the scope of inquiry to contexts outside marriage (and the household) and raise the issue of whether sexuality, as a set of ideas or a type of behavior, provides the basis of gender in a plurality of contexts. To what extent is a person's sexual orientation a determinant factor of her or his gender identity?[1] This set of questions gives

---

[1] See the analysis of gender crossing in native North America and its comparison with

us the opportunity to review the ethnographic literature on the subject. Some tentative hypotheses emerge as the comparison between the contexts under consideration is pursued. And previously unexplored aspects of sexuality, particularly pre- and extramarital sexual behavior, will be added to the agenda of future research in Greece.

THE DOMESTIC MODEL OF GENDER AND SEXUALITY

It is within holy matrimony that most mature men and women may legitimately express their sexuality, for procreation is part of God's plan (du Boulay 1986), and we are reminded that Campbell (1965) presented central aspects of the Sarakatsani discourse on sexuality in a paper called "Honour and the Devil." The message was twofold. First, "honor" and the values of kin integrity and domestic welfare implicate men and women as *sexual* human beings.[2] Adequacy of sexual behavior is a vital social achievement in a stratified prestige system: it is index and symbol of a rank that ultimately relies on sexual contest between men (Pitt-Rivers 1977).[3] In fact, "sexuality is a form of social power" (Gilmore 1987b:4). Second, in this value system sexualities are presented in a dichotomous manner, as opposed moralities (Brandes 1981:219). Men's sexual drives are regarded as "natural," nobler and stronger than women's,[4] and symbolically identified with male genitals (Campbell 1964:269–270; Brandes 1981:230–231). Despite the overwhelming belief that sex is dirty, men's pursuit of it is symbolic proof that they can effectively make and guard their own and their family's reputations.

But women's sexuality aligns them with the devil, at least in terms of Old Testament and androcentric discourse.[5] Women are regarded as sen-

New Guinea practices by Whitehead (1981) for an application of the thesis that variation in sexuality rests on differences in gender construction ideology (83).

[2] Yet the degree to which they are implicated varies depending on economic specialization, social rank, and the relative stress on kinship. In the classical "honor and shame" communities, this suggests heavy dependencies between male and female sexualities (Peristiany 1965a; Pitt-Rivers 1977; Schneider 1971). In more sex-segregated societies and in low-class contexts, there is more room left for women to administer their own sexualities (Wikan 1984; Goddard 1987; Papataxiarchis 1988).

[3] Sexual politics are often symbolically enacted. The bullfight in Andalusia (Douglas 1984; Corbin and Corbin 1987:110) or animal-theft and card playing in Crete (Herzfeld 1985a) act metaphorically as sexual contests. They suggest domination, and therefore masculinity, through symbolic effeminization.

[4] The superiority of male over female sexuality could be linked to a parallel stratification of creative powers between the sexes. In some parts of Greece and Anatolia, we encounter a monogenetic theory that portrays men as seed givers who fertilize a female field (Delaney 1986; Papataxiarchis 1988). According to this image, men hold superior genetic powers.

[5] In this regard beliefs about witches (Pina-Cabral 1986:89–91) or demons and other supernatural beings (Stewart 1985:52–53) suggest the potential threat of female sexuality.

suous and weak and in effect a threat to male reputations. The values of concealment and particularly the sentiment of *dropi* (shame) apply to women whose sexuality, especially in a patrilocal context, is subject to control by the kin group. Yet women speaking of their sexuality are reported to insist that they "contain themselves" for a long time, and not to emphasize the ease with which they might be seduced, but rather the danger to them that the compromising intentions of men represent (Hirschon 1978:70). This variation is indicative of gender ideologies that are specific to different types of marriage.

Most of these themes have been widely explored in Greek and Mediterranean ethnography.[6] The point to be stressed here is that women are, to varying degrees, penalized for their sexual identity; and they are expected either to conceal it in an attitude of shame and gradually negate it, and/or channel an otherwise stigmatized and supposedly controllable desire toward legitimate procreation.[7] According to the conjugal model of gender, gender and kinship mix in the definition of the person, and in the same context the sexual identity of women is subordinated to their kinship role as mothers and guardians of the domestic order.

In any case, men and women are haunted by the cultural stress on, and the social value of, their respective sexualities.[8] Conceptually and morally the domestic model implicates them in a state of heavy sexual dependence, from which only women can redeem themselves. Women gradually relax from the moment they first give birth: motherhood morally protects their sexuality. Men, on the other hand, live in constant fear of being tainted by feminine attributes, an identification that results from losing control or entering a passive role (Brandes 1981; Herzfeld 1985a).

In the dominant conjugal gender model, there is an indissoluble link between women's sexuality and the "natural" task of legitimate procreation. This can be seen in the (largely unexplored) attitudes toward con-

---

[6] On the sexuality of Greek men and women from the perspective of married life, see Campbell (1964); du Boulay (1974); Hirschon (1978:67–76); Handman (1983:86–94, 119–123). On other southern European communities see Brandes (1981); Pina-Cabral (1986:82–124); Corbin and Corbin (1987:35–40); Goddard (1987:173–179). For Turkey, see Delaney (1987:41–43).

[7] Pouriotes think that for men sex is a physiological need perceived on equal footing with food or sleep. Women have no sexual needs, and only the prospect of procreation legitimizes sex in the eyes of women over the age of thirty-five (Handman 1983:87–88, 172). In Yerania women's power to control their sexual drives is stressed (Hirschon 1989:149). The close link of women's sexuality to procreation is also stressed in Andalusia (Corbin and Corbin 1987:35–36). For an opposite conception of women as having strong sexual appetites, see Pina-Cabral (1986:89).

[8] It is very interesting to note that in Pouri, sex is referred to as *doulia* (work), an activity that leaves no scope for pleasure (Handman 1983:87)

traception and abortion. Despite the fact that we lack baseline data on this issue and statistical evidence hardly exists, as ethnographers we have strong indications that in various settings abortion is employed as a contraception technique alternative to the more traditional coitus interruptus (Presvelou and Teperoglou 1976, 1980).[9] In contrast to the figures for other Western European societies, the extremely high rate of artificially disrupted pregnancies in Greece might even be termed an abortion syndrome.[10]

To approach this syndrome even provisionally we will have to place it into social context. First, it occurs in a climate of greater sexual permissiveness, amply testified to in current ethnographic work (Cowan, this volume; Papataxiarchis 1988). Sex before marriage becomes increasingly possible for both men and women and a necessary ingredient of courtship behavior. Second, it is linked to an atmosphere of demographic "conservatism" and lowered birth rates that prevails in postwar Greece and that has established the three- or four-member conjugal family as the norm (McNeill 1978:237).[11] Loizos was frequently given to understand by male informants that "the doctor said it would be dangerous for my wife to have another child," the statement being accompanied by a grin and a wink. Third, it is a partial outcome of public condemnation of illegitimacy and procreation outside marriage.

However, given all this, we must ask why women deal with the prospect of undesirable birth, not through contraconception, but only after pregnancy is a fait accompli. Female informants in Athens who had themselves had abortions maintain that "proper sex is natural sex." These women are against mechanical means of contraception that disrupt the tempo of the sexual act and the very "free" expression of sexuality, and they are skeptical of the application of chemical methods. Their views are compatible with the widespread "technique" of coitus interruptus, which

[9] The analysis of data from a 1972 survey in the metropolitan area of Athens has shown that "abortion is part of everyday life and experience" (Presvelou and Teperoglou 1980:340) and it is approved by more than half the women and men interviewed. This is a remarkably high rate of approval given that abortion was illegal, yet tolerated, at that time. Equally impressive are the results of the 1966–1967 "abortion survey" showing that abortion, practiced by 35 percent of the interviewed women, and withdrawal, practiced by 33 percent of them, were the two most popular methods of birth control (Valaoras, Polychronopoulou, and Trichopoulos 1969:40–41).

[10] An estimated 150,000 abortions per annum were performed in Greece in the late sixties (Valaoras, Polychronopoulou, and Trichopoulos 1969). The Greek feminist journal *Dine*, in an issue on abortions, makes an estimate of 300,000 abortions per annum in Greece during the seventies.

[11] Examples of extreme demographic conservatism are found in the countryside. Arnold (1982) reported on a Cypriot village where a single child per marriage had become the norm.

passes the responsibility of birth control to men (Papataxiarchis 1988; Pina-Cabral 1986:89).[12]

Our hypothesis is that the theory of "natural sex" reveals the tendency of many women to treat sex and conception as inseparable. From the women's point of view what makes sex "natural," pleasurable, and desirable is that it leaves the door to conception open. And therefore, the eventuality of an undesirable birth is left to be dealt with in the course of pregnancy.[13] Sexuality in itself, sealed off from the prospect of pregnancy by contraceptive devices, is seen as undesirable. This point needs to be further explored since it will provide us with key insights into Greek women's attitudes toward their bodies and their sexuality.

MEN'S VARIED SEXUALITIES

Context-specific variations are also encountered in images of male sexuality. As elsewhere in the Mediterranean (Brandes 1981:230–231, 237), the contrast is between the possessive sexuality of the family man, whose masculinity centers on the testicles, and the more expressive sexuality of the man of the coffee shop, whose symbolic masculinity conceptually derives from the heart and is of spiritual composition (Papataxiarchis, this volume). This second version is encountered in neolocal and matrilocal contexts and is linked to a vocabulary of motive organized around the notion of *kefi*. The coffee shop style of sexuality is more open: it is not committed by definition to procreative conjugality nor necessarily to sexual congress with women. Certain of its aspects are present in commensal encounters among men. Its expression can be self-centered—i.e., through masturbation—as well. In other words, the context of the coffee shop gives refuge to a concept of male sexuality wider than the hetero-

---

[12] The inhabitants of the southern Italian town of Montebruno prefer the condom and coitus interruptus (which they call "reverse gear"), yet women use the pill as well, if inconsistently. Doubts about the pill's effectiveness and safety are accompanied by its contradictory connotations of modernity, freedom, and female companionship, on the one hand, and of male impotence, female guilt, and the undermining of family values, on the other (Korovkin 1986). In the Basque provinces of France, the main contraceptive method is coitus interruptus. The pill and the coil are feared and only few women use diaphragms or have opted for sterilization (Ott 1981:203–204). The preference given to coitus interruptus suggests the emphasis on the man's capacity to control his orgasm (Pina-Cabral 1986:89). For Greece, see Handman (1983:120).

[13] This is where the theme of fertility could be introduced. Fertility is a test point of womanhood. Infertility is highly stigmatized and in the case of a childless marriage it is the woman who is thought of as principally responsible (see Handman 1983:127; Corbin and Corbin 1987:38). Therefore, a woman's place in society ultimately rests on her ability to biologically reproduce, and the proof of that is pregnancy. Marriage concludes and sanctions this prospect once it has been demonstrated. From this angle we can understand the widespread phenomenon of "pregnant marriages."

sexual conjugal norm. Despite their differences, both sets of ideas treat men's sexuality as natural.

So far we can locate two forms of sexual behavior that deviate from the heterosexual stress of conjugal ideology. The first is a male sexuality that is self-centered, the other, a sexuality directed toward a member of the same sex. To these we can add a third: heterosexuality that is motivated by kefi, that does not accord with the values of the household and is not compromised by any form of obligation. These forms of sexual behavior are conceptually recognized and to a certain degree accommodated in the orbit of the coffee shop.

Kano kefi means "I desire something" and suggests a mixture of the sexual and the nonsexual.[14] Kefi is the spirit of desire that derives from the heart. The object of the kefi-centered desire may be another person, an object, or a project. Kefi itself includes commensal friendships free of explicitly erotic content, as well as properly erotic heterosexual liaisons. The desire itself as well as its relational outcome is qualified by its emotional basis: it is spontaneous, it can be ephemeral, and it effectively transforms the real into the imagined. It is also very individualistic and resists its assignment to corporate goals or collective responsibilities (Papataxiarchis 1988, 1985).

Mature men, in the anticonjugal discourses of the coffee shop, can speak of *yinekes* ("women," not "wives") and seek their company as partners who would respond naturally and spontaneously to the imperatives of bodily expressiveness.[15] In such discourses a life can be imagined in which men and women come together for the natural pleasure of each other's company, and without the corporate demands of householding. Perhaps "living together" catches the essence of the Greek word *spitoma* for such an irregular union, but the passé American usage "shacking up" is closer to the Greek.

Women who are available as erotic partners, "just for pleasure," to the men of the coffee shop are strongly condemned by married women. They are bracketed with "women of the road." Prostitutes are morally denigrated since they deviate from the "natural" propensity of their sex, which is to seek sexual congress only for procreative purposes (and in the context of marriage).

The Greek popular word for masturbation is *malakia*. Despite its high profile in Greek popular speech, it has been hardly mentioned in ethnography. Men present themselves as having powerful "physical needs," yet in practice they must control these, since most of the women in their

[14] Kefi and the ability of men to give seed underlie men's special creative powers and allow for self-motivation and autonomy. In transcending their domestic identities women can also be agents of kefi. Also see Caraveli (1982, 1985).

[15] Yet we should also note that in other contexts *yineka* means wife.

social universe are, of course, the wives, sisters, and daughters of other men, men whose self-respect enjoins them to "protect" these women from seduction. Yet when men discourse upon their own sexuality, they do not emphasize their self-control; rather, images of "natural drives" and an idiom of the positive virtues of sexual expressiveness dominate their speech. *Malakas* is probably the most widely used term of reference or address in male contexts. Young unmarried men, but often married men as well, greet each other in a joking bittersweet manner by the term *malakas*, which implies consciousness of a common predicament. It probably suggests the dangers of any attempt to act out sexuality either with unmarried women or with other men. Masturbation, as self-expression, is a kind of safety valve for what are perceived as the "natural" forces of men's sexuality.

The mentioning of masturbation further suggests male fraternity and equality at the lower, yet honorable, levels of male humanity. It involves men who, despite the fact that they lack proper erotic partners, do not give up their masculine right to desire in the holistic way that kefi dictates and by necessity opt for a minimalist solution. It is doubtful, however, that masturbation's primary meaning is to emphasize a functioning penis, nor do we have evidence of it performed collectively and in a sort of contest (Gilmore 1987b:133).

The practice of masturbation is circumscribed by more general ideas about men's sexual behavior. Semen, as a life-giving substance, should be spent carefully. Men are aware of women's (corroding) power to consume their masculinities through excessive sexual demands. Even more, the mindless nonfertile loss of semen at masturbation puts masculinity at risk (see also Brandes 1981:226). Boys are warned that masturbation causes mental illness, an association which can be traced to Victorian medical ideology (Caplan 1987a:4; 1987b:286–289).[16]

Many ethnographers of the Mediterranean have spotted an "exaggerated horror at homosexuality" (Gilmore 1987b:12), which is seen as involving an "active" or supermasculine man with a "passive" or "woman-like" one (Campbell 1964; Brandes 1981:233).[17] As Caplan (1987a:2) notices, nonconformity to heterosexual norms posits a threat to the view that sex is innate. This hardly explains the moral stigma attached to the *poushtis* (passive homosexual) in the Greek context: he is strongly denigrated as someone who fundamentally lacks full humanity, and his moral

---

[16] For a more ambivalent attitude toward the spending of semen as both good for men's health and an acceleration of the course to impotence, see Pina-Cabral (1986:94).

[17] This sharply contrasts with ethnographic evidence from New Guinea according to which the ritualized practice of homosexuality confirms masculinity to both partners (Herdt 1981). Notice here Currier's (1974:174) remark on the occurrence of premarital male homosexuality.

weakness exposes him to all sorts of evil dispositions (du Boulay 1974:105; Herzfeld 1985a:77). *Poushtis* comes to be a synonym for liar or thief, a man without dignity, and it strongly contrasts with the characterization of the man who adopts the "male" role and who may claim a "supermale" reputation, much as he might if he consorted with a prostitute.

Linked to exaggerated displays of masculine identity (machismo), the hierarchical version of homosexuality can be approached in terms of psychological theories that stress gender ambivalence in men (Gilmore 1987b) and unresolved bisexuality (Gilmore and Gilmore 1979), or in terms of more sociologically minded hypotheses that focus on men's weak position in socioeconomic status (Driessen 1983), or even vis-à-vis women (Brandes 1981:235). However satisfactory these approaches may be, they overlook the fact that, as in the Greek coffee shop, masculinity is a moral category. The poushtis lacks the natural propensity of his sex toward kefi; in effect, he is without a core attribute of personhood that would otherwise place him in normative equality to male consociates. He represents a sexual transformation with heavily negative moral implications.

The hierarchical content of homosexuality strongly contradicts the code of moral equality in the coffee shop. If, from the perspective of normative egalitarianism, masturbation is a legitimate option and an effective outlet of male sexuality, homosexuality is totally undesirable since it implies a fundamental state of dependence and subordination to fellow men.[18]

WOMEN'S SEXUALITY IN TRANSFORMATIONAL CONTEXTS

When we turn to women's alternative forms of sexuality, we find a striking contrast with men. First, while men conceptually, and sometimes in practice, engage in forms of sexual expression other than "normal" heterosexuality, such alternatives seem to be unacknowledged in concept and unattained in practice among women. Second, many men seem to have their first sexual experience before marriage and outside the household, under the influence of coffee shop norms. Conjugal heterosexuality is a phase that concludes a process of sexual maturation which involves sexual self-expression, a symbolic play with the prospect of homosexuality, and forms of heterosexuality that lack the commitment of marriage. Women, on the other hand, at first sight seem to realize their sexualities in the prospect and course of marriage and in the context of households. Their sexual expression appears to be largely framed by the domestic

[18] Hirschon (1978:67) suggests that in Greece masturbation and homosexuality are on equal footing, as morally denigrating deviations from the heterosexual norm.

imagery of gender. Let us consider the accuracy of these impressions in the light of recent ethnography and certain of the contributions in this volume.

Women do not have a sexual term of address, in the way that boys greet each other with *malaka*, because they are not thought to have the same sort of "nature" and "physiological" problems. Indeed, they commonly address each other as *kori* (daughter, maiden), which suggests a subordinate kinship status. But the contrast between men and women runs still deeper, for we are aware of no commonly used term to suggest the possibility of sexual attraction between women in rural Greece. Not only is there no female counterpart to the poushtis, but there is no common term for a woman who would wish to take a "male" role, either. Robinette Kennedy (1986:135) reports specifically that in fieldwork which focused on women's friendships, she found no "adult female homosexuality."[19] It is as if the linking of female sexuality to fertility is so powerful that there can be no perceived need for women to "express" sexuality in contexts which cannot lead to procreation. Since women are to be seen embracing each other in friendship and mutual support, we suggest that quite simply the possibility of sexual love between rural Greek women is "unknown" in the sense of unconceptualized, and so unrecognized. Sexual practices that may occur are in some sense unseen, or unperceived (Sheena Crawford, personal communication). None of this holds good, we must stress, for the larger cities, where lesbian identities are to be seen.

These assumptions, however, are subject to change in certain transformational contexts that include systematic adultery, intercultural courtship leading to ethnically mixed marriages, and intersex friendships that are based outside the house and that leave room for sex without procreation.

Papataxiarchis (1988:116–117) reports a form of adultery that usually involves married women—who, for various reasons but primarily because their husbands stay away from the village for long periods of time, are not sexually satisfied—and unmarried men. These illicit sexual liaisons take place in the "wild" or in the nearby town, and they are often known and discussed. The involved women are treated with sympathy, mainly by men, if it is known that the husbands are not for various reasons doing their sexual duty.[20]

---

[19] Handman (1983:122) notices as well that affection and bodily intimacy among women do not develop into open female homosexuality. Also see Corbin and Corbin (1987:39).

[20] In contrast to other Mediterranean communities, the husband is not stigmatized and ridiculed as a cuckold (*keratas*) as long as his sexual potency is not brought in question. Also see Handman (1983:167–168). We should note, here, the existence of an urban pattern of adultery that distinguishes between the *sizigos* (spouse) or *kira* and the *aisthema*, meaning

Adultery suggests an attitude of negotiating sex between male and female conjugal partners who are both recognized as sexually active human beings, dealing with their respective sexualities and needs in a balanced exchange (see Hirschon 1978:67; Pina-Cabral 1986:89).[21] Women's sexual activity outside marriage is also manifested in sex during courtship and the frequent occurrence of pregnant marriages. The female protagonists of adultery are usually outsiders who have no kin in the community. The behavior of *xenes* (outsiders) is less circumscribed by kinship norms, yet their greater freedom makes them vulnerable to gossip and moral criticism by their insider counterparts.[22]

Zinovieff discusses in this volume the "hunting" idiom in courtship. The erotic partners of the *kamaki*, the victims who sometimes turn into conjugal partners, are tourists who usually come from northern Europe. These outsiders are ready to participate in a "game" that local women find distasteful and unpleasant. The sexual attitudes of female tourists are not explored, although it is implied that what they seek from their male hosts is sex and pleasant company. From the men's point of view, these women are poor victims of masculine competence and cunning. They are equivalent to "women of the road," a characterization that accords with local women's view and places them at the bottom of a hierarchy of reputations. Marriage, when that interethnic courtship is successful, merges opposed definitions: men want to pursue the extreme intersexual hierarchy of "hunting" within marriage, while their foreign counterparts envisage a more balanced companionship that fits the "trapping" idiom in courtship (Brandes 1981:224).[23] Yet marriage hardly opens the door to approval and local participation for the xenes. The female tourist turned local wife is limited in her role as agent of "Western" conceptions about self, sex, and marriage: with women of the same origins she shares a state of disillusion (Zinovieff, personal communication).

In both extramarital sex and interethnic courtship, women enter erotic partnerships with men who act out their coffee shop sexualities: in effect

---

"emotion" and referring to the mistress, usually the permanent recipient of male sexual desire. These relationships are conceptually acknowledged in discourse (stories, songs, jokes, movies) and are positively received since they combine a double stress on the permanence of marriage and male sexuality.

[21] For the general condemnation of unproductive sex, see Corbin and Corbin (1987:37–38).

[22] On the frequent occurrence of premarital pregnancies, see Handman (1983); Pina-Cabral (1986:53, 57). Village adultery occurs in a climate of greater sexual permissiveness. Sex before marriage is tolerated for women, and reference to chastity has a rhetorical value (Herzfeld 1983). On the transformation of female chastity codes, see Giovannini (1981:70–72); also Goddard (1987:175–176).

[23] Premarital sex is an essential ingredient of the "trapping" strategies in female courtship (Herzfeld 1983:171).

these women bear a sexuality void of kinship role and enter these relationships as yinekes. Yet their ability to pursue sex for pleasure and not for procreation seems to be dependent on their otherness vis-à-vis the moral codes of local domesticity. From the local women's point of view, their sexual attitudes symbolize the very immorality of the outside world and confirm the local assumption that moral standards are preserved only in the locality. These deviant attitudes can hardly put their mark on mainstream sexual behavior: they lack institutional space and they symbolically remain unacknowledged, of little influence on the insiders.

This is not the case with the attitudes of intersexual friendship that Cowan reports as occurring in the context of the *kafeteria*, an institution gradually spreading from the big cities to the smaller towns. The kafeteria opens the scope of the coffee shop to young, mostly unmarried women and men for purposes of leisure, and leisure connotes availability of sex in itself and not within the framework of marriage.

As Cowan vividly demonstrates, using the medium of "local voices," the kafeteria is viewed in contradictory terms: as a place where men's predatory sexuality puts the women, whose aggressive pursuit of sex brought them there, into danger; or as an institution in which a woman can have a pleasurable time and be an *anthropos*, a fully human being. There is no doubt that this institution provides the terrain for organized courtship. It promotes definitions of female personhood that are thought of as "Western" in origins and primarily focus on the body. Women are fully acknowledged as autonomous human beings; they bear their distinctive, active sexual desires, which are the very core of their independence from the standards of domesticity. The attitudes of the young attendants at the kafeteria come close to the feminist discourse of the cities and to images of women as "whole persons," in control of their sexuality (and their bodies).

Institutional spaces such as the kafeteria, the urban *zacharoplastio* (sweetshop), and the *spiti ton yinekon* (women's club) emerged in the urban centers after 1974 to promote undomesticated expressions of women's sexuality, which focus on the person, her body, and not on the *domus*. In these transformational contexts, women defend versions of their personhood that are total, i.e., that include their sexuality as an independent variable instead of concealing it or merging it within procreation.

SEXUALITY, GENDER, AND THE PERSON

However, besides the points of contrast, some of the contributions in this volume suggest certain points of similarity in the ways female and male sexualities are articulated outside marriage. These similarities emerge when men or women engage in relations with members of the same sex.

What has become evident so far is that convent and coffee shop are loci of ideas that are openly juxtaposed to or transcend domestic kinship. The theme that remains to be considered is how sexuality and gender are implicated in personhood when kinship is not involved. The approach to this subject is through the metaphor of body versus spirit opposition.

This is the core of Iossifides's contribution. She argues that nuns adopt idioms of kinship in order to effectively transcend it. Marriage with Christ marks membership in the convent, as marriage with Saint Constantine symbolizes entry into the *anastenaria* cult group (Danforth, this volume). These usages certainly confirm conjugality as a powerful idiom of structural relatedness. Yet what characterizes these "unions" is their spiritual content. The practical denial of biological sexuality in the convent leads to celibacy. Further, female spiritual hypergamy aims to transcend secular marriage in the first case, to correct the content of affinal relations in the anastenaria case.

Monastic ideology requires that the salvation of the soul be achieved through the elevation of the body into a state of spiritual purity. Women can reach this pure state by "the love of Christ" that assists them in transcending bodily functions and sexual desires and negates the core symbol of the body. Iossifides captures this point in the local image of salvation as a pyramid: at the base are disciplined Christians, then come the virgins, and the angels and saints who bear a "spiritual body" appear at the top. And the ranking is ordered with precise numbers.

In coffee shop ideology, on the other hand, a dimension of spirituality is achieved not in opposition to the (biological) body but by means of it.[24] The spirit of commensal joy and desire does not negate the materiality of the body but includes it and dominates it. Kefi elevates the body in this world. This is captured in the image of the big man who dances solo. The supreme male dancer is likened to a worldly angel (Papataxiarchis 1985). His spirited body seems to represent the achievement of immense pleasure and joy, a state of salvation in this world, one could say.

This is not to say that monastic and coffee shop spiritualities are the same, nor do we mean to imply that they relate similarly to sexuality. The spirit of commensality is heavily gendered and acknowledges male sexuality through bodily expression other than sex. The spirit of removal from this world, on the other hand, transcends all requirements of the body, including sexuality. Indeed, monastic spirituality seems to be androgynous and incompatible with sexual expression.

However, the comparative stress on the dimensions of spirituality in convent and coffee shop is indicative of articulations of the self outside

---

[24] On the "spiritual qualities" of those who can convey true kefi in ritual celebration, see Caraveli (1985:263–265).

marriage. Flesh and the concerns of the body unite members of opposite sexes in heterosexual encounters that usually aim at procreation. These bonds of heterosexuality should be sanctified and mixed with domestic kinship. On the other hand, spirit and the concerns of the soul unite members of the same sex either in sisterhood in Christ or in friendships of the heart. To put it another way, in convent and coffee shop, people realize a sense of the self as moral entities through their spiritual attributes: love that is not sexually consummated and does not lead to biological kinship, on the one hand; kefi that does not necessarily lead into sexual congress, on the other.[25] And although admittedly in the contexts of convent and coffee shop, sexuality and gender relate differently to the moral person, both are still informed by the most inclusive concept, desire. In both social contexts gender is not shaped by a single pattern of sexuality but by codes of conduct that either confirm, or deny, desire.

To summarize: From the households' point of view, women need men and men need women in order to become persons. Heterosexuality is the link, yet one that in adultery threatens the very stability and solidarity of its conjugal outcome. Heterosexual behavior has to be circumscribed by the rule of domestic kinship, and, as we saw in the introduction, must adopt kinship as a symbol of personhood. Men, however, do not need women in order to achieve an identity that is meaningful in the coffee shop; nor do women need men in order to reach a state of spirituality. In both contexts personhood can be attained through exchanges that involve members of the same sex, made possible by encompassing notions of the spiritual. Yet when the cultural meaning of gender is linked to notions of spirituality, it may either stand in open opposition to domestic kinship or undermine the meaning of biological kinship.

It is worth noting that we have analyzed gender models that are either silent (convent) or ambivalent (coffee shop) on sexuality. Caplan (1987a:23) argues that ambivalent attitudes toward sexuality relate to flesh/spirit dichotomies which occur in societies of Eurasia. Our analysis so far confirms her view and further suggests that these linkages are more prominent in contexts where persons of the same sex are involved. The next step is to extend our investigations to universal religions and legal systems, not to say ethnicity (Ross and Rapp 1981).[26] In particular, we should have a closer look at definitions of sexuality and gender in the religious ideologies that historically shaped modern Greek culture, and

---

[25] Abstention from sex seems to be accepted if it is seen as the price of pursuing personal autonomy. On the values of male chastity, see Campbell (1964:280).

[26] For an argument that links state nationalism and sexuality, see Herzfeld (1987). Herzfeld (1987:11) argues that "the extreme sexual pudicity of rural folk is a phenomenon of the nineteenth century or not much before" and it is linked to the importation of Great Power models of state.

we should include in our investigations various strands of Christian and Islamic thought. The apparent rooting of the notions of *agapi* (of Christ) and kefi in both Orthodox Christian and Islamic mystical discourse is quite suggestive in this case.[27]

In this essay we have shown that there are forms of male and female sexuality other than the dominant ones in traditional and transformational contexts. Definitions of personhood that are centered upon the body or the spirit effect a challenge to the domestic model of gender. Ethnographic research will be needed to provide continuing close analysis of developments that are radically transforming the cultural map of gender in Greece.

ACKNOWLEDGMENTS

We wish to thank Alexandra Bakalaki, Marie-Elisabeth Handman, Roger Just, Maria Phylaktou, and Sofka Zinovieff for commenting on this essay.

[27] A number of scholars invite us to consider historically the formative influence of universalizing states and religions on sexuality and sexual behavior (see Davis 1987; Delaney 1987). For example, Gilmore (1983) sees in Marianism and Christian ideas on the sanctity of Mary a major factor to account for the contrast between Muslim and Latin Mediterranean views of sexuality.

CONTRIBUTORS

JANE K. COWAN, Ph.D. Indiana, currently teaches in the Department of Sociology and Anthropology, University College, Swansea.

LORING M. DANFORTH, Ph.D. Princeton, is Professor of Anthropology at Bates College, Maine.

JILL DUBISCH, Ph.D. Chicago, is Professor of Anthropology at the University of North Carolina.

JULIET DU BOULAY, Diploma in Social Anthropology, Oxford, is an Honorary Research Fellow of Edinburgh University.

MICHAEL HERZFELD, D.Phil. Oxford, D.Litt. Birmingham, is Professor of Anthropology at Indiana University.

A. MARINA IOSSIFIDES, Ph.D. London (L.S.E.) is Lecturer Designate in Social Anthropology at the University of the Aegean, Mytilene.

ROGER JUST, Ph.D. Oxford, is Senior Lecturer in Modern Greek at Melbourne University.

PETER LOIZOS, Ph.D. London (L.S.E.) is Senior Lecturer in Anthropology at the London School of Economics.

EVTHYMIOS PAPATAXIARCHIS, Ph.D. London (L.S.E.) is Assistant Professor Designate in Social Anthropology at the University of the Aegean, Mytilene.

SOFKA ZINOVIEFF, Ph.D. Cambridge, is working for the *Independent* newspaper, in London.

LITERATURE CITED

Abu-Lughod, J.
   1987 Bedouin Blues. Natural History 96(7):24–33.
Abu-Lughod, L.
   1986 Veiled Sentiments: Honor and Poetry in a Bedouin Society. Berkeley: University of California Press.
Aceves, J. B.
   1971 Social Change in a Spanish Village. Cambridge, Mass: Schenkman Publishing Co.
Alexakis, E. P.
   1980 Ta Yeni Ke i Ikoyenia stin Paradhosiaki Kinonia tis Manis. Athens.
Alexiou, M.
   1974 The Ritual Lament in Greek Tradition. Cambridge: Cambridge University Press.
   1983 Sons, Wives and Mothers: Reality and Fantasy in Some Modern Greek Ballads. Journal of Modern Greek Studies 1:73–111.
   1987 Review of Dubisch 1986a. To appear in Yearbook of Modern Greek Studies 3.
Allen, P.
   1976 Aspida: A Depopulated Maniat Community. *In* Dimen and Friedl 1976:168–198.
Anderson, B.
   1983 Imagined Communities: Reflections on the Origin and Spread of Nationalism. London: Verso.
Andromedas, J. N.
   1962 The Inner Maniat Community Type. Ph.D. diss., Columbia University.
Ardener, E.
   1971 Introductory Essay: Social Anthropology and Language. *In* Social Anthropology and Language, E. Ardener, ed., pp. ix–cii. ASA Monographs, 11. London: Tavistock.
   1975 Belief and the Problem of Women. *In* Perceiving Women, S. Ardener, ed., pp. 1–27. London: Malaby Press.
Ardener, S., ed.
   1978 Defining Females: The Nature of Women in Society. London: Croom Helm.
   1981 Women and Space: Ground Rules and Social Maps. London: Croom Helm.
Aries, P., and A. Bejin, eds.
   1985 Western Sexuality: Practice and Precept in Past and Present Times. Oxford: Blackwell.

Arnold, L. E.
   1982 Krasi: A Grape-growing Village in Southwestern Cyprus. Ph.D. thesis,
   University of Manchester.
Aschenbrenner, S.
   1976 Karpofora: Reluctant Farmers on a Fertile Land. *In* Dimen and Friedl
   1976:207–221.
Basso, K. H.
   1970 "To Give up on Words": Silence in Western Apache Culture. Southwestern Journal of Anthropology 26:213–230.
   1979 Portraits of "The Whiteman": Linguistic Play and Cultural Symbols
   among the Western Apache. Cambridge: Cambridge University Press.
Beaton, R. M.
   1980 Folk Poetry of Modern Greece. Cambridge: Cambridge University
   Press.
Beidelman, J. P.
   1980 The Moral Imagination of the Kaguru: Some Thoughts on Tricksters,
   Translation and Comparative Analysis. American Ethnologist 7(1):27–42.
Bennett, D. O.
   1989 Class in a Greek Village. *In* The Social Economy of Consumption, H. J.
   Rutz and B. S. Orlove, eds., pp. 177–209. Monographs in Economic Anthropology, no. 6. Lanham, Md.: University Press of America for the Society for
   Economic Anthropology.
Beopoulou, J.
   1987 Trajets du Patrimoine dans une Société Maritime Grecque: Lieux Mas-
   culins et Féminins dans l'Acquisition et la Circulation des Biens. *In* Femmes
   et Patrimoine dans les Sociétés Rurales de l'Europe Méditerranéenne. Mar-
   seilles: CNRS.
Bernard, H. R.
   1976 Kalymnos: The Island of the Sponge Fishermen. *In* Dimen and Friedl
   1976:291–307.
Bettenson, H., ed.
   1967 Documents of the Christian Church. London: Oxford University Press.
Bialor, P.
   1976 The Northwestern Corner of the Peloponnesos: Mavrikion and Its Region. *In* Dimen and Friedl 1976:222–235.
Bloch, M.
   1987 Descent and Sources of Contradiction in Representations of Women and
   Kinship. *In* Gender and Kinship: Essays toward a Unified Analysis, J. F.
   Collier and S. J. Yanagisako, eds., pp. 324–337. Stanford: Stanford Univer-
   sity Press.
Bloch, M., and J. H. Bloch, eds.
   1981 Women and the Dialectics of Nature in Eighteenth-Century French
   Thought. *In* MacCormack and Strathern 1980:25–41.
Bloch, M., and J. Parry
   1982 Death and the Regeneration of Life. Cambridge: Cambridge University
   Press.

Bottomley, G.
    1986 A World Divided? Studies of Gender Relations in Modern Greece. Mankind 16:181–189.
Bourdieu, P.
    1977 Outline of a Theory of Practice. Translated by Richard Nice. Cambridge: Cambridge University Press.
Brandes, S.
    1973 Social Structure and Interpersonal Relations in Navanogal (Spain). American Anthropologist 75:750–765.
    1979 Drinking Patterns and Alcohol Control in a Castilian Mountain Village. Anthropology 3:1–16.
    1980 Metaphors of Masculinity: Sex and Status in Andalusian Folklore. Philadelphia: University of Pennsylvania Press.
    1981 Like Wounded Stags: Male Sexual Ideology in an Andalusian Town. In Ortner and Whitehead 1981:216–239.
Brenneis, D.
    1987 Performing Passions: Aesthetics and Politics in an Occasionally Egalitarian Community. American Ethnologist 14:236–250.
Brettell, C. B.
    1985 Male Migrants and Unwed Mothers: Illegitimacy in a Northwestern Portuguese Parish. Anthropology 9:87–110.
Bruner, E. M., and J. P. Kelso
    1980 Gender Differences in Graffiti: A Semiotic Perspective. Women's Studies International Quarterly 3:239–252.
Campbell, J. K.
    1963 The Kindred in a Greek Mountain Community. In Mediterranean Countrymen: Essays in the Social Anthropology of the Mediterranean, J. Pitt-Rivers, ed., pp. 73–96. Paris: Mouton.
    1964 Honour, Family and Patronage: A Study of Institutions and Moral Values in a Greek Mountain Community. Oxford: Clarendon Press.
    1965 Honour and the Devil. In Honour and Shame: The Values of Mediterranean Society, J. Peristiany, ed., pp. 139–170. London: Weidenfeld and Nicholson.
Caplan, P.
    1987a Introduction. In The Cultural Construction of Sexuality, P. Caplan, ed., pp. 1–30. London: Tavistock.
    1987b Celibacy as a Solution? Mahatma Gandhi and Brahmacharya. In The Cultural Construction of Sexuality, P. Caplan, ed., pp. 271–295. London: Tavistock.
Caraveli, A.
    1982 The Song Beyond the Song: Aesthetics and Social Interaction in Greek Folksong. Journal of American Folklore 95:129–158.
    1985 The Symbolic Village: Community Born in Performance. Journal of American Folklore 98:259–286.
    1986 The Bitter Wounding: The Lament as Social Protest in Rural Greece. In Dubisch 1986a:169–194.

Carrithers, M., S. Collins, and S. Lukes, eds.
  1985 The Category of the Person: Anthropology, Philosophy, History. Cambridge: Cambridge University Press.
Casselberry, S. E., and N. Valavanes
  1976 "Matrilocal" Greek Peasants and a Reconsideration of Residence Terminology. American Ethnologist 3(2):215–226.
Cesara, M.
  1982 Reflections of a Woman Anthropologist: No Hiding Place. London: Academic Press.
Chock, P. P.
  1987 The Irony of Stereotypes: Toward an Anthropology of Ethnicity. Cultural Anthropology 2:347–368.
Christian, W.
  1972 Person and God in a Spanish Valley. New York: Seminar Press.
  1981 Local Religion in Sixteenth-Century Spain. Princeton: Princeton University Press.
  1984 Religious Apparitions and the Cold War in Southern Europe. In Religion, Power and Protest in Local Communities, E. Wolf, ed., pp. 239–266. Berlin: Mouton.
Clark, M. H.
  1982 Variations on Themes of Male and Female: Reflections on Gender Bias in Fieldwork in Rural Greece. Women's Studies 10:117–133.
Clifford, J.
  1986 Introduction: Partial Truths. In Clifford and Marcus 1986:1–26.
Clifford, J., and G. E. Marcus, eds.
  1986 Writing Culture: The Poetics and Politics of Ethnography. Berkeley: University of California Press.
Cohen, E.
  1977 Arab Boys and Tourist Girls in a Mixed Jewish-Arab Community. Oxford: Clarendon Press.
Collier, J. F., and S. J. Yanagisako, eds.
  1987 Introduction. In Gender and Kinship: Essays Toward a Unified Analysis, J. F. Collier and S. J. Yanagisako, eds., pp. 1–13. Stanford: Stanford University Press.
Connolly, W.
  1974 The Terms of Political Discourse. Oxford: Martin Robertson.
Constantinides, P.
  1977 Ill at Ease and Sick at Heart: Symbolic Behaviour in a Sudanese Healing Cult. In Symbols and Sentiments: Cross-Cultural Studies in Symbolism, I. Lewis, ed., pp. 61–84. London: Academic Press.
Corbin, J. R., and M. P. Corbin.
  1987 Urbane Thought: Culture and Class in an Andalusian City. Aldershot: Gower.
Cott, N. F.
  1978 Passionlessness: An Interpretation of Victorian Sexual Ideology, 1790–1850. Signs 4:219–236.

Couroucli, M.
1985 Les Oliviers du Lignage. Paris: Maisonneuve et Larose.

Cowan, J. K.
1988 Embodiments: The Social Construction of Gender in Dance Events in a Northern Greek Town. Ph.D. diss., Indiana University. Forthcoming (1990) as Dance and the Body Politic in Northern Greece. Princeton: Princeton University Press.

Crapanzano, V.
1973 The Hamadsha: A Study in Moroccan Ethnopsychiatry. Berkeley. University of California Press.

Culler, J.
1983 On Deconstruction: Theory and Criticism after Structuralism. Ithaca: Cornell University Press.

Currier, R. L.
1974 Themes of Interaction in an Aegean Island Village. Ph.D. diss., University of California.
1976 Social Interaction and Social Structure in a Greek Island Village. In Dimen and Friedl 1976:308–313.

Danforth, L. M.
1983 Power through Submission in the Anastenaria. Journal of Modern Greek Studies 1(1):203–223.
1989 Firewalking and Religious Healing: The Anastenaria of Greece and the American Firewalking Movement. Princeton: Princeton University Press.

Danforth, L. M., and A. Tsiaras
1982 Death Rituals of Rural Greece. Princeton: Princeton University Press.

Davis, J.
1964 Passatella: An Economic Game. The British Journal of Sociology 15:191–207.
1977 People of the Mediterranean: An Essay in Comparative Social Anthropology. London: Routledge and Kegan Paul.
1987a Libyan Politics: Tribe and Revolution. London: I. B. Tauris.
1987b Family and State in the Mediterranean. In Honor and Shame and the Unity of the Mediterranean, D. Gilmore, ed., pp. 22–34. A special publication of the American Anthropological Association, no. 22.

Delaney, C.
1986 The Meaning of Paternity and the Virgin Birth Debate. Man (n.s.) 21:494–513.
1987 Seeds of Honor, Fields of Shame. In Honor and Shame and the Unity of the Mediterranean, D. Gilmore, ed., pp. 35–48. A special publication of the American Anthropological Association, no. 22.

di Leonardo, M.
1987 The Female World of Cards and Holidays: Women, Family and the Work of Kinship. Signs 12(3):440–453.

Dimen, M.
1986 Servants and Sentries: Women, Power, and Social Reproduction in Kriovrisi. In Dubisch 1986a:53–67.

Dimen, M., and E. Friedl, eds.

1976 Regional Variation in Modern Greece and Cyprus: Toward a Perspective on the Ethnography of Greece, 268:1–465. New York: Annals of the New York Academy of Sciences.

Douglas, C.

1984 Toro Muerto, Vaca Es: An Interpretation of the Spanish Bullfight. American Ethnologist 11:242–258.

Douglas, M.

1966 Purity and Danger: An Analysis of Concepts of Pollution and Taboo. London: Routledge and Kegan Paul.

Drakontaeidis, F. D.

1986 Chtapodhia kai Kamakia. Proti, 11 September. Athens.

Driessen, H.

1983 Male Sociability and Rituals of Masculinity in Rural Andalusia. Anthropological Quarterly 56(3):125–133.

Dubisch, J.

1972 The Open Community: Migration from a Greek Island Village. Ph.D. diss., University of Chicago.

1974 The Domestic Power of Women in a Greek Island Village. Studies in European Society 1(1):23–33.

1976 The Ethnography of the Islands: Tinos. In Dimen and Friedl 1976:314–327.

1983 Greek Women: Sacred or Profane. Journal of Modern Greek Studies 1(1):185–202.

1986a Gender and Power in Rural Greece. Ed. Princeton: Princeton University Press.

1986b Introduction. In Dubisch 1986a:3–41.

1986c Culture Enters through the Kitchen: Women, Food, and Social Boundaries in Rural Greece. In Dubisch 1986a:195–214.

1987 What Mother Is Crying: Suffering and the "Poetics of Womanhood" in Greece. Paper presented at the Annual Meeting of the American Ethnological Society, San Antonio, Texas.

1988 Golden Apples and Silver Ships: An Interpretative Approach to a Greek Holy Shrine. Journal of Modern Greek Studies. Forthcoming.

1989 Death and Social Change in Greece, J. Dubisch and L. Taylor, eds. Special Issue of Anthropological Quarterly 62(4):189–200 on the Uses of Death in Europe.

1990 Pilgrimage and Popular Religion at a Greek Holy Shrine. In Religious Orthodoxy and Popular Faith in European Society, E. Badone, ed. Princeton: Princeton University Press. Forthcoming.

du Boulay, J.

1974 Portrait of a Greek Mountain Village. Oxford: Clarendon Press.

1976 Lies, Mockery and Family Integrity. In Mediterranean Family Structures, J. G. Peristiany, ed., pp. 389–406. Cambridge: Cambridge University Press.

1982 The Greek Vampire: A Study of Cyclic Symbolism in Marriage and Death. Man (n.s.) 17:219–238.

1983 The Meaning of Dowry: Changing Values in Rural Greece. Journal of Modern Greek Studies 1:243–270.

1984 The Blood: Symbolic Relationships between Descent, Marriage, Incest Prohibitions and Spiritual Kinship in Greece. Man (n.s.) 19:533–556.

1986 Women—Images of Their Nature and Destiny in Rural Greece. In Dubisch 1986a:139–168.

EOT (National Tourism Organization of Greece)

1985 Tourismos '85. Athens: EOT Publications.

Felson-Rubin, N.

1987 Penelope's Perspective: Character from Plot. In Homer: Beyond Oral Poetry—Recent Trends in Homeric Interpretation, J. M. Bremer, I.J.F. de Jong, and J. Kalff, eds., pp. 61–83. Amsterdam: B. R. Gruner.

Fernandez, J. W.

1986 Persuasions and Performances. Bloomington: Indiana University Press.

Firth, R., J. Hubert, and A. Forge

1969 Families and Their Relatives: Kinship in a Middle-Class Sector of London. London: Routledge and Kegan Paul.

Flandrin, J.-L.

1979 Families in Former Times: Kinship, Household and Sexuality. Cambridge: Cambridge University Press.

Flax, J.

1987 Postmodernism and Gender Relations in Feminist Theory. Signs 12(4):621–643.

Forge, A.

1972 The Golden Fleece. Man (n.s.) 7:527–540.

Fortes, M.

1969 Kinship and the Social Order. The Legacy of Lewis Henry Morgan. Chicago: Aldine Publishing Co.

Foster, G. M.

1953 Cofradia and Compradrazo in Spain and Latin America. Southwestern Journal of Anthropology 9:1–28.

1960 Interpersonal Relations in Peasant Society. Human Organization 19:174–178.

Foucault, M.

1978 The History of Sexuality. New York: Pantheon Books.

1979 Discipline and Punish: The Birth of the Prison. New York: Random House.

Friedl, E.

1962 Vasilika: A Village in Modern Greece. New York: Holt, Rinehart and Winston.

1970 Field Work in a Greek Village. In Women in the Field, P. Golde, ed., pp. 195–217. Chicago: Aldine Publishing Co.

1986 The Position of Women: Appearance and Reality. In Dubisch 1986a:42–52. (First published in 1967.)

Galt, A. H.
  1973 Carnival on the Island of Pantelleria: Ritualized Community Solidarity in an Atomistic Society. Ethnology 12:325–339.
Geertz, H., and C. Geertz
  1975 Kinship in Bali. London: University of Chicago Press.
Gellner, E., and J. Waterbury, eds.
  1977 Patrons and Clients in Mediterranean Societies. London: Duckworth.
Georgeles, F.
  1986 Me, You, Bed. Tachidhromos (magazine), June.
Gibson, T.
  1986 Sacrifice and Sharing in the Philippine Highlands: Religion and Society among the Buid of Mindoro. London: The Athlone Press.
Giddens, A.
  1976 New Rules of Sociological Method: A Positive Critique of Interpretative Sociologies. London: Hutchinson.
Gilmore, D.
  1975 Friendship in Fuenmayor: Patterns of Integration in an Atomistic Society. Ethnology 14:311–324.
  1983 Sexual Ideology in Andalusian Oral Literature: A Comparative View of a Mediterranean Complex. Ethnology 22:241–252.
  1985 Introduction. In Sex and Gender in Southern Europe: Problems and Prospects, D. Gilmore and G. Gwynne, eds. Special issue of Anthropology 9(1–2):1–10.
  1987a Aggression and Community: Paradoxes of Andalusian Culture. New Haven and London: Yale University Press.
  1987b Introduction: The Shame of Dishonor. In Honor and Shame and the Unity of the Mediterranean, D. Gilmore, ed., pp. 2–21. A special publication of the American Anthropological Association, no. 22.
Gilmore, M., and D. Gilmore
  1979 Machismo: A Psychodynamic Approach. Journal of Psychological Anthropology 2:281–300.
Gilsenan, M.
  1976 Lying, Honor and Contradiction. In Transaction and Meaning: Directions in the Anthropology of Exchange and Symbolic Behaviour, B. Kapferer, ed., ASA Essays in Social Anthropology, no. 4, General Editor, E. Ardener, pp. 191–219. Philadelphia: Institute for the Study of Human Issues.
Giovannini, M. J.
  1981 Woman: A Dominant Symbol within the Cultural System of a Sicilian Town. Man 16(3):408–426.
  1986 Female Anthropologist and Male Informant: Gender Conflict in a Sicilian Town. In Whitehead and Conaway 1986:103–116.
  1987 Female Chastity Codes in the Circum-Mediterranean: Comparative Perspectives. In Honor and Shame and the Unity of the Mediterranean, D. Gilmore, ed., pp. 61–74. A special publication of the American Anthropological Association, no. 22.

Goddard, V.
  1987 Women's Sexuality and Group Identity in Naples. *In* The Cultural Construction of Sexuality, P. Caplan, ed., pp. 166–192. London: Tavistock.
Goffman, E.
  1974 Frame Analysis. New York: Harper & Row.
Gough, K.
  1971 Nuer Kinship: A Re-examination. *In* The Translation of Culture: Essays to E. E. Evans-Pritchard, J. P. Beidelman, ed., pp. 79–122. London: Tavistock.
  1975 The Origin of the Family. *In* Toward an Anthropology of Women, R. R. Reiter, ed., pp. 51–76. New York: Monthly Review Press.
Gramsci, A.
  1971 Selections from the Prison Notebooks. London: Lawrence and Wishart.
Hammond, D., and A. Jablow
  1987 Gilgamesh and the Sundance Kid: The Myth of Male Friendship. *In* The Making of Masculinities, H. Brod, ed., pp. 241–258. Boston: Allen and Unwin.
Handman, M.-E.
  1983 La Violence et la Ruse: Hommes et Femmes dans un Village Grec. La Calade, Aix-en-Provence: Edisud (Mondes méditerranéens).
Hapgood, I. F.
  1975 Service Book of the Holy Orthodox-Catholic and Apostolic Church. New York: Antiochian Orthodox Christian Archdiocese of New York and All North America.
Harris, O.
  1985 Review of Herzfeld 1985a. The Times Higher Education Supplement.
Hattox, R. S.
  1985 Coffee and Coffeehouses: The Origins of a Social Beverage in the Medieval Near East. Seattle and London: University of Washington Press.
Heath, S. B.
  1983 Ways with Words: Language, Life, and Work in Communities and Classrooms. Cambridge: Cambridge University Press.
Heine, S.
  1987 Women and Early Christianity: Are the Feminist Scholars Right? London: SCM Press.
Herdt, G.
  1981 Guardians of the Flutes: Idioms of Masculinity. New York: McGraw Hill.
  1982 Rituals of Manhood. Ed. Berkeley: University of California Press.
Herzfeld, M.
  1976 Categories of Inclusion and Exclusion in a Rhodian Village. D.Phil. thesis, University of Oxford.
  1980 Honour and Shame: Problems in the Comparative Analysis of Moral Systems. Man (n.s.) 15:339–351.
  1981 Meaning and Morality: A Semiotic Approach to Evil Eye Accusations in a Greek Village. American Ethnologist 8:560–574.

1982 Disemia. *In* Semiotics 1980, M. Herzfeld and M. D. Lenhart, comps., pp. 205–215. New York: Plenum Press.

1983 Semantic Slippage and Moral Fall: The Rhetoric of Chastity in Rural Greek Society. Journal of Modern Greek Studies 1(1):161–172.

1985a The Poetics of Manhood: Contest and Identity in a Cretan Mountain Village. Princeton: Princeton University Press.

1985b Gender Pragmatics: Agency, Speech, and Bride-Theft in a Cretan Mountain Village. Anthropology 9:25–44.

1986 Within and Without: The Category of "Female" in the Ethnography of Modern Greece. *In* Dubisch 1986a:215–233.

1987 Anthropology through the Looking-Glass: Critical Ethnography in the Margins of Europe. Cambridge: Cambridge University Press.

1989 "As in Your Own House": Hospitality and the Stereotype of Mediterranean Society. *In* Honour and Shame and the Unity of the Mediterranean, D. Gilmore, ed., pp. 75–89. A special publication of the American Anthropological Association, no. 22.

1990 I Ritoriki ton Arithmon: Sinteknia ke Kinoniki Ipostasi stin Orini Kriti. *In* Fila ke Kinonia sti Sinchroni Elladha, E. Papataxiarchis and T. Paradellis, eds. Athens: Kastaniotis Publications. Forthcoming.

Hirschon, R.

1978 Open Body, Closed Space: The Transformation of Female Sexuality. *In* Ardener 1978:66–88.

1981 Essential Objects and the Sacred: Interior and Exterior Space in an Urban Greek Locality. *In* Ardener 1981:72–88.

1983 Women, the Aged and Religious Activity: Oppositions and Complementarity in an Urban Locality. Journal of Modern Greek Studies 1(1):113–130.

1984 Women and Property—Women as Property. Ed. London: Croom Helm.

1985 The Women-Environment Relationship: Greek Cultural Values in an Urban Community. Ekistics 52:15–21.

1989 Heirs of the Greek Catastrophe: The Social Life of Asia Minor Refugees in Piraeus. Oxford: Clarendon Press.

Hobsbawm, E.

1959 Primitive Rebels: Studies in Archaic Forms of Social Movement in the 19th and 20th Centuries. Manchester: Manchester University Press.

Hoch-Smith, J., and A. Spring, eds.

1978 Women in Ritual and Symbolic Roles. New York: Plenum Press.

Hoffman, S.

1976 The Ethnography of the Islands: Thera. *In* Dimen and Friedl 1976:328–340.

Holden, P., ed.

1983 Women's Religious Experience. London: Croom Helm.

Irigaray, L.

1974 Speculum de l'Autre Femme. Paris: Minuit.

Jackson, M.

1983 Thinking through the Body: An Essay on Understanding Metaphor. Social Analysis 14:127–149.

Jakobson, R.
  1960 Linguistics and Poetics. *In* Style in Language, T. A. Sebeok, ed., pp. 350–377. Cambridge, Mass.: MIT Press.

Joseph, S., and D. White
  1974 Excuse Me Miss, Have You Seen the Acropolis? Athens: Lycabettus Press.

Just, R.
  1980 Fathers and Fathers-in-Law. Journal of the Anthropological Society of Oxford 11:157–169.

Kabbani, R.
  1986 Europe's Myths of Orient: Devise and Rule. London: Macmillan.

Kakouri, K.
  1963 Dionysiaka. Athens.

Karp, I.
  1980 Beer Drinking and Social Experience in an African Society: An Essay in Formal Sociology. *In* Explorations in African Systems of Thought, I. Karp and C. S. Bird, eds., pp. 83–119. Bloomington: Indiana University Press.

Karp, I., and M. B. Kendall
  1982 Reflexivity in Fieldwork. *In* Explaining Human Behavior: Consciousness, Human Action and Social Structure, P. F. Secord, ed., pp. 249–273. Beverly Hills: Sage Publications.

Kenna, M.
  1976a Houses, Fields and Graves: Property and Ritual Obligation on a Greek Island. Ethnology 15:21–34.
  1976b The Idiom of the Family. *In* Mediterranean Family Structures, J. G. Peristiany, ed., pp. 347–362. Cambridge University Press.
  1990 Saying No. In press.

Kennedy, R.
  1986 Women's Friendships on Crete: A Psychological Perspective. *In* Dubisch 1986a:121–138.

Kleinman, A.
  1980 Patients and Healers in the Context of Culture. Berkeley: University of California Press.

Korovkin, M.
  1986 Oral Contraceptives in a Southern Italian Community. Current Anthropology 27:80–83.

Lever, A.
  1986 Honour as a Red Herring. Critique of Anthropology 6(3):83–106.

Lévi-Strauss, C.
  1963 The Effectiveness of Symbols. *In* Structural Anthropology, pp. 186–205. New York: Basic Books.
  1965 Le Triangle Culinaire. L'Arc 26:19–29.
  1973 Tristes Tropiques. Translated by J. Weightman. London: Cape.

Lewis, I. M.
  1971 Ecstatic Religion. Harmondsworth: Penguin Books.

Leyton, E.

1974 Irish Friends and "Friends": The Nexus of Friendship, Kinship and Class in Aughnaboy. *In* The Compact: Selected Dimensions of Friendship, E. Leyton, ed., pp. 93–104. Toronto: University of Toronto Press.

Lineton, M.

1971 Mina Present and Past: Depopulation in a Village in Mani, Southern Greece. Ph.D. thesis, University of Kent, Canterbury.

Lobel, M.

1985 Women's Creations for the New Creation: The Anastasi in Astoria. Master's thesis, New York University.

Loizos, P.

1975a The Greek Gift: Politics in a Cypriot Village. Oxford: Blackwell.

1975b Changes in Property Transfer among Greek Cypriot Villagers. Man 10(4):503–523.

1977 Politics and Patronage in a Cypriot Village, 1920–1970. *In* Gellner and Waterbury 1977:115–135.

Lukes, S.

1974 Power: A Radical View. London: Macmillan.

Lutz, C.

1988 Unnatural Emotions: Everyday Sentiments on a Micronesian Atoll and Their Challenge to Western Theory. Chicago: University of Chicago Press.

MacCormack, C. P., and M. Strathern, eds.

1980 Nature, Culture and Gender. Cambridge: Cambridge University Press.

McNeil, W. H.

1978 The Metamorphosis of Greece since World War II. Oxford: Blackwell.

Maltz, D. N.

1978 The Bride of Christ Is Filled With His Spirit. *In* Women in Ritual and Symbolic Roles, J. Hoch-Smith and A. Spring, eds., pp. 27–44. London: Plenum Press.

Marcus, G. E., and M. J. Fischer

1986 Anthropology as Cultural Critique: An Experimental Moment in the Human Sciences. Chicago: University of Chicago Press.

Mauss, M.

1985 A Category of the Human Mind: The Notion of Person; The Notion of Self. *In* The Category of the Person: Anthropology, Philosophy, History, M. Carrithers et al., eds. Cambridge: Cambridge University Press. (First published in 1938.)

Megas, G.

1961 Anastenaria ke Ethima tis Tirinis Defteras. Laografia 19:472–534.

Messick, B.

1987 Subordinate Discourse: Women, Weaving, and Gender Relations in North Africa. American Ethnologist 14:210–225.

Meyendoroff, J.

1984 Marriage: An Orthodox Perspective. 3d ed. New York: St. Vladimir's Seminary Press.

Miller, N. K., ed.

1986 The Poetics of Gender. New York: Columbia University Press.

Moerman, D.
1979 Anthropology of Symbolic Healing. Current Anthropology 20:59–80.

Moore, H.
1988 Feminism and Anthropology. Oxford: Polity Press.

Mosse, G.
1985 Nationalism and Sexuality: Respectability and Abnormal Sexuality in Modern Europe. New York: Howard Fertig.

Murphy, M.
1983 Emotional Confrontations between Sevillano Fathers and Sons: Cultural Foundations and Social Consequences. American Ethnologist 10:650–664.

Nicol, D. M.
1963 Meteora: The Rock Monasteries of Thessaly. London: Chapman and Hall.

Nilsson, M. P.
1961 Greek Folk Religion. New York: Harper Torchbooks.

Okely, J.
1978 Privileged, Schooled and Finished: Boarding Education for Girls. In Ardener 1978:109–139.

Olson, E.
1982 Duofocal Family Structure and an Alternative Model of Husband-Wife Relationship. In Sex Roles, Family and Community in Turkey, C. Kâğitçibaşi, ed., pp. 33–72. Bloomington: Indiana University Turkish Studies.

O'Neill, B. J.
1987 Social Inequality in a Portuguese Hamlet: Land, Late Marriage and Bastardy, 1870–1978. Cambridge: Cambridge University Press.

Ortner, S. B.
1974 Is Female to Male as Nature Is to Culture? In Rosaldo and Lamphere 1974:67–87.

Ortner, S. B., and H. Whitehead, eds.
1981 Sexual Meanings: The Cultural Construction of Gender and Sexuality. Cambridge: Cambridge University Press.

Ostrogorsky, G.
1956 The History of the Byzantine State. Translated by J. Hussey. Oxford: Blackwell.

Ott, S.
1981 The Circle of Mountains: A Basque Shepherding Community. Oxford: Clarendon Press.

Pagels, E.
1979 The Gnostic Gospels. New York: Random House.

Paine, R.
1969 In Search of Friendship: An Explanatory Analysis in "Middle-Class" Culture. Man (n.s.) 4:505–524.
1974 Anthropological Approaches to Friendship. In The Compact: Selected Dimensions of Friendship, E. Leyton, ed., pp. 1–14. Toronto: Toronto University Press.

Pantazopoulos, N.

1967 Church and Law in the Balkan Peninsula during the Ottoman Rule. Thessaloniki: Institute for Balkan Studies.

Papadopoulos, Th.

1967 Orthodox Church and Civil Authority. Journal of Contemporary History 2(4):201–209.

Papataxiarchis, E.

1984 Raki Is Thicker Than Water: Male Commensality and the Symbolism of Drink in Aegean Greek Coffeeshops. Paper presented in the seminar on the Anthopology of Drink, Department of Social Anthropology, School of Oriental and African Studies. Forthcoming as O Kosmos tou Kafeniou. *In* Fila ke Kinonia sti Sinchroni Elladha, E. Papataxiarchis and T. Paradellis, eds. Athens: Kastaniotis Publications.

1985 The Dancing *Efes*: Notions of the Male Person in Aegean Greek Fiction. Paper presented at the Modern Greek Studies Association Symposium on Greeks and Asia Minor, Anatolia College, Thessaloniki.

1988 Kinship, Friendship and Gender Relations in Two East Aegean Village Communities. Ph.D. thesis, University of London.

1990 The Cost of the Household: Social Classes, Marriage Strategies and Ecclesiastical Law in Nineteenth Century Lesbos. *In* Sociétés Sub-Européennes à l'Age Moderne, Adaptions et Resistances, S. Woolf, ed. Paris: La Découverte.

Pennington, M. B.

1979 O! Holy Mountain: Journal of a Retreat on Mount Athos. London: Cassell.

Peristiany, J. G., ed.

1965a Honour and Shame: The Values of Mediterranean Society. London: Weidenfeld and Nicholson.

1965b Introduction. *In* Peristiany 1965a:9–18.

1965c Honour and Shame in a Cypriot Village. *In* Peristiany 1965a:171–190.

Photiades, J.

1965 The Position of the Coffeehouse in the Social Structure of the Greek Village. Sociologia Ruralis 5:45–53.

Pidalion, The

1976 The Pidalion [Rudder] of the Orthodox Catholic Church. 8th ed. Athens.

Pina-Cabral, J. de

1986 Sons of Adam, Daughters of Eve: The Peasant Worldview of the Alto Minho. Oxford: Clarendon Press.

Pitt-Rivers, J. A.

1968 Pseudo-kinship, S. V. Kinship. *In* International Encyclopedia of the Social Sciences 8:408–413. New York.

1971 The People of the Sierra. 2d ed. (1st ed., 1954.) Chicago: University of Chicago Press.

1973 The Kith and the Kin. *In* The Character of Kinship, J. Goody, ed., pp. 89–105. Cambridge: Cambridge University Press.

1977 The Fate of Shechem or the Politics of Sex: Essays in the Anthropology of the Mediterranean. Cambridge: Cambridge University Press.

Politis, A.
1973 To Dhimotiko Traghoudhi: Kleftika. Athens: Ermis (Nea Elliniki Vivliothiki).

Presvelou, K., and A. Teperoglou
1976 Kinoniologiki Analysi tou Phenomenou tis Ektroseos ston Elliniko Choro. Greek Review of Social Research 28:275–285.

1980 Kinoniologiki Analysi tou Phenomenou tis Ektroseos ston Elliniko Choro. Greek Review of Social Research 39–40:324–341.

Rabinow, P., and W. M. Sullivan, eds.
1979 Interpretive Social Science: A Reader. Berkeley: University of California Press.

1987 Interpretive Social Science—A Second Look. Berkeley: University of California Press.

Rapp, R.
1987 Towards a Nuclear Freeze? The Gender Politics of Euroamerican Kinship Analysis. In Gender and Kinship: Essays Towards a Unified Analysis, J. F. Collier and S. J. Yanagisako, eds., pp. 119–131. Stanford: Stanford University Press.

Redfield, R.
1960 The Little Community/Peasant Society and Culture. Chicago: University of Chicago Press.

Reiter, R. R.
1975 Men and Women in the South of France: Public and Private Domains. In Toward an Anthropology of Women, R. R. Reiter, ed., pp. 252–282. New York: Monthly Review Press.

Rogers, S. C.
1975 Female Forms of Power and the Myth of Male Dominance: A Model of Female/Male Interaction in Peasant Society. American Ethnologist 1(4):727–756.

1985 Gender in Southwestern France: The Myth of Male Dominance Revisited. Anthropology 9(1–2):65–86.

Romaios, C.
1944–1945 Laikes Latries tis Thrakis. Arhion tou Thrakikou Laografikou ke Glossikou Thisavrou 11:1–131.

Rosaldo, M. Z.
1974 Woman, Culture and Society: A Theoretical Overview. In Rosaldo and Lamphere 1974:17–42.

1983 The Shame of Headhunters and the Autonomy of Self. Ethos 11:135–181.

Rosaldo, M. Z., and L. Lamphere, eds.
1974 Woman, Culture and Society. Stanford: Stanford University Press.

Ross, E., and R. Rapp
1981 Sex and Society: A Research Note from Social History and Anthropology. Comparative Studies in Society and History 23:51–72.

Rushton, L.
  1983 Doves and Magpies: Village Women in the Greek Orthodox Church. *In* Women's Religious Experience, P. Holden, ed., pp. 57–70. London: Croom Helm.
Sahlins, M.
  1972 Stone Age Economics. London: Tavistock.
Salamone, S. D., and J. B. Stanton
  1986 Introducing the *Nikokyra*: Ideality and Reality in Social Process. *In* Dubisch 1986a:97–120.
Sanday, P. R.
  1981 Female Power and Male Dominance: On the Origins of Sexual Inequality. Cambridge: Cambridge University Press.
Sant Cassia, P.
  (forthcoming) To the City: Kinship, Property and Family in 19th Century Athens. Cambridge: Cambridge University Press.
Sapir, J. D.
  1977 The Anatomy of Metaphor. *In* The Social Use of Metaphor: Essays on the Anthropology of Rhetoric, J. D. Sapir and J. C. Crocker, eds., pp. 3–32. Philadelphia: University of Pennsylvania Press.
Schneider, D. M.
  1969 Kinship, Nationality and Religion in American Culture. *In* Forms of Symbolic Action, V. Turner, ed., pp. 115–125. Proceedings of the 1969 Annual Spring Meeting of the American Ethnological Society.
  1980 American Kinship: A Cultural Account. [1968] 2d abridged ed. Chicago: University of Chicago Press.
Schneider, J.
  1971 Of Vigilance and Virgins: Honor, Shame, and Access to Resources in Mediterranean Societies. Ethnology 10:1–24.
Shepherd, G.
  1987 Rank, Gender and Homosexuality: Mombasa as a Key to Understanding Sexual Options. *In* The Cultural Construction of Sexuality, P. Caplan, ed., pp. 240–270. London: Tavistock.
Shorter, E.
  1982 A History of Women's Bodies. New York: Basic Books.
Showalter, E.
  1986 Piecing and Writing. *In* Miller 1986:222–247.
Stamiris, Eleni.
  1986 The Women's Movement in Greece. New Left Review 158:98–112.
Stavropoulos, D.
  1987 Awaiting AIDS. ENA (magazine), 9 April. Athens.
Steiner, G.
  1975 After Babel: Aspects of Language and Translation. London: Oxford University Press.
Stewart, C.
  1985 The *Exotika*: Greek Values and Their Supernatural Antitheses. ARV (Scandinavian Folklore Archives) 41:37–64.

Stone, L.
1979 The Family, Sex and Marriage in England, 1500–1800. Harmondsworth: Penguin.

Strathern, M.
1981a Culture in a Netbag: The Manufacture of a Subdiscipline in Anthropology. Man (n.s.) 16:665–688.
1981b Self-Interest and the Social Good: Some Implications of Hagen Gender Imagery. In Ortner and Whitehead 1981:166–191.
1988 The Gender of the Gift: Problems with Women and Problems with Society in Melanesia. Berkeley: University of California Press.

Tiffany, S. W.
1984 Introduction: Feminist Perceptions in Anthropology. In Rethinking Women's Roles: Perspectives from the Pacific, D. O'Brien and S. W. Tiffany, eds., pp. 1–11. Berkeley: University of California Press.

Tompkins, J. P.
1981 Sentimental Power: Uncle Tom's Cabin and the Politics of Literary History. Glyph 8:79–102.

Uhl, S.
1985 Special Friends: The Organisation of Intersex Friendship in Escalona (Andalusia), Spain. Anthropology 9:129–152.

Valaoras, V., A. Polychronopoulou, and D. Trichopoulos
1969 Abortion in Greece. In Social Demography and Medical Responsibility, pp. 31–44. Proceedings of the Sixth Conference of the International Planned Parenthood Federation, Europe and Near East Region. London.

Vassilikos, V.
1978 Ta Kamakia. Athens: Kaktos.

Vernier, B.
1984 Putting Kin and Kinship to Good Use: The Circulation of Goods, Labour, and Names on Karpathos (Greece). In Interest and Emotion: Essays on the Study of Family and Kinship, H. Medick and D. W. Sabean, eds., pp. 28–76. Cambridge: Cambridge University Press.

Whitehead, H.
1981 The Bow and the Burden Strap: A New Look at Institutionalized Homosexuality in Native North America. In Ortner and Whitehead 1981:80–115.

Whitehead, T. L., and M. E. Conaway, eds.
1986 Self, Sex and Gender in Cross-Cultural Fieldwork. Urbana: University of Illinois Press.

Wikan, U.
1984 Shame and Honour: A Contestable Pair. Man (n.s.) 19:635–652.

Williams, R.
1977 Marxism and Literature. Oxford: Oxford University Press.

Wolf, E.
1966 Kinship, Friendship and Patron-Client Relations. In The Social Anthropology of Complex Societies, M. Banton, ed., pp. 1–22. ASA Monographs 4. London: Tavistock.

Yanagisako, S. J.

1979 Family and Household: The Analysis of Domestic Groups. Annual Review of Anthropology 8:161–205.

1987 Mixed Metaphors: Native and Anthropological Models of Gender and Kinship Domains. *In* Gender and Kinship: Essays toward a Unified Analysis, J. F. Collier and S. J. Yanagisako, eds., pp. 86–118. Stanford: Stanford University Press.

INDEX

CPSIA information can be obtained at www.ICGtesting.com
Printed in the USA
LVOW100222180612

286529LV00001B/1/A